A History of Electric Cars

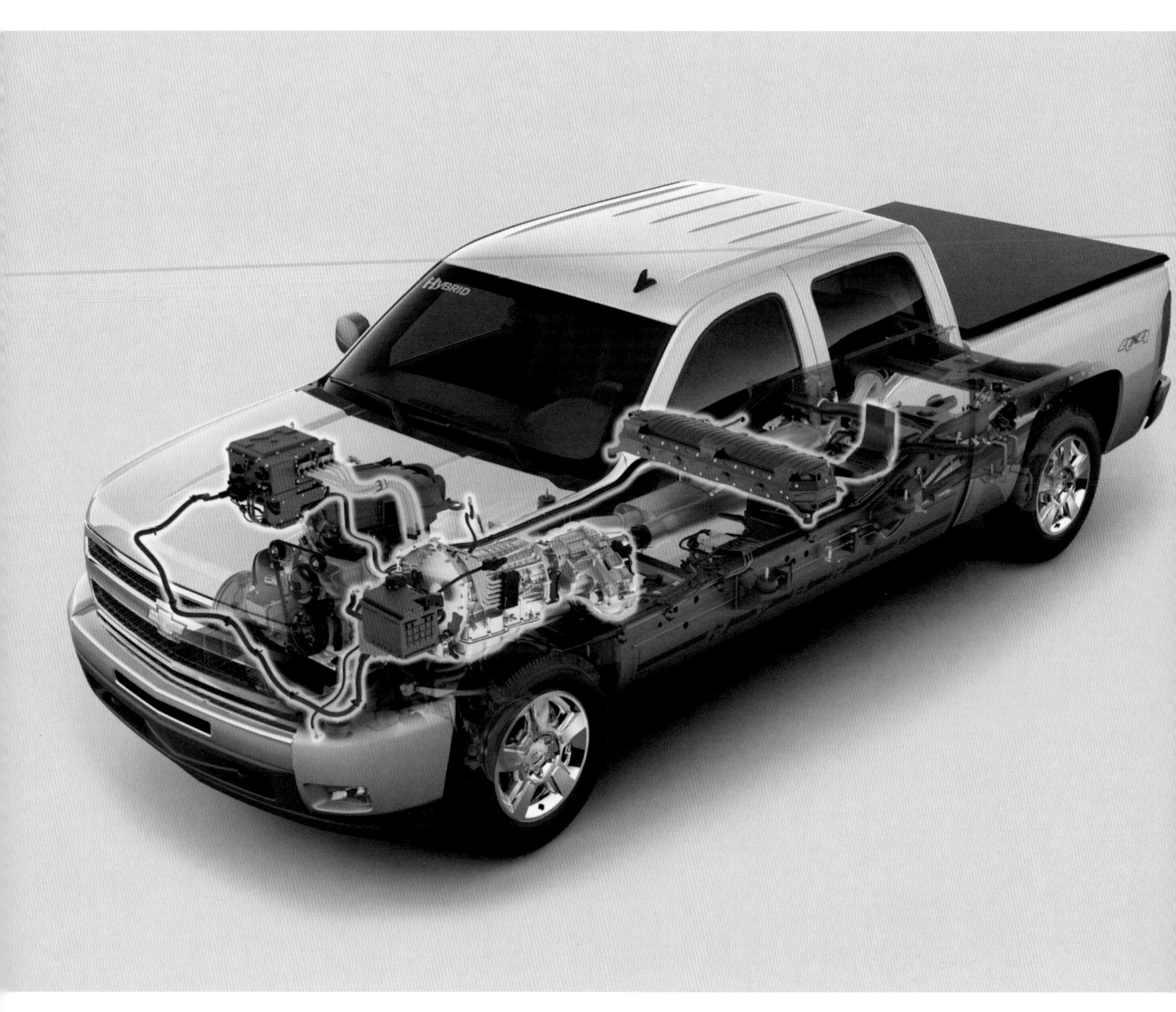
HYBRID

A History of Electric Cars

Nigel Burton

THE CROWOOD PRESS

First published in 2013 by
The Crowood Press Ltd
Ramsbury, Marlborough
Wiltshire SN8 2HR

www.crowood.com

British Library Cataloguing-in-Publication Data
A catalogue record for this book is available from the British Library.

ISBN 978 1 84797 461 7

Dedication
I would like to dedicate this book to my wife, Jane, whose encouragement and patience helped enormously, and my two children, Jack and Mia, who will hopefully grow up in a world where electric cars are not just curiosities. I am also indebted to the people who gave their time for interviews and provided rare documents for me. Special mention should go to Tony Wood Rogers for his help with the Sinclair C5 chapter, Gary Witzenburg, who provided valuable input on the EV1, and Clarence Milburn, who provided many of the documents and photos for the early chapters. Although the history of the EV is sparse, there have been a few earlier books. Three in particular, *The Electric Vehicle*, by Gijis Mom, *The Electric Vehicle and the Burden of History*, by David Kirsch, and *Electric and Hybrid Cars*, by Curtis and Judy Anderson, proved invaluable for cross-checking facts. *Monopoly on Wheels* by William Greenleaf, originally published in 1961, is the definitive account of Henry Ford's battle with the American Association of Licensed Automobile Manufacturers, as described in Chapter 2.

Designed and typeset by Guy Croton, Sevenoaks, Kent

Printed and bound in India by Replika Press Ltd

CONTENTS

1	BEGINNINGS	6
2	ELECTRIC CABS AND THE ELECTRIC VEHICLE COMPANY	18
3	THE GOLDEN AGE	32
4	THE DARK AGES	56
5	THE SIXTIES AND SEVENTIES	68
6	THE EIGHTIES AND NINETIES	96
7	A FALSE DAWN: THE GENERAL MOTORS EV1	120
8	A NEW BEGINNING: THE TOYOTA PRIUS AND THE HONDA INSIGHT	140
9	REBIRTH: NEW HYBRIDS AND THE NISSAN LEAF	158
10	FROM COMMUTER CARS TO SUPERCARS – ALL THE WORLD LOVES AN ELECTRIC CAR	194
	Epilogue: the More Things Change, the More They Stay the Same	220
	References	222
	Index	223

CHAPTER ONE

BEGINNINGS

Frogs' Legs and Batteries

At the dawn of the twentieth century, the car industry was in its nascent period. Cars were beginning to take over from the horse and carriage, but only the wealthy could afford to buy one. All over the world, hundreds of former carriage companies had diversified into building automobiles. Three propulsion technologies were competing for the emergent market, but only one appeared to have a winning hand: it offered pioneering motorists the quietest and smoothest drive; it powered cars to the land-speed record; it was easy to start and the cars that used it were so simple to drive almost anyone could get to grips with it in a few hours; what's more, the fuel it used was both cheap and widely available throughout the developed world. Yet, despite these apparently crushing advantages, the electric car failed to capture the buying public's imagination. Its failure left drivers with only one choice: the internal combustion engine. Indeed, so thoroughly was it routed, that the role electric vehicles played in the early development of the automobile has been largely expunged from history. Only a few grainy black-and-white photos remain of cars that, once upon a time, ruled the roads.

Fast-forward 100 years and the electric car is once again in the ascendency. Vehicles such as the Toyota Prius, the Nissan Leaf and the Chevrolet Volt are in the vanguard of a new generation of cars that use battery power. Some, like the Prius and the Volt, use electricity to reduce running costs; others, like the Leaf, to slash exhaust pollution, and a select few, like the Porsche 918, harness electric motors to boost their outright performance.

The Porsche 918: state-of-the-art application of petrol–electric hybrid technology promises supercar performance with the running costs of a large family saloon. But this isn't the first high-performance Porsche hybrid.

Car manufacturers have turned to electricity over fears of a looming environmental disaster. As Carlos Ghosn, chairman and chief executive of the Renault Group, says:

> *The Renault-Nissan alliance is targeting sales of 1.5m zero emissions vehicles by 2016, delivering a 20 per cent reduction in our carbon footprint and a 35 per cent improvement in our overall fuel economy. Beyond pure sales volumes the LEAF symbolises our wide-angled view of society. The world already has seven billion people and one billion cars. The Nissan LEAF shows that the automobile industry can contribute to sustainability without giving up our role as a source of unmitigated excitement and mobility. The electric car will represent a very big percentage of our industry in the future.*

Global warming has brought the electric car – and its close cousin, the hybrid – back from obscurity. However, the obstacles to sales success these new vehicles face are just the same as they have ever been. If the electric car is to accomplish in the twenty-first century what its predecessors so spectacularly failed to achieve a century ago, manufacturers must learn the lessons of the past.

Why did electric cars fail to catch on in the first years of the twentieth century, despite their early advantage? And how did the development of electric vehicles proceed so much faster than the competing technologies of internal combustion and steam power, only to come to a complete halt?

The early years of the electric car are filled with stories of snake oil salesmen, dubious speculators and patent trolls. Many of the outrageous claims made for horseless carriages were untrue. Motorists who found themselves stranded miles from anywhere with a flat battery had good reason to be angry when their car failed to achieve the range-to-empty figures they had been promised. Henry Ford, whose wife used an electric car, was so alarmed by the poor dependability of batteries that he even built a charging station just so he could be sure his wife would always be able to get home.

But, for all their drawbacks, electric cars did have many good points. Had the electric car industry found its own Henry Ford (and it almost persuaded Ford himself to be its advocate, see Chapter 3), history may have been very different.

And it all began with the battery – a ground-breaking discovery, which came about as a result of a friendly dispute over frogs' legs.

Alessandro Volta: Italian physicist who invented the first battery capable of supplying a reliable electric charge.

Although some historians believe the electrochemical cell was invented in Mesopotamia shortly after the crucifixion of Christ, the man most widely credited with the discovery of the modern-day battery was the Italian chemist and inventor Alessandro Volta.

Volta was born in Como, Italy, and was a physics professor at the city's Royal School. In 1775, he took an invention by a Swedish professor called Johan Carl Wilcke and refined it to create what he dubbed the electrophorus. The device consisted of a dielectric plate made from resinous material and a metal plate with an insulated handle. When the dielectric plate was charged, by rubbing it with fur or cloth, the resulting electrostatic induction process created a charge in the metal plate, which could be used for experiments.

Volta was fascinated by the potential of electricity. He did pioneering work on what is now known as electrical capacitance, developing a means to study both potential and charge, and experimented with very primitive ignition systems, burning methane via an electrically generated spark.

Around the same time as Volta was refining his electrophorus, one of his fellow countrymen, a physicist called Luigi Galvani who was Professor of Medicine at the University of Bologna, was making an even more important discovery. According to Galvani's notes, while conducting static electricity on a skinned frog, his assistant accidentally touched the animal's crural nerve with a steel scalpel, creating an electrical charge. The two saw the frog's leg kick out as though the (very dead) amphibian were suddenly alive.[1] Galvani was convinced that he was seeing the effects of what he dubbed 'animal electricity'. His experiments led many people at the time to conclude that electricity could be used in some way to revive the dead. This theory of reanimation was the inspiration for Mary Shelley's famous novel *Frankenstein*.

However, Volta was not convinced that animal tissue was necessary for the conduction of electricity. To prove this, he assembled plates of copper and zinc separated by pasteboard soaked in an electrolyte (a brine mixture of salt and water). When the top and bottom contacts were connected by wire he measured a continuous electric current. In doing so, Volta had invented the primary battery. In honour of his discovery, it was named the voltaic pile – because the primitive cells were literally 'piled' on top of one another.

The battery opened up infinite possibilities. For the first time, inventors could draw a continuous electric current for hours, instead of relying on the erratic sparks produced by the Leyden jar method, which 'stored' static electricity in a very primitive form of capacitor.

In 1821, English chemist Michael Faraday built two devices to demonstrate how a wire rod carrying a current from a voltaic pile would rotate around a fixed magnet if one end extended into a liquid conductor that completed the circuit. By reversing the elements, the magnet could be made to rotate around the wire. Faraday had invented the world's first electric motor. One (possibly apocryphal) story says that during a demonstration for the Prime Minister, Sir Robert Peel, Faraday was asked what possible use his discovery could be, to which he replied: 'Why Prime Minister, someday you can tax it'.

Faraday's peers were quick to seize on his breakthrough. A year later, English mathematician and physicist Peter Barlow produced an interesting variation on Faraday's motor, using it to turn a wheel, thereby demonstrating a practical use for the new discovery.

In 1831, Faraday created the world's first dynamo – called the Faraday disc – when he succeeded in moving a disc held perpendicular to a magnetic field, a technological breakthrough that led to renewed scientific interest in using mechanical means to create electrical energy. Faraday's work was the cornerstone of understanding that underpins all electrical technology, including the motors and generators that power electric vehicles in the twenty-first century.

Four years later, a blacksmith from Vermont, New England, in the United States, built a small drifter operated by an electric motor – proving that electricity could be put to work. Then, in 1838, a Scots chemist named Robert Davidson unveiled an electric locomotive. Sadly, its practical value was limited. The top speed of just four miles per hour had been roundly trumped almost a decade earlier by Stephenson's Rocket steam loco, which achieved 30mph (48km/h) during the Rainhill Trials. However, the principal of electric propulsion was sound and, in 1840, a patent was issued for the use of rails as conductors of electricity.

Davidson, who came from Aberdeen, set to work on a larger loco, which was the star exhibit at the Royal Society of Arts Exhibition in 1841. He named his creation the Galvani in honour of Lugi Galvani. The impressive 7-ton loco was hauled by two direct-drive motors, which used fixed electro-magnets acting on iron bars that were attached to a wooden drive cylinder mounted on each axle. The following September, Davidson demonstrated his invention on the Edinburgh and Glasgow Railway, where it managed to haul a 6-ton load one-and-a-half miles before the batteries were exhausted.

Economically, however, the electric locomotive couldn't hold a candle to the steam engine. The invention of the rechargeable battery was more than a decade away and disposable batteries were more expensive than coal. Davidson's invention was viewed with suspicion, and outright hostility, by workers on the railway who though electricity might put them out of a job. Things came to a head when, in a fit of unprecedented industrial unrest, a group of angry railwaymen broke into the Galvani's engine shed and destroyed it. Davidson's hopes came to nothing.

The First Electric Horseless Carriage

As Davidson was beavering away on electric trains, another Scotsman was examining the possibilities of an electric horseless carriage. Little is known about Robert Anderson's invention – sadly the details of his vehicle have been

The first electric horseless carriage: Sibrandus Stratingh's battery-powered carriage was a breakthrough in electric propulsion.

lost – but sometime between 1832 and 1839 he designed, built and tested a battery-powered horseless carriage. Unfortunately for him, Anderson had no alternative but to use non-rechargeable cells as the lead-acid rechargeable battery wasn't invented until 1859, thus making his carriage nothing more than an interesting oddity and the smallest of footnotes in history, rather than a ground-breaking invention. Despite this, Anderson can still be said to be one of the pioneers of the electric car. The other was a Dutchman.

Sibrandus Stratingh was a Dutch chemistry professor and keen inventor with a yen for speed. He was convinced technology would make the horse-and-carriage redundant. Stratingh and his friend, German instrument maker Christopher Becker, were at the forefront of steam power development.

On 25 March 1834, *The Provincial Groninger Courant*, a newspaper published in the Dutch province of Groningen, reported:

> *In the early hours of this morning, 22 March, the first test journey was made by messrs Stratingh and Becker on their steam vehicle, which made a journey through the city's undulating and curving streets with a positive result. The designers were so happy with the test that they feel that some small improvements will enable the vehicle to not only travel over new stone and rock roads, but also the bumpier cobbled streets, without problem...*

On 8 September, the papers carried a report of a trip the friends made outside the town, passing through several villages and 'moving with the speed of several running horses' for more than four hours.

Although Stratingh's invention attracted crowds wherever it went, the professor was unhappy with it. The carriage was uncomfortable, smoky and noisy. The solution, as Stratingh saw it, was to switch from steam power to electricity.

In 1835, Professor Stratingh gave a lecture to the Royal Physics Society, in Groningen, entitled: 'Electromagnetic moving force and the use of this to an electromagnetic carriage...'. The idea for a small-scale electric cart came to him after reading reports of the work of Moritz von Jacobi, who had designed an electromagnetic motor at the Academy of Sciences in St Petersburg, Russia.

What they came up with was a very basic wooden platform to carry a galvanic battery, consisting of two plates, one zinc and one copper, rolled together and divided by wooden rods sitting in a porcelain jar filled with dilute

The precarious nature of Professor Stratingh's vehicle is obvious. The porcelain jar was filled with dilute acid.

The sole remaining Stratingh electric carriage is held at the Museum of the University of Groningen.

Professor Stratingh's carriage could run for about 15min before the battery was exhausted.

acid. This cocktail was precariously mounted on the front to provide the current. Professor Stratingh described the vehicle as his 'electric motor'.

The carriage weighed about 6.6lb (3kg) and could drive for about fifteen minutes loaded with half its own weight before the current was exhausted. Professor Stratingh made several electric horseless carriages and a number still survive. Most of them are on display at the *Museum Boerhaave*, in Leiden, the Netherlands, and can be said to be the oldest electric vehicles still in existence.

The ultimate development of the professor's ideas had eight magnets, instead of four, so that in its positive position there are twelve poles on twelve poles working on each other to give maximum power. In 1934, this vehicle was donated to the Museum of the University of Groningen. Today, it is one of the museum's most important and valuable exhibits.

Professor Stratingh was a leading advocate of electric power. At his urging Becker began building larger magnets and Stratingh stated confidently that an electric carriage would easily outrun a steam-powered rival. Electric vehicles were simpler, lighter, carried no heavy fuels and offered no danger of explosion or fire.

As well as his carriages, Professor Stratingh also built a model electric boat, which he sailed in the pond near his home. Sadly, his experiments in electric propulsion were curtailed by ill-health and he died in February 1841. Nevertheless, Professor Stratingh had demonstrated that electricity was a viable means of vehicle propulsion – an idea that was enthusiastically taken up by others.

Britain and the First Rechargeable Electric Horseless Carriages

However, it wasn't until 1881 that the first electric vehicle to be powered by a rechargeable battery was unveiled. French inventor Gustave Trouve had developed an engine for marine applications – the first practical outboard motor. Trouve, who had taken to cruising the river Seine with friends aboard his electrically powered 17ft (5m) launch, adapted it to power a Coventry-Rotary pedal tricycle. In November 1881, he demonstrated a working three-wheeled automobile at the International Exhibition of Electricity, held in Paris. Trouve used the second cell design, invented by Gaston Plante, a Belgian, who had found a way to discharge and recharge batteries – thus overcoming the problem of what to do when a battery was exhausted.

A year later, Professors William Ayrton of London and John Perry from Garvagh, County Londonderry, in Ireland, combined their knowledge to create their version of the electric trike. It used ten lead/acid Plante-type rechargeable batteries in series, which supplied 20V to a half-a-horsepower electric motor mounted beneath the plank-like driver's seat. The vehicle, which had two large spoked bicycle wheels at the front and a small wheel at the rear, was also the first to feature electric lights. These small bulbs were not, however, to allow anyone stupid enough attempting to drive after sundown to see where they were going, but to illuminate the trike's instruments, a small ammeter and voltmeter. Its speed was governed by switching between the batteries in series. Ayrton and Perry claimed their rickety contraption was good for a maximum speed of 9mph (14km/h) and could cover a remarkable 25 miles (40km) – depending on the terrain – before the power was exhausted.

Responding to the growing demand for electric propulsion, financier Paul Bedford Elwell and engineer Thomas Parker, formed a company to manufacture rechargeable batteries in Wolverhampton, England, in October 1882. The Elwell–Parker company quickly expanded its range to include dynamos, motors and controllers.

All this was going on three years before Carl Benz unveiled the first automobile to be powered by a gasoline internal combustion engine – an event that ushered in the beginning of the motoring age.

But in Britain development of cars of all kinds had already been dealt a major blow by a piece of government legislation designed to curb 'excessive speeds' made possible by new methods of propulsion (mainly steam, although electric vehicles and the internal combustion engine would also fall foul of the notorious Red Flag Act).

The Locomotive (Roads) Act of 1865 famously stipulated that a locomotive should be preceded by a man on foot waving a red flag as warning. The same person was expected to calm horse-drawn traffic ahead of the locomotive's appearance.

The act (and its 1878 amendment) also laid down regulations for lights (two at the front, one on each side), a primitive highway code (locomotives to give way to horse-drawn traffic and give as much room as possible to other vehicles) and even created the world's first official speed limits – 2mph in town and 4mph in open country – punishable by a hefty £10 fine. Large towns and cities were also given special powers to set their own rules on hours of operation and top speeds. This Draconian law would cripple development of new automobiles in Britain until politicians finally saw sense and repealed it in 1896.

Trikes aside, the first primitive electric vehicles were in every way just horseless carriages – just a wooden body riding on wood-spoke wheels and solid tyres. The 'conversion' consisted of a battery mounted on the chassis, an electric motor and a means of steering. This hybrid design was far from ideal. The crude suspension and solid tyres transmitted all the bumps and potholes from poorly surfaced roads directly to the chassis, with predictably dire consequences for the fragile battery plates sitting in containers filled with acid. Worse still, electric vehicles were considerably faster than their horse-drawn counterparts and a carriage chassis would become unstable at high speeds. The advantages of electric propulsion – smoothness and refinement – were entirely negated by the crudity of the design. As all the forces acting on a car do so through the contact patches of the tyres, the adoption of pneumatic tyres (perfected by Irish vet John Boyd Dunlop for his son's bicycle in 1887) proved a breakthrough in making electric cars more comfortable to drive.

By the time the automobile industry really began to flourish in the 1890s, the electric vehicle appeared to have an unassailable lead. The DC motor and its ancillaries were well-developed thanks to trams, such as the Volk's Electric Railway, which ran along the eastern seafront at Brighton. Lead-acid batteries, too, were rapidly reaching maturity after more than a decade of commercial development. Although the battery was still the weakest link in the electric car layout, commercial success would drive research into new materials and better designs. By the turn of the twentieth century, lead-acid batteries were durable enough to be used with confidence in automotive applications.

America

In America, the famous inventor Thomas Edison was working on a new type of battery – which used nickel-iron and promised even greater gains – specifically for electric vehicles.

According to an article in *Electric World* magazine, published in 1925, between 1910 and 1925 battery technology progressed in leaps and bounds. Storage capacity increased by 35 per cent, service life by an impressive 300 per cent and maintenance costs fell by 63 per cent.

A century before the Toyota Prius and the Nissan Leaf became the poster boys for supporters of a sustainable green method of transport, electric vehicles were advertised as the environmentally friendly alternative to traditional transportation. Horse-drawn carriages and wagons were sturdy and dependable but the accumulation of horse manure and urine in large towns and cities was a serious problem. The electric vehicle was clean technology with none of the smell and mess associated with horse-drawn carriages. Not only that, but the electric car produced far less noise than an internal combustion engine, started more easily and had no need of a complex crash gearbox. It was also more convenient than steam, which needed time to light up and build a head of steam.

At the Chicago World's Fair, held in 1893, six electric vehicles vied for the public's attention. Interestingly, the only American exhibit was a twelve-seater designed by William Morrison of Des Moines, Iowa, the rest being European in origin. The Morrison machine used twenty-four cells to power a 4bhp motor – enough for a top speed of 14mph (22km/h). The battery charging time was around ten hours.[2]

The American Battery Company of Chicago had bought the rights to the fringe-topped contraption in the hopes of manufacturing it. At the World's Fair, company president George Burroughs gave his youngest son, Edgar Rice Burroughs, the job of ferrying potential customers around the grounds. Edgar, of course, would go on to become a famous novelist and the creator of Tarzan. The vehicle certainly wowed the crowds who gathered to watch its progress.

On 28 November 1895, company secretary Harold Sturges entered a modified electric in a race organised by the *Chicago Times Herald*. Unfortunately, the combination of a 54-mile route (87km), from Chicago to Evanston and back again, and terrible weather, conspired against him. Despite having extra batteries, his vehicle was ill-prepared for several inches of fresh snow and drifts. It came to a halt in the slush and ice having covered less than a quarter of the route.

Another electric car – the Electrobat made by Henry Morris and Pedro Salom from Philadelphia – fell victim to the same malady and the race was won by a petrol-powered Duryea. The first automobile race had laid down an ominous marker: for all their smoothness and refinement, only an internal combustion engine could be relied upon to battle through to the end.[3]

Europe

From the earliest days, the French were enthusiastic supporters of electric power. At the time, France was the world's pre-eminent motor manufacturing nation, with literally dozens of car companies pandering to the whims of rich clients. One of the best known was Jeantaud, named after founder Charles Jeantaud, a coach-builder who made his first electric horseless carriage – fashioned from a Tilbury-style buggy – with the help of inventor Camille Faure. His first successful electric car was launched in 1894. *La Nature* magazine described it as a two-seat carriage and said the batteries, which weighed a not inconsiderable 450kg (992lb), were mounted beneath the seat. The 4hp motor was slowed by leather brake shoes acting on solid tyres. The driver steered via a tiller. Jeantaud's carriages used Fulmen accumulators that were protected by boxes. On a full charge the Jeantaud carriage was capable of an impressive 13mph (21km/h) top speed (about half that up a hill).

In 1895, *Scientific American* magazine quoted Jeantaud as saying: 'The electric carriage has a future, and already in London there is a firm which displays a sign saying they are prepared to charge accumulators of all sizes at any hour of the day or night.'

By the turn of the century his business was thriving and a Jeantaud was highly prized among wealthy Parisians. Anyone who couldn't afford their own Jeantaud could always experience one by hailing one of the company's electric taxicabs, which plied for trade on the city's streets and could carry two or three passengers. In a presentation to the prestigious Society of Civil Engineers of France, Jeantaud claimed the efficiency of electric cabs could solve the problem of travel in busy cities.

Jeantaud was keen to prove his vehicles in early competitions and a Jeantaud four-seater took part in the 1895 Paris–Bordeaux race, the only electric vehicle to enter. As the race involved a round trip of more than 700 miles (1,100km), the considerable problems of range had to be overcome. The company arranged for supplies of new batteries to be available at battery stations every 24 miles (15km), rather like a simple pit-stop.

Sadly, exhausted batteries proved to be the least of Charles Jeantaud's problems. His car was ruled out of the race early on when it encountered axle trouble near Orleans.

The company's competition cars were more successful in other speed and distance tests when Jeantaud showed them to be capable of covering 37 miles (60km) in less than four hours.

Jeantaud's cabs sat the driver up front – exposed to all weathers – while his passengers enjoyed a luxurious carriage behind. His two-seater phateon moved the driver high to the rear. The Frenchman was an innovator who experimented with separate motors driving the rear wheels and front wheel drive. According to *Scientific American* (November 1899), the latter used a single motor fixed in the centre of the chassis with a differential driving the two front wheels via bevel gearing. He was also an early pioneer of aerodynamics.

By the turn of the century, however, the internal combustion engine had developed to the point where it was a serious rival to the electric car. Determined not to see his vehicles eclipsed, Charles Jeantaud linked up with a dashing French racing driver and together they made history.

The Fastest Man on Earth

In 1898, magazine publisher M. Paul Meyan, who was also a founding member of the *Automobile Club de France*, persuaded the editor of *La France Automobile* to sponsor a timed hill climb competition at Chanteloup, 20 miles (32km) north of Paris. The event was held on 27 November 1898, over a tortuous course – more than a mile up a winding gradient as steep as one-in-twelve at certain points. Fifty-four cars turned up for the inaugural event.

Having seen what lay before them, seven pulled out on the spot leaving forty-seven drivers to fight for overall honours. The winning vehicle was driven by a Belgian named Camille Jenatzy, who had entered on impulse. His average speed was 17mph (27km/h) and the car was electric. In second place was a Bollee petrol-powered car.

Meyan was delighted by the time trial and the following week *La France Automobile* announced an international speed competition 'at the request of one of our distinguished friends'. The distinguished friend was, in fact, the swashbuckling Count Gaston de Chasseloup-Laubat, the younger brother of the Marquis de Chasseloup-Laubat, who had founded the *Automobile Club de France* with his friend the Count de Dion to indulge his passion for motor racing.

The date was set for 18 December but the course would be very different. The contest would be no hill climb. Instead, the contestants would fling their cars around a 1.2-mile (2,000m) stretch of the smoothest road in France in Acheres Park, between the towns of St Germain and Constans. Thanks to Napoleon, France was well blessed with long, straight roads, perfect for top-speed runs. The crowds that gathered that chilly morning would bear witness to history: the world's first land-speed record attempt.

Count Gaston Chasseloup-Laubat was confident of victory. His chain driven rear-wheel drive Jentaud electric racer made 40bhp – an enormous amount of power for 1898 – and, with its aerodynamic torpedo-shaped body, nothing was expected to touch it. To record his glorious triumph, the organizers laid on six timekeepers, each holding a carefully synchronized stopwatch, and a meticulously measured and marked stretch of road. The strip was divided into two. The first kilometre was for setting a standing start record, while the second was for a flying start figure. To ensure absolute accuracy, the organizers doubled up with two timekeepers at the start, two after the first kilometre and two at the end.

Four cars arrived to take up the challenge. They included a de Dion tricycle and two Bollees, but all eyes were on the menacing electric car. Although the bodywork was shaped like a boat, Chasseloup-Laubat didn't sit inside it. He actually perched on top of it, exposed to all manner of danger, with only his legs actually inside the tub. As the contenders prepared themselves the organizers explained the rules: all four would be timed over one standing kilometre and then, provided they were all still running, over the flying kilometre.

The Count was the last up and Paul Meyan himself gave the signal for the record attempt to begin. Hunched low over the horizontal steering wheel, Chasseloup-Laubat unleashed the full power of his car's Fulmen batteries and it whistled up the track, bouncing precariously on its quarter and half-elliptic springs front/rear and terribly thin tyres on coach-type wheels. The wait had been worth it. Chasseloup-Laubat cracked the kilometre in 57sec at an average speed of 39.34mph (63.13km/h) – shattering the record set just minutes earlier by a 3-litre Bollee by 6mph (9.6km/h). An electric car had shown itself to be superior to a noisy and smelly gasoline rival. The French were ecstatic and so was Charles Jeantaud. They had claimed an official record and Chasseloup-Laubat was hailed as the fastest man on earth.

Not everyone was so happy. News of the record enraged the winner of the Chanteloup hill-climb event, the Belgian inventor and electric car pioneer Camille Jenatzy.

Known to his friends as the *Le Diable Rouge*, or 'Red Devil', in honour of his formidable-looking ginger beard, Jenatzy came from a wealthy family. His father, Constant Jenatzy, was a successful manufacturer of rubber products and he had studied engineering. Jenatzy was a strong proponent of electric vehicles and had opened a manufacturing plant to build electric carriages and trucks for the fast emerging market in Paris. Following his success in the Chanteloup hill climb he was smitten by the thrill of motor racing.

When news of the French record reached him, Jenatzy responded with a challenge. In an open letter to *La France Automobile* he expressed dissatisfaction at not being at Acheres Park when Chasseloup-Laubat set his record time. Going further, he expressed certainty that had he been competing then a Belgian would hold the world record, not a French dandy. He was sure his car would have the legs on Chasseloup-Laubat's Jentaud. Jenatzy asked if the count would be prepared to pit his electric racer against one of his own creation? Naturally, the count accepted.

The stage was set for an epic duel between the pre-eminent electric cars of the day with a new world record as the prize. What followed was a series of high profile face-offs between the two drivers. Their record-breaking runs also helped publicize the cars manufactured by Jeantaud and Jenatzy. The first took place on 17 January, 1899.

As the challenger, Jenatzy went first. His confidence appeared well place when his car broke the standing kilometre at a stunning speed of 41.42mph (66.65km/h), comfortably faster than the count's car had managed a month earlier. Witnesses said the batteries in the Red Devil's car were exhausted as it crossed the line – in the best tradition of great racing cars they only lasted as long as was necessary to finish. Nevertheless, the world record had been broken for the first time and Jenatzy was the man to have done it. His celebrations were short-lived, however.

Within minutes, the Frenchman saddled up and sent his car bowling down the road recording an elapsed time of 43.69mph (70.31km/h). Many in the crowd feared Chasseloup-Laubat would die in his pursuit of the record, the human body having never travelled so fast. The count survived but the motor in his Jeantaud didn't – it was destroyed in the attempt.

Undaunted, Jenatzy vowed to return with an even more powerful electric car and wrest the record back for Belgium. Chasseloup-Laubat assured him he would defend French honour.

The Red Devil was true to his word and, when the bitter rivals next met at Acheres ten days later, Jenatzy took the honours (and the record) with a 49.92mph (80.33km/h) time. By this time, the battle for supremacy had become an international talking point. *The Automobile Club de France* appointed officials and marshals to scrutinize the trials and avoid any accusations of cheating.

With national honour at stake, Chasseloup-Laubat raised the bar to 57.60mph (92.69km/h) in March 1899. For his part, Jenatzy was confident he had a secret weapon, one that would put the count in his place once and for all. His car had a sophisticated chassis with semi-elliptic leaf springs front and rear. Its lightweight cigar-shaped wind-cheating body was designed around the aerodynamic principles used by airship manufacturers – although any wind-cheating benefit was largely invalidated by the driver sitting in the air stream and by the exposed

La Jamais Contente *(Never Satisfied): daredveil racer Camille Jenatzy built a streamlined record-breaker in his bid to become the fastest man alive.* MICHELIN

Jenatzy was an early pioneer of aerodynamic streamlining. The torpedo-like shape of La Jamais Contente, *manufactured from a lightweight aluminium, tungsten and magensium metal alloy called Partinium, can clearly be seen here.* MICHELIN

Jenatzy laps up the applause of the crowd after setting a new land-speed record of 105km/h. MICHELIN

Camille Jenatzy

Belgian civil engineer, Camille Jenatzy, was an early believer in the adage that 'racing improves the breed'.

Camille, who was born in 1865, advertised his electric cars by pitting them in competitions. He made his racing debut in 1898, winning a rain-soaked Chanteloup hill-climb by covering the 1,800m (1.1 mile) course at an average speed of 17mph (27km/h).

Jenatzy did not take part in the first speed trial held at Acheres, west of Paris, which set a new world land-speed record. When he heard the record had been set by the Count Gaston de Chasseloup-Laubat behind the wheel of a car built by Jeantaud, his bitter manufacturing rival, Jenatzy challenged the dashing French count to a rematch.

The two men traded speed records throughout the winter of 1899 – a contest finally decided in Jenatzy's favour when he became the first man to break the 100km/h (62mph) barrier – a record that would stand for three years.

Jenatzy's love of speed exceeded his love of electric vehicles. Realizing an electric racer would never be viable over a long distance, he turned to petrol–electric hybrid powertrains and competed in the 1900 Gordon Bennett Cup in a Bolide hybrid of his own design. He also patented a magnetic clutch, used by Rochet–Schneider for a short time.

Jenatzy led something of a charmed life, walking away from several massive accidents, including a huge crash at the Circuit des Ardennes in 1902 when his car slewed off the track and into a ditch.

He drove for Mercedes in 1903 and would probably have won the Paris–Madrid race but for (of all things) a fly in the carburettor. Putting that disappointment behind him, the same year he won the Gordon Bennett Cup for Germany, coming home twelve minutes ahead of the second-place car.

The Belgian had a very successful racing career and retired from international events in 1908.

Jenatzy also had a wicked sense of humour and his fondness for practical jokes cost him his life. In 1913, during a hunting party with friends in the Ardennes, Jenatzy decided to frighten his fellow hunters by creeping up to their lodge, hiding behind a bush and imitating the grunt of an angry wild boar. His impression was rather too good. One of the fearful guests leaned out of the window and shot the practical joker dead.

Doug Lambert attempts to speed record for an electric car at Elvington air field, near York, in 1989.

In January 2010, more than a century after Jenatzy set his record, Michelin used La Jamais Contente *at the Detroit Motor Show to publicize its part in the development of electric vehicles.*

chassis beneath. It was fashioned from 'partinium' – a new metal alloy of aluminium, tungsten and magnesium invented by a Frenchman called Henri Partin – and powered by a pair of DC Postel-Vinay 33hp (25kW) motors. The Michelin brothers, Edouard and Andre, pitched in with special pneumatic tyres designed to run on the car's 55cm (21.7in) wooden-spoked wheels.

Certain that he had the beating of his bitter rival, Jenatzy named his new challenger *La Jamais Contente* ('Never Satisfied') perhaps after his own frame of mind.

The high-speed battle commenced on 1 April, 1899. Perhaps it was over-confidence that led Jenatzy to start his first run too soon, or maybe he just couldn't wait to try his new machine out.

Whatever the reason, *La Jamais Contente* whistled down the timed kilometre before the officials were ready. Jenatzy was certain he had broken the psychologically important 100km/h (62mph) barrier, but due to his impatience there was nothing to prove it. Worse still, he did not have the luxury of a second run, having no spare batteries to hand. Jenatzy had to watch as the count set a new time. The Red Devil had a notoriously fiery temper (in his obituary *The New York Times* said that he raced with 'demonical fury') so one can only imagine his confrontation with the embarrassed timekeepers. Humiliated and angry, he vowed to return.

He did so on 29 April when, in front of a large crowd (including the Count Chasseloup-Laubat) he raced his car down the track. When the run was finished, Jenatzy, who was still smarting from the embarrassment of the debacle earlier in the month, jumped down from the car and strode over to the flustered timekeepers who were still working out his speed. After the timepieces were double-checked they announced he had set a new record of more than 105km/h (65mph). Jenatzy was ecstatic – he had become the first man to break the 100km/h (62mph) barrier and had done so with ease.

La Jamais Contente was a remarkable vehicle for its time – a pioneer of electric propulsion, direct drive (to reduce friction losses the motor was directly mounted on the driven axle) and aerodynamics, although not everyone was impressed. The author W. Worby Beaumont wrote with eery prescience:

> *This is without doubt a higher speed than any other human being has ever travelled on roads, but it was only for about three-quarters of a mile that it was maintained. This vehicle was of no use in any way as a guide for any other class of vehicle.*

Beaumont's prediction would prove to be correct – although that did not prevent other land-speed pioneers copying the bullet-shape of *La Jamais Contente* in a bid to grab the record for themselves. Jenatzy held the record for three years, until another Frenchman (Leon Serpollet) broke it in a steam-powered racer. However, his time for an electric car stood for more than half a century – a reflection, perhaps, of the electric vehicle's spectacular fall from grace in the subsequent two decades.

In 1989, the spirit of *La Jamais Contente* was resurrected for an attempt on the land-speed record for electric cars. A replica – called *Toujours Vitesse* – was driven by British enthusiast Doug Lambert at Elvington Air Field, near York.

The car was sponsored by Exide and the Merseyside and North Wales Electricity Board. However, that was to occur in the future. In 1899, electric cars were literally on top of the world.

CHAPTER TWO

ELECTRIC CABS AND THE ELECTRIC VEHICLE COMPANY

The Electrobat: the Electric Cab

Although electric cars were popular with wealthy private individuals, as the twentieth century dawned they enjoyed their greatest sales success as electric cabs. Electric 'horseless carriages' plied for trade in major cities across the world – and America in particular. For a time, their advantages of smooth running, reliability and simplicity appeared to be a winning combination and led to the first attempt to creation a truly nationwide personal transport infrastructure.

In America, the story really began in 1894 when business associates Henry Morris and Pedro Salom designed and built an electric vehicle in a mere two months. Morris, who was a mechanical engineer, based the design on lessons he had learned while working on battery-powered trams. He used a modified motor taken from a ship, a lead-acid battery slung as low as possible and carriage-style wheels. The vehicle, which was completely open rather like a wagon, had plenty of room for Morris and Salom and was steered via a tiller arrangement that controlled the rear wheels. It had carriage-style spoked wheels and side-mounted lamps. The first stunned pedestrians who saw it bouncing down the road in Morris's home city of Philadelphia must have though it looked like a runaway crate on four wheels. It certainly didn't have the attractive lines of a horse-drawn carriage.

Morris was the first to admit that his first electric carriage had allowed form to follow function – making the vehicle more attractive to prospective customers would come later. Instead, the duo's first electric vehicle was a proof-of-concept lash-up – a way of refining the mechanical design before moving on to more ambitious things.

The Electrobat: designed by Henry Morris, who used his knowledge of work on battery-powered trams to create a horseless carriage capable of transporting two people. The tiller-type steering can clearly be seen. AMERICA ON WHEELS MUSEUM, ALLENTOWN, PA

Altogether, the car weighed a hefty 4,250lb (1,927 kg), including the 1,600lb (725kg) battery pack. The claimed performance was 15mph (24km/h) and it had a scarcely believable 50-mile (80km) touring range.

For the first test ride on 31 August 1894, the two business partners had to apply for a special permit from City Hall and, rather like the red flag act in England, a policeman was detailed to walk in front of the whirring vehicle to warn horse-drawn carriages and pedestrians of what was coming their way.

Morris and Salom patented their idea the same day they took to the Philadelphia streets and their vehicle went into production the following year. Each vehicle was hand-built, rather like a horse-drawn carriage, and the partners were continually refining their ideas with the result that no two Electrobats were exactly the same (automobile mass production was still some way off). Later Electrobats used two 1.5bhp motors that were good for a 25-mile (40km) range and a top speed of 20mph (32km/h), which was plenty fast enough on the roads of the day. They were considerably lighter, too, thanks to a significant reduction in the weight of the battery from 1,600lb (725kg) to 640lb (290kg) – the fourth, and final, Electrobat ran on a battery that weighed a 'mere' 350lb (158kg). The reduction in weight meant the Electrobats were able to run on pneumatic tyres, rather than steel, for a more comfortable ride. The bodywork was built by the Charles Caffrey Carriage Company, in Camden, New Jersey, just across the Delaware River. The Caffrey Carriageworks also built steam vehicles including, in 1895, an intriguing four-wheel drive version with steam motors on each wheel. The motors could be selected together or individually via a lever.

The Electrobat was a modest success – despite not finishing, the second-generation Electrobat took the judges' medal at the Chicago Times-Herald Chicago-to-Evanston race in 1895 – but Morris and Salom had bigger plans for it. In 1896, they founded the Morris and Salom Electric Carriage and Wagon Company and continued to refine their design. They reckoned their invention would be the perfect inner-city hansom cab and set out to corner the market. By early 1897, a small fleet of Electrobat cabs were competing for business on the streets of New York. The passenger sat at the front, accessed via two outward swinging doors, and the driver sat on top and behind rather like his predecessor, the coachman. New Yorkers came to know the drivers as 'lightning cabbies' denoting the fact that their vehicles were powered by electricity. The novelty factor alone made battery-powered cabs popular with trendy travellers and they could be hired for a single trip, a day or even (if you really wanted to show off to your friends) an entire month. By June 1897, the Electrobats were doing steady business – making 632 journeys carrying 1,580 passengers and covering an impressive 4,603 miles (7,406km) in a single month.[4] The charges were the same as for a horse-drawn carriage: a dollar for the first two miles and fifty cents for each subsequent mile. If hired by the hour, a cab cost $1 per 60min. Soon electric cabs built by Morris and Salom were operating on the streets of London and Paris, too. Maximizing operational time was vitally important for a cab – lengthy recharge times would have made them financial non-starters – so the battery box was fitted to a roller tray. Entrepreneur Issac L. Rice, who took over in September 1897, refined the system. When the batteries ran low, the driver simply called into a charging station where it was removed and replaced in one smooth operation. The cab backed into a charging dock. Hydraulic rams lifted it up and held it in position with a loading table while the battery pack was rolled out. At the same time, an overhead crane swung a fresh battery pack into place on the table directly behind the cab. When everything was ready, a hydraulic ram pushed the 1,250lb (567kg) battery pack into the cab, where it automatically connected. A maintenance operator slammed the doors of the battery compartment closed before waving the cabbie on his way. If the operation went smoothly, an electric cab could be turned around and back on the streets in a few minutes. The contacts were made automatically as the tray locked into place and the circuit was completed by the driver turning a switch. A hand lever governed the top speed, which was a maximum of 15mph (24km/h). A conventional plug socket was also provided for recharging in an emergency or overnight.[5]

A feature in *American Machinist* on 8 July 1897, claimed:

> *The electric hansoms, offered for public use only since March 15th of this year, are meeting with public favour to the extent it is claimed of paying current expenses and leaving an actual profit, the rates of hire being the same as those of horse-drawn hansom cabs in New York City.*

Four months after they first took to the streets of New York, the business was already making money. Electric cabs were a hit.

Bersey Electric Cabs

Walter Bersey, a precocious 20-year-old who had designed his own dry battery, was the first businessman to introduce a 'self-propelled' vehicle for hire on the streets of London. His early cabs resembled horseless carriages with twin 3.5bhp Lundell-type motors, a two-speed gearbox (with clutch) and chain final drive. They were capable of a steady 9mph (14km/h) – more than enough to give them an edge over horse-drawn carriages. The forty-cell battery box was designed to slide out for quick changes – having encountered a problem, Bersey had found a way to engineer around it.

The public had their first glimpse of Bersey's cabs at a motor show in South Kensington in 1896 and a dozen were working for a living by August 1897. They even took part in the London to Brighton Emancipation Run in November 1896, but could not complete the route. Their batteries exhausted, the cabs ignominiously completed the route by train. Bersey contracted out the manufacture of his cabs to the Great Horseless Carriage Company (the bodies were made by Arthur Mulliner, of Northampton), and, at its peak, his company had more than seventy. His rates were competitive with horse-drawn cabs but the electrics boasted a level of luxury hitherto unknown – although the provision of electric lighting was not universally welcomed. Some passengers felt the internal lighting made them too conspicuous. They were nicked-named 'humming birds' for the sound their motors made as they drove by and their yellow and black paintwork.

A Bersey electric cab from 1897. The yellow and black coachwork made them a distinctive sight on the streets of London.

Unfortunately the business got off to a rather inauspicious start when, just three weeks after the humming birds first took flight, a cabbie was charged with driving while drunk. The intoxicated driver was trying to negotiate one of the busiest thoroughfares in London – Bond Street – when he hit a wall. Magistrates fined him 20 shillings.

Less than a month later, a far greater tragedy struck when a 9-year-old boy, who had hopped on the back to hitch a ride, was pulled under when his coat was snagged by the drive chain. The poor youngster became the first child in Britain to die in a motor accident. Edward Nichol, the cabbie, told the inquest at Hackney Coroner's court that the Bersey was doing no more than 5mph. A juryman suggested fitting guards between the wheels and the chassis. The cabs were operated by the London Electric Taxicab Co. and could carry four passengers plus a substantial amount of luggage" after "Taxicab Co."

Nor were the cabs a model of reliability. Long hours and heavy use exacted a heavy penalty on the batteries, which quickly wore out and ruined tyres with their weight.

In a bid to balance the books, Bersey was forced to charge drivers more to lease their electric cabs. The daily rate of six shillings (30p) soared to more than double that – prompting many cabbies to quit in disgust.[6]

Bersey responded by withdrawing the original fleet and replacing them with a new design that had improved batteries, but another highly publicized accident, when a Bersey ran out of control and crashed outside Hyde Park, was the final nail in the coffin. Faced with a hostile press, rising costs and fewer passengers, Walter threw in the towel. Some of his cabs were sold off at a cut price to independent cabbies, the rest were scrapped.

Other companies stepped into the breach. The Lambeth-based British Electromobile Company sought to take over where Bersey left off. It ordered a fifty-strong fleet of electric cabs. A Leeds engineering company built the chassis, which were fitted with bodies crafted by the famous Gloucester Wagon Company (among others). The cabs were operated by the London Electric Taxicab Co. and could carry four passengers plus a substantial amount of luggage.[7]

Originally, Electromobile – which also furnished the City of London police with an electric ambulance stationed at St Bartholomew's hospital – hoped to run a fleet of 200 such cabs and, for a while, they were rather successful, but the advent of petrol-engined cabs with their vastly improved range drove the electric taxi fleet off the roads by the 1920s.

Sadly, Bersey's dream of London taxi-cab domination was foiled by poor batteries and bad luck.

The Electromobile taxi service was popular among wealthy residents of London.

Here an Electromobile taxi is at the head of a queue in London 1907.

The Electric Vehicle Company

The early success of electric cabs in America brought Morris and Salom's invention to the attention of Isaac Leopold Rice, president of the Electric Storage Battery Company, of Philadelphia. Rice, a brilliant lawyer who had made his name saving ailing railroad companies from financial ruin, had snapped up many of the most promising patents on battery technology (at the turn of the twentieth century many American inventors made money by patenting ideas and selling them, rather than actually manufacturing anything). His company held more than 500 such patents, including Charles F. Brush's highly-prized patent on lead storage batteries, and had acquired them by snapping up rivals such as the Car Lighting and Power Company, the Lindstrom Brake Company and the Consolidated Railway Electric Lighting and Equipment Company. This relentless consolidation had made the Electric Storage Battery Company a highly successful enterprise, grossing its first million dollars in 1895 and installing batteries in the central power generating stations for cities across America. Rice enjoyed almost total domination of battery manufacturing and saw electric vehicles as a potential goldmine ripe for consolidation. Accordingly, he made Morris and Salom an offer they couldn't refuse and, on 27 September 1897, the Electric Carriage and Wagon Company became the Electric Vehicle Company.

Rice was in the perfect position: he manufactured the batteries and the vehicles. The Electric Vehicle Company had a guaranteed supply of discounted batteries from the Electric Storage Battery Company. Soon, improved Electrobat cabs were plying for trade in several major cities. In New York, operations were run out of an old indoor cycling rink on lower Broadway. The headquarters was hugely impressive, boasting a degree of integration hitherto unknown. The upper floor had space for 100 cabs and the lower was converted to be the charging area with space for 200 battery packs that were held in wooden racks. The company's business offices were located at the front of the building, while off-duty drivers had a place to relax at the rear. At each end of the battery room were massive elevators for raising and lowering cabs to the storeroom above. If a driver had finished his shift, and his carriage wasn't needed, it was moved aside in the battery room, washed and cleaned before being transferred to the upper floor via the rear elevator. The station eschewed its own electricity generator, preferring to take a supply from the Edison service. Rice took the company's consolidation a stage further when he bought the Consolidated Rubber Tire Company and was able to supply the vehicles with discounted tyres – something they required frequently due to the fact that the 3-inch pneumatic tyres of the day struggled to cope with the great weight of an electric vehicle. By 1899, the EVC's cabs were using 5-inch tyres made from half-inch robber hose and pumped to 60psi (414kPa).

Development of the cabs continued apace. *The Electric World* magazine noted:

> *Of the external and visible improvements over the old type, one is an increase in the height of the hood, the older vehicles being so low as to have an unprepossessingly 'squatty' appearance compared with horse drawn cabs.*

But a programme of near constant upgrades took their toll on the hard-pressed fleet managers. Cabs were built in batches of fifty and each batch was different. Nothing was interchangeable – not even the batteries – leading to on-going maintenance problems and a looming spare parts headache.

Then Rice had a stroke of good luck. New York was hit by blizzards in December 1897 and the bad weather continued into January 1899. The snow and hard-packed ice made it impossible for horse-drawn cabs to operate but their battery-operated rivals had no such problems. The heavy battery packs and 5-inch tyres meant they could carry on no matter how inclement the conditions. Dejected horse-drawn cab companies were forced off the road. They even advised desperate customers to try their electric rivals. Suddenly, everyone needed an electric cab. *Electrical World* magazine noted:

> *The cars ran through the whole night, the last coming in about 6 o'clock in the morning, by which time the snow had reached an average depth of about eight inches, and much more where drifted. Other cab companies turned over orders to the electric service rather than fill them themselves.*

Although the cabs seemed to be working fine, management cut down on their mileages as a precaution. The drivers were ordered to return to base for fresh batteries every 10 or 12 miles (16–20km). As one contemporary writer noted, the battery-operated vehicles were 'literally coining money'.

The EVC employed drivers to man its cabs – rather than lease the vehicles to owner-operators – and this seems to have caused problems because many of them had no prior experience of driving an electric cab. Battery maintenance was often neglected leading to high failure rates. The drivers were paid $2 a day, plus whatever tips they picked up from well-heeled passengers. In a bid to encourage greater productivity, the company also introduced a bonus scheme for drivers.

For all his acquisitive nature, Rice was, by most accounts, something of a benign business magnet. He was a keen chess player (the Rice Gambit is named after him) and a founder of the Poetry Society of America. When his electric submarine business ran aground during the financial panic of 1907, he covered many of its debts with his own money. Long after his death, the submarine business, and several others, would be consolidated into a new company called General Dynamics, which still remains one of the largest defence contractors in the world. Rice bought companies to combine them into a greater whole and had high hopes that the Electric Vehicle Company would be his greatest success. However, a syndicate of so-called electric-streetcar 'traction magnets', led by the politician, lawyer and businessman William C. Whitney, saw even greater potential in the EVC.

Whitney's crew was made up of very powerful men. Whitney himself was a former United States Secretary of the Navy and his associates included Peter A. B. Widener, the former city treasurer of Philadelphia, and the Wall Street financier Thomas F. Ryan. Whitney had a home on New York's exclusive Fifth Avenue and, as he sat looking out of a window during yet another blizzard in the big freeze of January 1899, he took note of how the electric cabs kept running when everything else was forced off the streets. The success of the little battery-powered cabs set Whitney thinking – could they be a beneficial adjunct to the syndicate's streetcar interests?

No doubt, they were also keen to get their hands on Rice's slew of battery patents in the hopes of creating another transport monopoly to go with their streetcar combine. Whitney envisaged creating a transport colossus with electric cabs and streetcars at its hub. The snow was still on the ground when Whitney and Ryan made their move and made Rice an offer he couldn't refuse.

On 21 February 1899, the Electric Vehicle Transportation Company was incorporated with a notional working capital of $25m. Whitney's consortium had to move quickly because it was already facing unwelcome competition from the Anglo-American Rapid Vehicle Company, a British syndicate that had held talks with the Studebaker Brothers about using their expertise to establish an electric taxi and light truck service in New York. With no time to lose, the EVC announced immediate plans to launch satellite operations in Chicago, Boston, Philadelphia (having incorporated the Philadelphia Motor Wagon Co. into the burgeoning EVC portfolio), as well as international services in London and Paris. To get the US franchises up and running as quickly as possible, cabs were sent from the existing fleet. Around forty were distributed between Chicago, Boston and Philadelphia. At the same time, the EVC was cranking out electric cabs as fast as it could make them at its New York factory. Motors were bought in from the Westinghouse company (they had a capacity of 2bhp at 700rpm) and Studebaker provided the bodies, meaning the production process was both fast and effective. By December 1899, the factory had completed an impressive fleet of 200 cabs built to the very latest specifications. In the same year, Whitney and his fellow financiers pulled off a deal to acquire the electric vehicle interests of the Pope Manufacturing Company of Hartford, Connecticut.

Colonel Albert Augustus Pope had made a mint from building bicycles and collecting on a number of cycle patents he held that forced other bicycle manufacturers to pay him royalties. At the height of cycling's popularity, Pope's factory was manufacturing around 250,000 bicycles every year under the Columbia brand name. Bicycles were more than just a business for Col. Pope. He was also a keen cyclist and a political lobbyist who fought for better roads on behalf of his fellow riders. Pope had started his business by importing Penny Farthings from Europe. Legend has it that during one trip to Paris he was shown a gasoline-powered car. Shaking his head in disbelief he turned to a friend and asked: 'Who would willingly sit atop an explosion?'. Other accounts attribute his comment to the moment when he was shown a prototype horseless carriage by one of his young engineers, Hiram Percy Maxim, who believed gasoline engines were the future. Whichever story is correct, there seems no doubt the Colonel was unconvinced by the internal combustion engine's commercial potential until it could be perfected. Maxim later claimed that Pope told him 'I believe this horseless carriage business will be one of the big businesses of the future' and said one of his biggest regrets was

A Riker electric taxi cab c.1900.

the fact the bicycle baron had died before he saw his prediction come true.

Pope was sufficiently impressed by Maxim to give him the go-ahead to begin design work on an electric car. As part of his research, Maxim crewed an Electrobat, built by the enterprising Philadelphia duo Henry Morris and Pedro Salom, in the Chicago Times–Herald race. Although the race was won by a gas car, Maxim concluded that 'only courageous men well equipped with tools, knowledge and spare parts' could take on such a crude machine.

Maxim had a working electric prototype ready the following April. Tests were conducted only at night in conditions of total secrecy and the Colonel set a provisional on-sale date of May 1897 for the first Columbia Electric Motor Carriage.

Despite the mounting excitement, Maxim, who was appointed chief engineer of the Columbia and Electric Vehicle Company, never really gave up on the internal combustion engine. Later, he would become famous as the inventor of the car exhaust muffler, which did so much to make noisy gasoline engines bearable. He also invented the pistol silencer – the sinister-looking black canister screwed on to the nose of pistol-packing assassins in dozens Hollywood thrillers.

The Columbia factory, located in Hartford, Connecticut, was the first commercially viable electric car concern. When the first electric carriages were ready – bang on the Colonel's provisional date of May 1897 – the unveiling was attended by celebrities such as John Jacob Astor and reported in newspapers and magazines as far afield as Great Britain. But the electric carriages were nothing without a charging infrastructure and so a service station was hurriedly opened in Newport. Wealthy motorists could hire a vehicle for $150 a month and were allotted a mileage allowance of 600 miles (960km). Drivers were also available for those too nervous, or too lazy, to get behind the wheel themselves. This was before any notion of a driving test and the results were predictably disastrous with accident write-offs aplenty. The design was also licensed for overseas production in Germany, France, Belgium and Austria. Between 1897 and the summer of 1899, Columbia manufactured several hundred vehicles for domestic and overseas markets.

Pope was the country's largest bicycle company and a prolific electric car manufacturer and, tantalizingly for Whitney and his backers, it had the capacity to build many more at its factory in Hartford. The deal – which came about after Whitney approached Col. Pope to discuss an order for several hundred cabs, then offered him a deal for the entire business – was concluded in April 1899. Pope split the automobile division of his company into a separate firm, the Columbia and Electric Vehicle Company, and then sold half of it to Whitney. The scale of the deal became apparent in the EVC annual report the same year, which said:

> *The Columbia and Electric Vehicle Company is in a position to furnish during the coming year an output of at least 8,000 automobiles, representing at present prices a gross business of $20,000,000. The exclusive right to purchase the entire output is assured by contract to the Electric Vehicle Company. By its half ownership of the stock of the Columbia and Electric Vehicle Company, the EVC becomes entitled to one half of the profits of manufacture, which in all cases are fixed at twenty per cent above cost, making the profit accruing to the EVC 10 per cent on the entire product.*

The next year Col. Pope sold out completely and the Columbia and Electric Vehicle Company became part of the rapidly expanding EVC empire, which also acquired the entire capital stock of the New Haven Carriage Company and its factory at New Haven. On 5 May 1899, the EVC purchased the Siemens and Halske Electric Company of America and *The New York Times* announced that the Chicago works would supply electrical components to its other plants for the construction of electric cabs.

Although Isaac L. Rice's New York factory had proved up to the job of batch production, the EVC consortium had much larger numbers in mind. Pope's Hartford manufacturing plant had both greater capacity and a more experienced workforce, giving it the edge over the cramped quarters in New York. If the EVC was to monopolize the market, Whitney and his investors needed overwhelming numerical superiority – a doctrine Whitney probably learned while serving as the US Secretary of the Navy under President Cleveland from 1885 to 1889 – so, in February 1900, the decision was taken to move production to Connecticut. The Hartford plant also had capacity to manufacture electric trucks and buses, another market identified by the EVC as ripe for exploitation. Whitney's grand vision was for Hartford to build electric taxis, buses, wagons and light trucks, the Electric Storage Battery Company (which later became Exide) would supply the batteries and the Electric Vehicle Company would operate them in towns and cities across North America and Europe. It was an ambitious plan but Whitney and his fellow investors had backed the wrong technology. Big strides were being made in the development of the internal combustion engine and, soon, the EVC would face formidable competition.

New York-based EVC continued to sell the Columbia and, by 1900, the Columbia and Electric Vehicle Company was based in the former Hartford bicycle factory, as well as the factory of the former New Haven Carriage Company, where the large proportion of bodies was made. According to an article in *Electrical World and Engineer* magazine, the company employed 1,500 men and it couldn't satisfy orders fast enough. The magazine commented:

> *It is an excellent commentary on the growth of the electric automobile business to note that the facilities... are crowded to their utmost capacity and, at present, there is not even a department of the Columbia works for the storage of finished vehicles. The product is shipped as fast as it is ready.*

Ever ready to bang the drum for electric automobiles, the article concluded:

> *In this country the electric automobile was the first to prove its claim for consideration on the score of convenience, economy and other desirable features. It is generally conceded that the electric vehicle in urban service, or for use where the mileage limitations of storage batteries need not be considered, has no rival. In this field it is not probable that either gasoline or steam vehicles can trespass.*

Consolidation Continues: the Riker Electric Motor Vehicle Company

The EVC continued its remorseless policy of consolidation. Before the end of the year the Riker Electric Motor Vehicle Company, of New Jersey, had been bought out.

Andrew Lawrence Riker had lashed together his first electric car by cannibalizing two Remington bicycle frames in 1894 with a metal cradle and a motor. Two years later, in 1896, he finished second to an electric vehicle entered by Morris and Salom in a heat for a closed-circuit dirt-track race held at Narragansett Park in Rhode Island. Despite bad weather, a crowd of 5,000 spectators gathered to watch the event. Riker's entrant made the fastest mile time of 2min 13sec, but the Morris and Salom vehicle had greater endurance. Scientific American magazine reported that Riker received the first prize of $900 and the runner-up prize of $450 went to Morris and Salom. Its report of the race went on:

> *The success of the electric carriages created some surprise, as it has been thought lately that motors using some form of petroleum were best adapted for horseless carriage use, and the electric motor has been somewhat discounted. The electric carriage has made a record for speed, and the great ease of control and the absence of noise and odour will commend it to those who are anxious to purchase horseless carriages, but whether they are adapted for long runs or not still remain to be proved.*

Riker was bitten by the racing bug. His electric vehicle performed with distinction in Boston (where it won the braking contest) and the first race meeting of the New York Automobile Racing Association held at Aquidneck Park on 6 September 1900.

However, Riker was not blind to the drawbacks of electric vehicles. *The Electrical World* magazine of 23 January 1897, reported an address Riker made to the American

Institute of Electrical Engineers in which he sounded a note of caution that contemporary battery technology was not sufficient for the electrically powered vehicle. Summing up, he told distinguished guests that such vehicles 'did not appear to be suitable for long-distance travelling, but would be principally successful as pleasure vehicles, where the short-lasting qualities would not be objectionable and where their many superior advantages would place them in a very superior position'. Riker set up a company to manufacture electric motors based on ideas he had patented, then quickly moved on to full-scale vehicle production. He used bicycle frames for light weight and strength.

Anxious to prove his inventions in competition, on 16 November 1901, his torpedo racer (named after its torpedo-like nose) set a new world speed record for electric cars in a speed trial held at Coney Island, New York. Riker managed to drag his car down the 1-mile dirt track straight in just 63sec. His record was unbroken for 10 years.

His company also manufactured a number of straightforward runabouts that could seat two people and were driven by two electric motors connected to the rear axle by spur gearing. Their maximum speed was 10mph (16km/h) and the battery pack was good for a range of 25 miles (40km). The wheels were shod with pneumatic tyres and the controller gave three forward speeds and two reverse. The upmarket phaeton deluxe model had been shown at the 1898 Paris automobile show. Riker also built four-seater carriages that were propelled by a pair of 3bhp motors of his own design, which gave a 12mph (19km/h) top speed. *The Electrical Engineer* of 9 September 1896 commented:

> *The carriage is admirably contrived and balanced and, while light to look at, moves with wonderful steadiness. It turns easily, moves forward or backward at a touch, and by having two motors is able to get along very well even if one of them should break down.*

By 1898, Riker had a full range – a two- and four-passenger trap, the posh phaeton, a victoria, a surrey, a wagon and a tricycle. With typical American modesty the vehicles were advertised as 'the last step in the perfection of automobiles'. The ads went on:

> *Vibration has been completely overcome; absolute control of speed and direction has been secured, every requirement of pleasure or business, every demand for beauty and service is supplied by the Riker electric vehicle.*

Not everyone was able to testify to the Riker's 'absolute control' as one amusing story in the London-based *Motor Car Journal* of 21 July 1899, attested. The writer, having bor-

An advert for Riker electric vehicles. The reality was sometimes rather different.

rowed a Riker from a Mr Frost-Smith, was travelling downhill by Highgate Station and overtaking another vehicle when a cyclist suddenly appeared in front of him. The innocent biker panicked at the sight of two horseless carriages charging toward him and tried to pass between them but, as the article put it, 'an accident was inevitable'. The report continues:

> *Our brake was jammed hard, the vehicle swerved, caught the kerb, travelled on two wheels for a yard or two, and then the driver and writer were both sent flying.... Quickly picking ourselves up and finding no bones broken, we gazed around, saw the car had been turned on its side, one wheel buckled, spokes bent and broken in another; the acid was pouring out in gallons and the wheels were revolving at great speed.*

The poor cyclist was pulled to his feet having suffered a severe scalp wound and lost the sole off one of his shoes. Luckily for all concerned the article concludes:

> *The accident happened opposite the Winchester Arms [a pub], and the landlord did all that a man could do to assist, and performed nobly the work of a 'Good Samaritan'.*

Presumably with free pints of beer all round.

It seems most likely that Whitney and the Electric Vehicle Company were interested in Riker's commercial vehicles. According to a feature in *The Horseless Age* (October 1898), the truck consisted of a tubular steel frame and a motor mounted on the rear axle, which rode on elliptic springs. The batteries were modular – fitted in crates that could be varied according to distance and load. Recharging was simple and the batteries cut themselves off when full. An automatic circuit-breaker beneath the seat disconnected the batteries in the event of an overload on the motor. Riker claimed a range of 25–30 miles (40–48km) and a top speed of 15mph (24km/h). The following year, the firm introduced a real workhorse: a delivery wagon which rode on wooden wheels and 3-inch solid rubber tyres (presumably because its weight would have burst conventional pneumatic tyres). The weight of the vehicle, which had a 68-inch wheelbase, was 3,600lb (1,633kg) and its carrying capacity 1,000lb (453kg), in addition to the driver and delivery man. Top speed from the twin motor set up was a modest 9mph (14km/h) and the range was

10 THE HORSELESS AGE.

INTERIOR OF BATTERY ROOM IN STATION

ELECTRIC HANSOM, SHOWING HYDRAULIC RAM FOR SIDE ALIGNMENT AND BATTERY IN POSITION FOR LOADING.

An article in Horseless Age *magazine shows the EVC's impressive charging station.*

said to be 30 miles (48km). Riker also marketed a mail wagon for postal deliveries, some of which were used in Washington DC for a time, and a delivery wagon, which was used to transport carbonated water in New York.

Such a tempting array of commercial vehicles made the company a natural fit for the EVC and at a meeting of the board of directors on 6 December 1900, Riker agreed to sell the company. Reporting the deal, *The New York Times* said:

> *The absorption of the Riker Company will give the Electric Vehicle Company, according to the statements of its officers, a complete monopoly of all the patents for manufacturing electric vehicles in this country, and will probably also give it control of all the patents for gasoline vehicles.*

No money changed hands. The takeover was a simple exchange of stock. As part of the deal, George H. Day, the former president of the Columbia Electric Vehicle Company, became president of the newly enlarged EVC.

The Rise and Fall

The EVC wasn't slow to put its grand plan into effect. Hartford was soon working on orders for thousands of electric vehicles and the company was expanding abroad.

To satisfy demand in Paris, the EVC built a charging station at 54 Avenue Montaigne, in the centre of the city, and acquired land for a second near the Arc de Triomphe. In March 1901, The Automobile Review reported how this second station would be capable of handling 150 carriages, as well as charging and conditioning hundreds of batteries. The cars were all privately owned, their drivers paid a fee for accommodation and maintenance.

In London, the company's agents were doing good business selling a range of vehicles to wealthy clients and even royalty (see Chapter 3). Hartford and Elizabethport built the running gear, while the bodies were sourced locally.

Back home in America, wealthy industrialists, socialites and politicians had taken the Columbia cars to their hearts. Indeed, when President Roosevelt took part in the first US presidential motorcade, in August 1902, he did so in an open Columbia Electric Victoria Phaeton. The President sat up front, accompanied by chairman Jacob L. Greene, with the nervous driver and a fellow footman perched behind them. The close protection security detail was provided by four policemen mounted on Columbia pedal cycles.

The cab business seemed to be doing well, too. As *The Horseless Age* commented:

> *Many aristocratic people have become partial to the motorcabs and employ them altogether for business and social routine. Some of them are so enthusiastic that they declare they will not bring their horses to the city for another winter, but will leave them at their country places.*

Despite the outward appearance of success, the EVC was in trouble. The taxi fleets were proving troublesome with a high rate of battery failures contributing to higher than expected running costs. They were also coming under pressure from gasoline-powered competitors that could run for hours, in marked contrast to the electric cabs, which needed regular battery swap outs at a convenient station. The first hint of difficulty came in 1900 when the company was forced to seek a capital injection to keep the business afloat. Shareholders, who had received an 8 per cent dividend the previous year and believed the business was in rude health, were shocked by the sudden reversal of fortunes. Nevertheless, the company was able to raise a significant amount of money via the syndicate's own State Trust Company.

As time went on it became more and more obvious that electric vehicles had been nothing more than an interesting development in the transition from horse-drawn carriages to cars powered by internal combustion engines. Even supporters of electric vehicles were forced to concede that their drawbacks would limit them to work in towns and cities, leaving longer out-of-town trips to the gasoline-powered competition. It looked as though the game was up. However, the EVC had one last ace card up its sleeve.

George Selden was a patent lawyer and a keen amateur inventor. During the day he worked for his father's legal firm, by night he disappeared into his basement workshop where he spent hours tinkering. Inspired by George Brayton's internal combustion engine, which was one of the major exhibits at the Philadelphia Centennial Exposition in 1876, Selden attempted to design a smaller, lighter and more reliable version. On 8 May 1879, he filed a patent application for not only the engine, but the idea of using an engine in a car. It wasn't until 5 November 1895, that the 17-year patent was finally granted but, when it was, the decision added legitimacy to Selden's claim to having invented the motor car. The delay in issuance, which was largely Selden's own doing, was important because it gave the fledgling motor industry time to catch up with Selden's ideas. By the time the patent was granted, cars were being built by small manufacturers throughout the United States and Selden believed he could demand a royalty payment on every one that used an internal combustion engine.

The Selden patent, which ran for 17 years, was a cause of some concern to Herman F. Cuntz, the engineer in charge of the patent department at the Pope Manufacturing Company. He warned management that its gasoline-powered vehicles, developed alongside the company's range of electrics, could be in violation of the patent.

However, Cuntz's fears were largely ignored until 1899 when Whitney arrived to discuss the terms of a merger. According to Cuntz, as the talks began to wind up Whitney asked if there were any outstanding patents that might cause trouble for the soon-to-be enlarged EVC, whereupon Cuntz produced a three-page list, which included details of the Selden patent.

However, Hiram Maxim, the brilliant inventor and engineer who was in charge of Pope's motor vehicle division, always maintained that his research into internal combustion engines led directly to the company taking an interest in the patent. Whichever story one chooses to believe, in late 1899 the EVC bought Selden's patent for a cash payment, a promised share of the royalties and a minimum payment of $5,000 a year. Whitney swooped when he heard that five other Wall Street speculators were planning to offer Selden $250,000 for the rights to his patent.

When the EVC ran into financial difficulties, Whitney dusted down the patent and used it as a legislative weapon against gasoline-powered rivals. The Horseless Age magazine, which never had a good word to write about the EVC, which it dubbed the 'Lead Cab Trust' due to Whitney's control of the Electric Storage Battery Company, condemned the move as 'grotesque'. In a damning editorial the magazine's editor wrote: 'If they have any saving sense of honour they will retire and leave the field to the mechanics and manufacturers to whom it rightfully belongs'. As John B. Rae, associate professor of history at the Massachusetts Institute of Technology, wrote in his paper on the EVC ('The Electric Vehicle Company: A Monopoly That Missed'), 'the EVC combine did not intend to enter the gasoline automobile field, but if it could levy a toll on all those who did produce such cars, then it stood to gain regardless of which type of automobile won out'.[8]

The consortium wasted no time in flexing its new legal muscles. In 1900, the EVC filed a lawsuit against the Winton Motor Carriage Company and the Buffalo Gasoline Motor Company in the US District Court. The choice of 'victims' was no accident. Founded in 1896 by Scotsman Alexander Winton, the Winton Motor Carriage Company was by 1900 the largest automobile manufacturer in America. The Buffalo Gasoline Motor Company was a major manufacturer of engines for marine, industrial and commercial applications. In a particularly mean-spirited move, the EVC also sued two firms chosen for their inability to fight back because they were little more than hobbyist ventures. It also sued a New York company, Smith and Mabley, which imported cars from Europe. By doing so the consortium had covered all bases.

Although both defendants resisted, by 1902 Winton's funds were running low and, having lost the first round, the company sued for peace. At the same time, the Manufacturers Mutual Association (MMA), a group of independent motor manufacturers that had banded together in a bid to ameliorate the threat of the Selden patent, opened negotiations. In March 1903, Winton and Buffalo Gasoline caved in and accepted the validity of the Selden patent. Winton became a member of the newly named Association of Licensed Automobile Manufacturers (ALAM), along with more than twenty other motor companies, and duly paid a discounted royalty on all its cars. Among the companies that coughed up were Packard, Cadillac, Oldsmobile, Peerless and Knox.

The ALAM and the EVC came to a cosy agreement. The EVC would collect the royalties and would pay two-fifths to the ALAM, one-fifth to Selden and keep the rest for itself. Any motor manufacturer wanting a Selden license, and a favourable royalty payment system, had to become a member of the ALAM. However, the group's high-handed attitude towards potential new members would prove to be its undoing.

In February 1903, Henry Ford applied for a license and membership. He was turned down flat. Ford tried again in the summer, around the same time as the Ford Motor Company was incorporated, but the result was the same. The official reason was that because Henry bought in components, his company was merely an assembler and not a true manufacturer. Ford's earlier ill-fated car companies were also cited as reasons for his unsuitability and questions were asked of his ability to meet the association's lofty manufacturing standards. The reasons were obviously spurious: almost every member of the ALAM used component suppliers in much the same way as Ford. The more likely explanation for the rejection is that Ford's plan to build an affordable automobile had his rivals running scared, particularly Frederick L. Smith, the ALAM's president, who was also secretary-treasurer of the Olds Company which was firmly in Ford's sights.

The decision to blackball Ford would prove to be an enormous mistake. The ALAM seized the initiative, taking out newspaper advertisements hailing its members as the true pioneers of the automobile and promising to prosecute anyone manufacturing, selling or even buying an unlicensed automobile. A lawsuit was filed on 22 October

1903, but, unlike Winton Motor, Ford had the resources to put up a fight. In the face of the association's aggressive advertising, Henry replied with a series of ads that promised to indemnify sales agents and buyers against prosecution for patent infringement – a guarantee backed by the company's $12m assets. In his biography, written in 1922, Ford claimed fewer than fifty buyers took him up on his offer. Taking a leaf out of the ALAM's book the ads weren't afraid to bend the truth, hailing Ford as a true pioneer and the first man to make a car in Detroit and only the third in the United States. Ford rejected the patent as 'a freak among alleged inventions'. He also enjoyed widespread public support. Many car buyers believed, correctly, that the patent fee was being passed on to them via higher prices and could see no reason why they should fund the EVC.

Ford became the bulwark with which other independent auto-makers resisted the ALAM and the EVC. In 1905, Ford and nineteen other car companies formed the American Motor Car Manufacturers' Association (AMCA) to defend the ALAM's litigious actions. The case dragged on for years. In 1907, the two opposing forces even built their own automobiles. The ALAM created a vehicle designed to the Selden patent to demonstrate that such a machine was viable. The defendants produced a similar machine with an engine designed to specifications patented by a French inventor in 1860 to show that the patent was spurious. Finally, after six years of argument, on 15 September 1909, presiding Judge Hon. C. M. Hough sided with Selden.

Summing up, the judge said:

> *Patents are granted for inventions. The inventor may use his discovery, or he may not, but no one else can use it for 17 years. That 17 years begins whenever the United States so decrees by its patent grant.*
>
> *Avoiding for the present the language of his original application, and the effect of the numerous changes therein during its many years in the Patent Office, was the thing fairly revealed by the model and drawings, and conceived under the circumstances above set forth,–the embodiment of a combination patentable in 1879?*
> *I think the answer is emphatically, yes.*

Discussing Selden's invention, the judge added:

> *[Mr Selden] does assert that he selected, adapted, modified, co-ordinated and organized the enumerated parts (including the usual mechanical adjuncts of each part) into a harmonious whole capable of results never before achieved, and of an importance best measured by the asserted fact, that after 30 years no gasoline motor car has been produced that does not depend for success on a selection and organization of parts, identical with or equivalent to that made by him in 1879.*
>
> *If I have correctly apprehended it, there was clearly room for a pioneer patent, and it must now be held that on its face and in view of the art, Selden's is such a patent. This means that Selden is entitled to a broad range of equivalents, and this rule as applied here results in this crucial inquiry: was Selden (or anyone else) entitled in 1879 to appropriate as one of the elements of any patentable combination a liquid hydro-carbon gas engine of the compression type?*
>
> *I think he was, and so was any other inventor, but he was the first so to do.*

Undaunted, Ford announced an immediate appeal but his determination to fight on was not shared by many of his AMCA partners. Within weeks, eight of them had signed deals with the ALAM. Five months later, the AMCA folded but Ford fought on alone. The Detroit Free Press labelled him 'Ford the fighter'.

Everything changed on 9 January 1911, when the appeal court handed down its decision: overturning the original judgement and handing Ford a stunning victory. Ironically, the battle had taken so long that Selden's patent only had one more year to run.

As for the Electric Vehicle Company, it didn't survive long enough to enjoy either the victory or suffer the ultimate agony of defeat. The financial panic of 1907, and the failure of its electric cab scheme, which more than swallowed up any income it received from royalties, saw both the EVC and the Pope Manufacturing Company collapse. The company had been living on borrowed time for several years. When Selden royalties failed to generate the bountiful income stream that had been anticipated (its best year was 1906 when income from the patent was $217,683.66), the EVC was a busted flush. When it threw in the towel, the company had cash assets of just $12,000.

The patent passed to the Columbia Motor Car Company, of Hartford, which went into receivership in 1912 after an ill-judged merger with the Maxwell–Briscoe Motor Company.

History has not treated the EVC sympathetically.

George Selden's 'explosive' motor wagon. The EVC turned patent troll in a bid to stave off impending financial disaster.

Author and historian Allan Nevins, who wrote a critically acclaimed biography of Henry Ford, condemned the Selden patent battle as the work of businessmen who had backed the wrong technology and tried to hold back the competition by litigation.[9] Historian John Rae was even more scathing. The EVC, he said, was a 'parasitical growth on the automobile industry, and its demise was regretted only by those unfortunate enough to hold its securities'.

Whatever the truth, when the EVC collapsed, any hopes of electric cars winning a large share of the emerging car market went with it. However, although the EVC had been the boldest electric vehicle company, it was far from the only one. At the turn of the century, dozens of small manufacturers were churning out electric cars and some were working on innovative ways of overcoming the problems associated with primitive batteries – the world's first hybrid vehicles.

CHAPTER THREE

THE GOLDEN AGE

Electric Cars: By Royal Command

The decade from 1900 to 1910 represented the Golden Age of electric cars. In the first year of the new century, nearly 40 per cent of the cars sold in the United States, the world's largest market, were electric. Gasoline-powered cars accounted for just 22 per cent.

Although development of the internal combustion engine was progressing swiftly, and manufacturers like Jenatzy and Jeantaud were well aware of the threat they posed, the electric car still held the upper hand, particularly in ease-of-use and refinement. The majority of car journeys took place in built-up areas, so early drivers had no range anxiety worries.

Electric cars had already seen off the challenge of steam-power, which required drivers to keep a close eye on the pressure gauge and needed regular top-ups to keep going.

The limited range of electric cars would only become an issue when smooth roads were built to link towns together – making longer trips not only viable, but also desirable. In 1900, routes outside urban areas were generally in poor condition and unsuitable for early automobiles of whatever persuasion.

Electric cars were also easier to drive. Manual transmissions of the era were sticky and difficult to master because they used straight-cut gears and had heavy clutches. Electric vehicles offered a largely fuss-free solution for pioneering motorists because they had no need of complex transmissions. They were relatively advanced, reliable and well-liked.

'The electric automobile is managed easily, is docile, has a noiseless motion and the motor itself is mounted in a very simple manner,' wrote *The Automobile* in 1905. 'Over petrol cars it has the advantages of easier starting, greater cleanliness and, perhaps, lower cost of upkeep. There is but little vibration with the electric automobile, no bad odour, and no consumption of energy whilst the car is stopped.'

Drawbacks? 'The inconveniences of electricity as automobile motive power are increase in dead weight carried, maintenance and renewal of accumulators. These... are lessened greatly in cars for town work.'

In May 1900, *The British Daily News* proclaimed electricity to be the future for automobiles. 'One cannot help thinking that the automobile carriage is destined to produce a change in the customs, character and ideas of society similar to that which the [replacement] of the stagecoach by the railway brought about,' began a report from the World's Show, held in Paris. 'Here [in Paris], for instance, is a comfortable, handsome carriage, seated for four people, and capable of doing nearly 40mph. [However] the family parties must be few who would care to fly over a country road at the rate of an express train. Half that speed might well content them.

'Of the four-wheeled variety of large electric carriage there are several examples, lightly and strongly built, tastefully designed, provided with hoods, splash-boards, footman's box and all the necessary apparatus. The guiding instrument (the steering) is placed on the right-hand side of the carriage.'

The paper was in no doubt electric cars would soon be good enough to tour Europe, replacing the traditional stagecoach-and-horses. '[The automobile] needs no horses, and it is cheap,' it went on. 'Your electric machine, of course, gets exhausted after a time, and must be replenished, but it never is tired and never needs a doctor.' For this prediction to come true, though, there would have to be established 'here, there and everywhere' depots for the supply of electrical energy.

Dozens of manufacturers sprang up to satisfy the demand for electric cars. Some, such as Oppermann, of London, Steinmetz of Baltimore, and the unlikely sounding Swiss company Triblehorn, only produced a small number of vehicles before they went bust, were taken over or gave up. Others, such as Columbia, Baker, Waverley, Studebaker, Rauch and Lang and Milburn, were among the largest motor manufacturers of the day. A few, like Lohner and Pieper, pioneered technology that would be refined by Toyota for the Prius hybrid nearly a century later.

All of these car manufacturers had two things in common: they were sure that electrical power was the future and that a breakthrough in battery technology was 'just around the corner'.

Indeed, by 1901 the electric car had become the first choice of Royalty. In 1896, the British company Thrupp & Maberley had built an electric 'carriage' for the Queen of Spain. Jeantaud received orders from Prince Strozzi, in Milan, the duchess of Alva, in Madrid, and Prince Galitzin, in St Petersburg.[10]

In Britain, Queen Alexandra took delivery of her first car in May 1901, from the City and Suburban Electric Carriage Company of Denman Street, Piccadilly Circus, in London. Edward VII's wife had the 'Electric Votiurette' shipped to Norfolk where she used it as her personal transportation in the grounds of the royal Sandringham estate. She even taught herself how to drive. Reporting the Queen's first drive, *The Evening Post* remarked:

> *Anything less like a Royal carriage it would be difficult to imagine. The floor level was several inches above the tops of the 28-inch wheels, and the vehicle looked top heavy and unsafe. There was no wind-screen, and practically no dash, but an enormous leather hood afforded moderate protection in bad weather.*[11]

Autocar was somewhat kinder. 'We understand that Her Majesty is in the habit of driving the vehicle herself, and is delighted with the ease and simplicity of control and manipulation,' it wrote on 25 May 1901.

The Queen's two-seater was luxuriously appointed. It was upholstered in dark green leather with a folding hood of polished grain hide lined with a dark green cloth. The black bodywork was highlighted with red pinstripes and the dashboard was also trimmed with patent leather. It

Queen Alexandra's electric car used as personal transportation on the Sandringham estate.

rode on bicycle pattern wire-spoked wheels with 3-inch pneumatic tyres and weighed, together with the batteries, 12cwt (612kg). According to *Autocar*, Her Majesty's car had a top speed of 12mph (19km/h) and a range of 40 miles (64km). Although the price isn't known, The Star newspaper stated on 27 September 1901, that: 'From a perusal of the builders' catalogue, such a vehicle could not be duplicated under a cost of £400'.

The Queen was so pleased with her choice that a couple of years later her son, the Prince of Wales (later to become King George V), acquired a town brougham, also manufactured to special order by City and Suburban. This vehicle benefited from developments in battery technology, which gave it increased capacity, a better range and a top speed of 16mph (25km/h).

Queen Alexandra's car was used by City and Suburban for publicity purposes, including an appearance on its stand at the 1901 show at the Agricultural Halls, in London. Thanks to royal patronage, the company reported that it had 'a number of orders in hand from members of the nobility of both sexes'.

Indeed, it had built a new seven-storey works in the heart of London's West End to sell, house and service its cars. The impressive 19,000ft^2 (1,765m^2) building, in Denman Street, close to Piccadilly Circus, had space for more than 100 electric carriages. The firm offered a premium service to wealthy clients similar to the horse-drawn carriage companies of the day. It not only sold electric cars outright, but for an annual fee of between 12 and 25 guineas, depending on the size of the vehicle, held them in storage, undertook all regular maintenance and took care of charging the batteries.

An article, written for the 1901 Automobile Club Show, explained the door-to-door service:

> *The cars will be run round to the house of the owner immediately on receipt of a telephone message, and will be run back to the station when the owner alights, fresh accumulators [batteries] put in, or fresh charge, as may be necessary. In the case of the theatre, the cars will not wait outside the theatre; the station will have notice when the piece is nearly over, and the car will be run round, or it can be had by telephone at any time. The charge is uniform for all sizes of vehicles and for all classes of users. The company propose to open depots wherever trade allows.*

The state of Britain's earthen roads was a source of royal consternation, however. Apparently, the dust kicked up by Queen Alexandra's car left Her Majesty in need of a good bath after every drive. As a result, the King and Queen decided they could only use the car when the roads were damp, which led to some hilarious attempts to solve the problem.

The *Evening Post* of Saturday, November 6 1926, reported:

> *Numerous patents were taken out, the most popular idea being to fit a large water-percolator on the back of a car. Some inventors were quite blind to the fact that dust was raised by air disturbance as well as by tire friction, and proposed to end the trouble by damping pads of absorbent material which should rest lightly on the tires, keeping the rubber mildly moist. Others regarded the problem as insoluble, and were content to suggest huge horizontal screens behind the car.*

Luckily for other road users, none of these crazy suggestions went beyond the patent stage.

City and Suburban manufactured vehicles under license from an American company – the Electric Carriage Company, of Hartford, in Connecticut – one of several that had made up the empire of Colonel Albert Augustus Pope. Although based on the popular Columbia design, in the UK they were mainly fitted with British-built bodies.

City and Suburban were popular with the upper-classes in London but the best-known British marque at the turn of the century was Electromobile, in Lambeth. Rather like City and Suburban, Electromobile licensed a foreign design – in this case a French front-wheel drive vehicle manufactured by Krieger – before refining the concept for British customers. The London-based company ditched front-wheel drive in favour of a motor in each rear wheel. This complex system was simplified for 1903 with a single motor mounted on the rear axle.

Limited sales led Electromobile to pursue a contract-hire scheme – although at an annual cost of £325 for a brougham (including batteries and maintenance) it was still beyond the reach of all but the very wealthy. Eventually the company gave up and moved into the London electric taxi business that had been recently vacated by Bersey. Its cabs continued to run well into the 1920s, long after demand for electric cars in Britain had dried up.

Big and Brash: the Battle for America

It was a very different story in America, where electric cars kept pace with the internal combustion competition until Ford's game-changing Model T arrived. Why was this? The greater urbanization of American cities made getting about in an electric car far easier and the electric car industry made a more determined effort to create a viable charging infrastructure. Electricity was widely available and recharging a battery overnight was a minor inconvenience compared to hand-cranking a cold internal combustion engine into life first thing on a morning.

As the world's largest manufacturer of horse-drawn carriages and harnesses, it was inevitable that Studebaker should take an interest in automobiles. The company built its first 'horseless vehicle' in the spring of 1897, when Frederick Fish, chairman of the executive committee, persuaded the company to put up $4,000 in development funds. By 1899, Studebaker was building bodies for third parties on a contractual basis. An early customer was the bicycle baron, Colonel Albert Augustus Pope, whose Columbia brand was one of the biggest names in electric cars. Three years later, Studebaker launched its own range of cars and trucks. The first electric carriage was sold to a Mr F. W. Blees, of Macon, on 12 February 1902. Its second customer was Thomas Edison. The vehicles, which were based on the company's earlier carriage designs, were manufactured at a factory in South Bend, Indiana.

In its first year Studebaker Electric sold a mere twenty 'electric runabouts'. Initially they only seated two people sitting side-by-side, but a larger four-passenger model was introduced in 1904 when production was in full swing. The handsome 1905 Victoria Phaeton was offered in gas and electric variants, the electric being for city and suburban driving with its softer springs, which gave a smoother drive on rough roads. The gasoline version was aimed at the adventurer who longed for a life on the open road.

Between 1904 and 1911, Studebaker Electric sold 1,841 electric vehicles (including electric buses) before abandoning the concept. The decision was announced in a terse statement that read:

> *The production of electric automobiles at South Bend has ended. It has been conducted for nine years without much success and, ultimately, the superiority of the gasoline engine is apparent.*

In Chicago, entrepreneur Clinton E. Woods founded the Woods Motor Vehicle Company in 1898, although its early attempts at building a carriage-style electric were flawed, to say the least. In 1900, it unveiled the curiously-named Spider, a horseless hansom carriage powered by a small electric motor mounted ahead of the rear wheels. The power was transmitted through a chain drive with differential pulleys.

Steering was via the front wheels and the driver nominally controlled the Spider via a curved tiller, which connected to the front wheels via two long rods running beneath the bench seat. As with so many horseless carriage designs of the period, the Spider's steering control was rudimentary at best. As the driver sat above and behind the passengers, the steering rods were both too long and too flexible. What worked well with a horse, didn't work with an electric motor set-up.

Several manufacturers noted this problem and moved the driver closer to the steering wheels. Later designs added gearing and extra linkages to better translate the driver's hand movement into steering effort.

As if the vague steering wasn't handicap enough, the Spider had another drawback. As it was a convertible, the driver's view of the road ahead was limited to a small window when the hood protecting the passengers was in place. In cold weather and rain, condensation made it

A City and Suburban electric Victoria from 1902.

A magazine advert for the Studebaker Victoria Phaeton.

almost impossible to see through. Woods quickly realized its mistake and revised the design, putting the driver ahead of his passengers. This was ironic given that the company's adverts for the original Spider said:

> *Don't wait for lower prices or 'improvements'! The Woods electrics today are reasonable in price and thoroughly effective twentieth-century automobiles – noiseless, odourless, free from danger. Their method of construction cannot be surpassed and the workmanship and material are of the finest quality.*

Buyers who fell for the sales pitch must have been annoyed when the company introduced a significantly improved model less than 12 months later.

Regardless of the Spider's drawbacks, Woods became well-known for applying its fine coach-building skills to electric vehicles. Many had electric side-lights (or lanterns), an illuminated interior and even electric 'foot warmers' for those chilly mornings. In other ways, however, Woods was behind the times. Its vehicles used wooden carriage-style wheels, when rivals like the Columbia were already exploiting the advantages of pneumatic tyres. Indeed, the heavy duty pneumatic tyres fitted to the Columbia Motor Carriage were a major selling point. Said to be good for 3,500 miles (5,600km), they were practically immune to the possibility of a puncture.

Columbia went head-to-head with Woods at the top of the market. Its electric brougham cost $3,500 and was fashioned from the finest materials for discriminating buyers. Silk curtains, a mirror, speaking tube (for communicating with the driver who sat outside like coachman) silver perfume bottles and an umbrella holder were standard. To avoid embarrassing breakdowns, there was a simple meter (dubbed the wattmeter) on the dashboard indicating the condition of the batteries. The company also devised a crude ignition key system – an aluminium safety plug, a bright red cap about the side of a cricket ball that was inserted into the main circuit, which, when removed, prevented the carriage from starting. It also doubled up as an emergency 'kill switch' in the event of an accident.

Colonel Pope, of course, sold Columbia to the Electric Vehicle Company – but he wasn't done with cars. He tried to re-enter the car market by acquiring several smaller vehicle companies and built several impressive models. Some, such as the Pope–Waverley Battery Wagon, used Edison batteries, which were more robust than other lead-acid designs. Others placed a greater emphasis on performance. The Pope–Waverley Tonneau of 1904 was fitted with twin electric motors that could produce 12bhp in a special 'overload mode' giving a top speed of 15mph (24km/h).

Despite these innovations, the colonel's new company never regained the market position he had once enjoyed. The days of low volume/high price production were drawing to a close and Pope declared bankruptcy in 1907, when his company could not pay debts of $4,306.30. Ironically, the Electric Vehicle Company also called in the receiver the same year.

Disaster on Staten Island: the Baker Torpedo

Just as a disillusioned Pope was contemplating bankruptcy, another American company, the Baker Motor Vehicle Company, in Cleveland, Ohio, was claiming to be the world's biggest manufacturer of electric cars. Founded by Walter C. Baker in 1899, with money from two businessmen who had made their fortunes selling sewing machines, the first Baker Runabout was a two-seater. It had a 0.75bhp motor that was fed by ten batteries. An early customer was Thomas Edison who was working on a new battery specifically for automotive applications. Having sampled the Runabout's measly 20-mile (32km) range, he redoubled his efforts.

Baker, however, was no slouch as an inventor himself and is credited with many discoveries, including the fully floating rear axle and the steering knuckle joint. New models followed and Baker's reputation for exceptional vehicles soon spread far and wide. The company was even commissioned to build a special for the King of Siam. No expense was spared: the side panels and front carried the royal crest, the body was finished in ivory and the folding soft-top was fashioned from white leather. All the metalwork was silver plated and the handles for the levers were crafted from pearl. Inside the finest clothes and materials were used, including lace tapestry and silk. No wonder Baker called its buyers: 'The aristocrats of motordom'.

Like Jenatzy in Europe, Baker hoped to prove the supremacy of electric power by setting a new land-speed record. The Baker Torpedo (which was built to Baker's own specifications and dubbed a 'freak' by newspapers) had a small tube-like pine body that was covered with a stretched oil-cloth skin. There was just enough room for the driver and a mechanic who sat in tandem in hammock-style seats. Their heads poked up above the shapely body into a fully enclosed cockpit and Baker looked out of a conning tower on the top with a six by two inch opening glazed with isinglass. His co-pilot, company chief mechanic C. A. Denzer, was kept very much in the dark. His job was to switch the battery as the car gained power.

The cells fed a Elwell–Parker motor, placed behind the cockpit rather like a modern Formula One racing car, which transmitted 12bhp to the rear wheels via a chain drive. The forty batteries were liberally scattered around the chassis. Most of them sat in front of the crew but lack of space dictated that some were behind their backs near the motor, and still more were sited behind the rear suspension. Sitting on its 36-inch wheels shod with 3-inch pneumatic tyres, the sleek-looking Torpedo was 18ft (5m) long and weighed a hefty 3,100lb (1,406kg). A coat of sinister black paint was probably good for an extra 10mph (16km/h).

Baker confidentially predicted that the Torpedo wouldn't so much break the world speed record as shatter it into little pieces, and chose the Automobile Club of America's speed event, at Staten Island Boulevard, in New York, to prove it.

Having witnessed record-breaking runs by twenty-four motorcycles and steam cars earlier in the day, the large crowd's anticipation was at fever pitch when the Baker Torpedo rolled up to the start line. With a quick salute and a pat on the back from Denzer, the Torpedo accelerated away down the mile-long straight.

Further down the track disaster awaited. Just below a slight kink in the road, at the junction of Lincoln Avenue and South Boulevard, the organizers had covered trolley lines with heavy layer of loose dirt that had been kicked up by the earlier runs. As the rails became exposed, the bikes and cars racing down the straight would buck and jolt as they crashed over them. Records were being smashed but gradually the crowd drifted to the place where, as one spectator put it, the cars 'were taking the hurdles'. Everyone was looking forward to seeing 'the demon' from Cleveland.

Another advertisement for the Studebaker range with prices starting at $1,110 for an electric 'runabout with top'.

Suddenly someone shouted 'Here she comes' and in the distance a cigar-shaped object appeared in a whirlwind of dust.

The New York Times of 1 June 1902 took up the story:

> *It was like a torpedo striking the water on leaving the tube of a battleship but it was apparent, even to the most inexperienced, that there was something the mat-*

Baker Torpedo

Motor: Elwell–Parker driving the rear wheels
Max power: 12bhp
Top speed: 130mph (208km/h) (claimed)
Drive: twin chain
Length: 216in (5,486mm)
Weight: 3,100lb (1,406kg)

> *ter. The racing machine was not keeping a straight course... but swerving from side-to-side.*
>
> *The fraction of a second before the machine struck the rails it moved in a straight line. Then it made a leap in the air like a deer shot through the heart when in full flight. It turned to the right, straight for the greatest number of the crowd. The machine swept to the left in a wide circle and tore up the left bank, throwing people there into the air as it swept them and the small trees before it, and then stopped, the two wheels on the right side being torn to pieces.*

To the side of the wrecked demon, Andrew Featherstone, a tax assessor from New Brighton, lay dead and several others were injured. Sixty-eight year old John Bogart died of his injuries later in hospital. In a bizarre scene, rescuers were serenaded by a ragtime band that struck up a jolly tune unaware of the disaster that had taken place. The bandsmen only stopped when police threatened to club them into submission.

Luckily for Baker and Denzer, the Torpedo was one of the first cars to have seatbelts – a factor that probably saved them from serious injury. 'Otherwise their brains must have been battered out against the ceiling or the forward machinery,' observed *The Times*.

Accounts differ as to what caused the tragedy. Some suggest spectators had strayed on to the track to get a better view of the speeding car and the wheel failed when Baker applied the brakes. Others say that Baker over-corrected on a slight bend in the track, snagging a wheel in a streetcar track and wrenching it loose. After an emotional reunion with his wife, the shaken driver and his battered mechanic left the scene for a nearby hotel where they were arrested for homicide. The charges were dropped when it became obvious the crowd had pushed through barricades set up for their own protection.

Sadly, the tragedy meant Baker's efforts went unrecognized. The driver said he believed the torpedo had reached 80mph (129km/h) before the accident and some accounts put the speed even higher at more than 100mph (129km/h). If so, then Baker undoubtedly smashed the record – it would be another two years before such a speed was officially recognized as a record. In the right conditions, Baker said, the Torpedo was capable of 130mph (209km/h). Although it was repaired – and even exhibited at Crystal Palace, in London, in 1903 – the would-be record-breaker was retired from competition. Baker tried again with another vehicle, the smaller and lighter Torpedo Kid, which had a similar layout minus the enclosed cockpit, but his efforts were always dogged by misfortune. So many things went wrong that he was dubbed 'Bad Luck Baker'. After another crash into spectators during a race, Baker gave up his motorsports career for good.

In stark contrast to his efforts at breaking records, the car manufacturing side of things was enjoying great success. In 1906, Baker made 800 cars, making it the largest electric vehicle manufacturer in the world at that time. Its advertisements claimed its factory was the largest in the world devoted exclusively to making electric automobiles. It modestly described the Baker Electric Brougham as 'the most exquisite creation known to the automobile world'. By the following year the company offered a seventeen-strong line-up of cars ranging from the Stanhope, a simple upgrade of the original Runabout, to the 'Inside Drive' (so named because the driver sat behind a windshield) Coupé.

Baker's impressive 50,000ft2 (4,645m2) showroom stood on the junction of East 71st Street and Euclid Avenue, the heart of Cleveland's 'Millionaire's Row'. The Arts and Crafts-style brick building boasted large windows revealing the oak panel wall showroom, where the various Baker automobiles stood on a ceramic tile floor and were floodlit at night. On the second floor there were small 'sleeping rooms' where exhausted chauffeurs could rest. At the rear there was a workshop where wealthy owners had their vehicles recharged. The showroom would outlive the company. After a period as a finishing shop, then a printers, it was redeveloped as a bio-tech lab and, in November 2010, became the first building in Ohio to be fitted with a public charging station for electric cars.[12]

Baker went on to join General Electric, where he eventually became Vice President, and helped create America's first national television standard as founder of the National Television System Committee.

In 1913, Baker ceded market leadership to Detroit Electric, and in 1915 it merged with another Cleveland car manufacturer, Rauch and Lang to become Baker, Rauch and Lang. The merger was something of a shotgun wedding as R & L had infringed Baker's patents. The last cars to carry the Baker name were made in 1916, although industrial truck production continued.

In Paris, the other hotbed of electric vehicle development in the early twentieth century, the Hautier Cab Company solved the hansom cab problem by the simple expedient of jacking the driver's seat up so that his eye line was above the roof of the cab. Hautiers were highly popular among wealthy Parisians at the turn of the century for their surprising turn of speed, silent running and novelty.

However, the threat posed by internal combustion engines was now very real – after a good deal of development it was becoming clear that gasoline offered infinitely more possibilities than battery power. Ironically, the man who would do more to kill off the electric car than any other would start out working for a company owned by Thomas Edison.

Henry Ford grew up on a farm in Dearborn and took a job at the Edison Illuminating Company, in Detroit. Ford quickly rose through the ranks to become chief engineer. In August 1896, he attended an Edison convention held at the Old Manhattan Beach Hotel, in Manhattan Beach, just a few miles from Coney Island. The conventions had become an annual event for chief engineers and managers of Edison plants to get together and discuss ideas. The great and the good sat at a large oval table with Edison at the head. To his right sat Charles Edgar, President of the Boston Edison Company, and next to him sat Ford.

During the afternoon the discussions turned to horseless carriages and the commercial opportunities of using electric power. Suddenly, Alexander Dow, President of the Detroit Edison Company, pointed across the table to Ford and said: 'There's a young fellow who has made a gas car'. The various engineers urged Ford to outline his theories and, as he did so, he noticed Edison taking a keen interest. Eventually, Ford was ushered to the head of the table where he sat next to the great inventor (who was decidedly deaf). Ford was grilled for information and resorted to sketching out his designs on the table.

As he outlined his plans for a gasoline-powered car, Edison suddenly brought his fist down on the table with a bang and said:

> *Young man, that's the thing; you have it. Electric cars must keep near to power stations. The storage battery is too heavy. Steam cars won't do, either, for they require a boiler and fire. Your car is self-contained – carries its own power plant – no fire, no boiler, no smoke and no steam. You have the thing. Keep at it. … No man up to then had given me any encouragement. I had hoped that I was headed right, sometimes I knew that I was, sometimes I only wondered if I was, but here all at once and out of a clear sky the greatest inventive genius in the world had given me complete approval. The man who knew most about electricity in the world had said that, for the purpose, my gas motor was better than any electric motor could be – it could go long distances, he said, and there would be stations to supply the cars with hydro-carbon. And this at a time when all the electrical engineers took it as an established fact that there would be nothing new and worthwhile that did not run by electricity.* [13]

Whether he knew it or not, Edison's thump on the table had been a wake-up call for Henry Ford, and dealt the electric car a fatal blow.

Thomas Edison

Thomas Edison (1847–1931), the so-called Wizard of Menlo Park (the township of New Jersey where he built his first industrial research lab), was arguably the greatest inventor of his day. Among the many innovations he is credited with discovering or developing are the incandescent electric light bulb, the power station, the voice-recording phonograph, the carbon microphone and the motion picture camera.

When he met Henry Ford, Edison was already a rich man thanks to his inventions and the success of the Edison Electric Light Company.

Although his hopes of building electric cars came to nothing, he did see electricity used to power trains. Shortly before he died, he rode in the cabin of the very first electric train to leave Hoboken, Hudson County, and helped drive it all the way to Dover, in New Jersey.

Bizarrely, Edison's 'last breath' is supposedly contained in a test tube held at the Henry Ford Museum, Ford having convinced the inventor's son Charles to seal a container of air from the room shortly after he passed away.

Range Anxiety and the First Hybrid Drives

Manufacturers of electric vehicles were already well aware of the drawbacks imposed by storage batteries and work was going on both sides of the Atlantic to find a way of solving the biggest problem of them all: how to extend the range-to-empty.

At the World Exhibition in Paris, in 1900, k.u.k. Hofwagenfabrik Ludwig Lohner & Co. unveiled the Lohner–Porsche. The car, called the Toujours-Contente, was the work of Lohner's chief designer, a young man called Ferdinand Porsche. As a fresh-faced 18-year-old, Porsche had caught a train from North Bohemia for Vienna, where he landed his first job working for the Bela Egger Electrical company. Although he had no formal education in engineering, Porsche showed a flair for design that caught the eye of his new employer. He had developed an almost friction-free drivetrain by mounting electric motors in the front wheel hubs. By using the rotation of the wheel as the rotor of a DC motor, Porsche was able to do away with gears and drive shafts.

His novel approach resulted in a motor that was 83 per cent efficient – perfect for an automotive application where batteries were still struggling to keep up with the ambitions of car designers. Within four years Porsche was promoted to head of the company's test department, where his flair brought him to the attention of Jacob Lohner, a coachbuilder with ambitions to become a car manufacturer.

Lohner was looking to develop a car as a way of making up for a slump in orders for his coaches. After he was rebuffed by Karl Benz and Gottlieb Daimler, Lohner decided to go it alone. His first attempt, with a French-made internal combustion engine, ended in ignominy when the block cracked after less than 15 minutes. After briefly flirting with Rudolf Diesel's then radical ideas for an internal combustion engine, Lohner partnered with Bela Egger to design and build an electric vehicle. Possibly because of his early setbacks with the technology, Lohner became a vocal critic of the gasoline-powered internal combustion engine and an early environmentalist. In 1898 he wrote:

> *Leave us 'world villagers' the last remnants of oxygen and clean air that our wonderful society has bestowed on us. This air is polluted ruthlessly by the combustion products of the growing number of gasoline engines.*[14]

The Baker torpedo set a new speed unofficial speed record but tragedy dogged the efforts of its creator Walter C. Baker.

The Lohner–Porsche – its front wheel hub mounted motors can clearly be seen.

The Lohner–Porsche was a revelation for the time. Its motors were housed in the wooden-spoke front wheels – one of the reasons why they each weighed a hefty 253lb (115kg). Each one was good for 2.5bhp at a mere 120rpm – enough to accelerate the first Lohner–Porsche to its 23mph (37km/h) top speed.

In September 1900, Lohner built a high-power sports special for the English gentleman racer E.W. Hart. The 4-ton monster, which was personally delivered by Ferdinand Porsche himself, had two extra motors acting on the rear axle – making it the first electric four-wheel drive car – and an enormous battery pack that had to be suspended on coil springs to protect the delicate cells. The one-off cost Hart 15,000 Austrian crowns – almost twice the price he had paid for a standard two-wheel drive car a few months earlier. They named the car *Le Toujours-Contente* (Forever Satisfied) possibly as a light-hearted dig at Camille Jenatzy whose car, Jamais Contente, was never satisfied.

Hart, who also sold cars and acted as Lohner–Porsche's British agent, said the car was 'speeded from five to fifty miles an hour, has four speed forward and two reverse with two electrical brakes, and is fitted with a special switch for recuperation of batteries while running down hill'. It apparently displayed 'wonderful speed when it was allowed to sprint' but the weight of its batteries proved a significant drawback.

In November 1900, Hart pitched his car into battle with Porsche himself at the wheel. The Automobile Club of Great Britain and Ireland organized a speed trial for electric cars at the Chiselhurst Electric Light Station just outside London. The car was innovative in other ways, too. It had powerful brakes front and back – an electric front brake and a mechanical strap-type brake acting on the rear wheels – so it stopped as well as it went. There was also a ratchet-type handbrake that operated on the rears to prevent the car rolling backwards when stopped on a hill.

Although the Lohner was fast, its vast weight exacted a terrible toll on the Continental pneumatic tyres. The test was run after torrential rain and the roads were "heavy in mud", according to a report. Porsche and his passenger rolled to a halt when the tyres burst after a disappointing 34 miles (54km). The winner, a French Krieger entered by the British and Foreign Electrical Vehicles Company, covered 59 miles (94.9km) at an average of 10mph (16km/h). Just to make things worse, Porsche came down with a terrible cold as a result of his efforts and could not continue the race.

Porsche built a high-powered version of his vehicle with four-wheel drive for competition but it proved too heavy for the pneumatic tyres.

Lohner sold around 300 all-electric vehicles to Porsche design.

The Semper Vivus was the world's first hybrid.

The hybrid's front-wheel drive motors can be seen in this photograph.

Nevertheless he bounced back in some style. He won the 1901 Exelberg Rally and a magazine reviewer commented the car showed 'no tendency to skid in sharp curves or on smooth, miry cobbles, or at least only momentarily, very much like being pulled by a horse, in which skidding is extremely short-lived and is rarely perceived as uncomfortable'.

Hart, who came from Luton, also produced his own light, electric two-seater called the Lutonia but its 2-bhp Bergmann electric motor paled beside the Lohner–Porsche. The motor was directly connected to the rear axle. Hart gave up on his own designs in 1901 to sell the Lohner–Porsche and Austro-Daimler electric vehicles before switching allegiance to cars powered by internal combustion.

Lohner company built around 300 all-electric Lohner–Porsche cars. Depending on the options, a wealthy owner specified they cost between 10,000 and 35,000 Austrian crowns. Lohner marketed it as a prestige vehicle only available to rich clients. Owners included the wealthy banker Baron Nathan Rothschild, early cinema pioneer Ludwig Stollwerck, Prince Egon von Furstenberg and the Viennese coffee magnet Julius Meinl.

However, the problems of weight and range vexed Porsche and in Autumn 1900 he set to work on a solution – a petrol–electric hybrid drive. The prototype, called the Semper Vivus (Always Alive), combined the electrical wheel-hub motors with two combustion engines, which drove an electric generator that supplied both the wheel-hub motors and accumulators. The twin-power solution required changes to the original layout. The original 74-cell accumulator was swapped for a smaller glass-bodied 44-cell battery, mounted on a separate sprung chassis, to free up enough room for a couple of water-cooled 3.5bhp de Dion single-cylinder petrol engines. These drove twin 2.5bhp generators, which provided 20A at 90V to power the wheel motors and charge the accumulator. Both engines operated independently and the generators could be used to start the petrol engines by the simple expedient of reversing their direction of rotation.

The Semper Vivus was hauled down from its theoretical maximum speed of 25mph (40km/h) by footbrake-operated external rear wheel-drum brakes. In an emergency, the current to the wheel motors could be reversed – albeit with catastrophic consequences for the front axle, as the torque abruptly changed direction.[15]

The Semper Vivus could run silently on battery power alone until they were drained, when the petrol engines could be engaged to recharge the cells.

Although the prototype was not without problems – it was heavy, the pneumatic tyres struggled to cope with the extra weight, the turning circle was 53ft (16m) and, because so much of the running gear was exposed to the elements, the accumulators suffered from dirt thrown up from the tyres – its potential was obvious.

Semper Vivus

Engine: 2 x single-cylinder de Dion combustion engines
Output: 2.5bhp per cylinder
Electric motor output: 2.7bhp per wheel
Top speed: 22mph (35km/h]
Range: 124 miles (200km)
Width: 73in (1,880mm)
Length: 132in (3,390mm)
Height: 72in (1,850mm)
Total weight: 1.7 tons
Front wheel weight: 598lb (272kg)
Track F: 53in (1,350mm)
Track R: 60in (1,540mm)
Wheelbase: 90in (2,310mm)
Ground clearance: 10in (250mm)

In 1901, the concept was ready for series production under the Lohner–Porsche Mixte name. An electrical generator beneath the front seats was connected via a driveshaft to a powerful 5.5-litre, 25bhp Daimler 4-cylinder combustion engine.

In the name of weight-saving, the Mixte used a relatively small battery, in a dust-proof housing, for intermediate energy storage and Porsche's wheel hub motors drove the fronts. In normal driving the petrol engine and generator ran at a constant speed, feeding the wheel-hub motors and battery with electricity at a constant voltage. The car also featured regenerative braking and, again, the generator also acted as a starter for the petrol engine. Incredibly, the Mixte weighed 1,322lb (600kg) less than just the battery pack in E.W. Hart's racer built just a year earlier. However, the reduction in battery size also reduced the car's ability to travel far solely on electrical power.

Lohner sold five Mixte cars in 1901 at a price of approximately 14,000 krone each. One of these early adopters was Emil Jellinek, the well-known agent of the Daimler engine company in Stuttgart-Untertürkheim and the inspiration behind the first Mercedes, which had been named after his daughter. Sadly, hopes of a Mercedes engine supply arrangement came to nothing and only seven Lohner–Porsches with Daimler engines were built. From 1903, the company switched to petrol engines from the French company Panhard et Levassor, which had licensed the Mixte design from Lohner for France, Great Britain and Italy.

Porsche continued to refine the concept, both for reasons of improved performance and reduced cost. The pure electric drive mode was dropped, the battery was cut down to a size required for the starter motor and the generator was fitted with an electro-mechanical speed regulator. A redesigned wheel hub allowed the kingpins to be located closer to the centre of the wheel, reducing steering effort and wheel deflection on poorly surfaced roads.

Porsche raced a two-seat Mixte car incorporating these improvements in 1902 and, in a mountain race at Exelberg, near Vienna, he emerged victorious in the large car class. In the Autumn of the same year, he acted as chauffeur to the infamous Austrian Archduke Franz Ferdinand who rode in a Lohner–Porsche with a touring body during military manoeuvres. His Imperial Majesty took the time afterwards to write a brief thank you letter to Porsche expressing his satisfaction at the drive.

Despite the publicity garnered by a successful racing campaign and high-profile demonstrations, sales of the

Lohner's hopes for the Mixte ultimately came to nothing but the car was a tantalizing glimpse of the future and Porsche's wheel-hub motors would be used by NASA.

The spirit of the Semper Vivus lives on in the twenty-first century with the Porsche Cayenne hybrid.

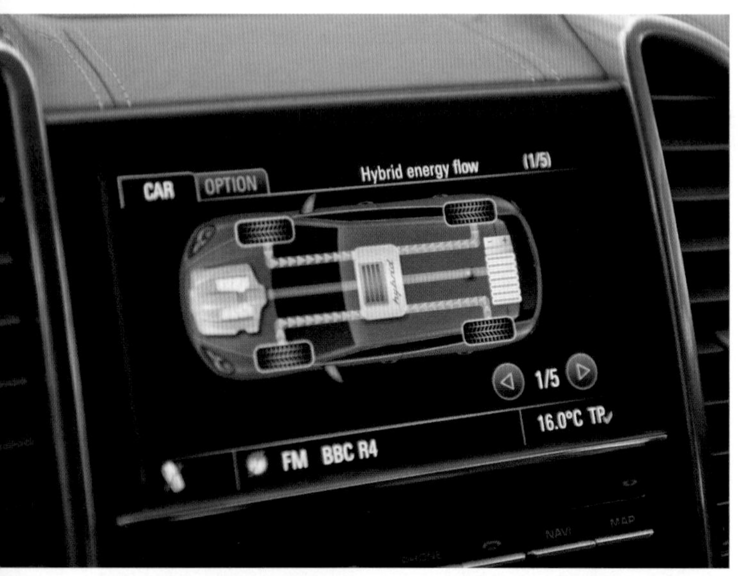

The Cayenne's hybrid drive is somewhat more sophisticated than the Semper Vivus.

Ferdinand Porsche

Ferdinand Porsche was born in Mattersdorf, in what was then North Bohemia, in 1875. He was an excellent mechanical engineer, although the only formal engineering education he ever had was sneaking into night classes at the Vienna Technical University.

After working for Jacob Lohner, the young Porsche spent time at Austro-Daimler and the Daimler parent company before he left to set up an automotive consultancy. Porsche created Germany's answer to the Ford Model T – the 'Volkswagen' – developed under a contract with the Third Reich. He also created the infamous Auto Union Grand Prix cars, which won races and set land-speed records.

After a spell in prison at the end of the war, when the company was run by his son, Ferry, Porsche returned and oversaw production of the Type 356 – the first Porsche sports car.

In November 1950, shortly after celebrating his 75th birthday, Porsche suffered a devastating stroke. He never recovered and died on 30 January 1952, leaving behind a sporting legacy that endures to this day.

Lohner–Porsche Mixte were way below the company's expectations. Only eleven examples were sold – a poor return for 5 years of hard work and a substantial investment. The car's technical excellence meant it was hideously expensive – depending on equipment, a Lohner–Porsche Mixte cost between 14,400 and 34,028 krone, making it twice the price of a conventional car. In addition, the complexity of the powertrain meant each one needed careful, and expensive, maintenance if it was to operate reliably.

If the Mixte was a sales flop at least Lohner saw a modest return on the full electric vehicle. Approximately sixty-five Lohner–Porsche electric cars were sold during the first 5 years of series production to the end of 1905.

Porsche himself had the last laugh: 60 years later his hub motor design would be revisited by NASA scientists and the concept was used in the lunar rover.

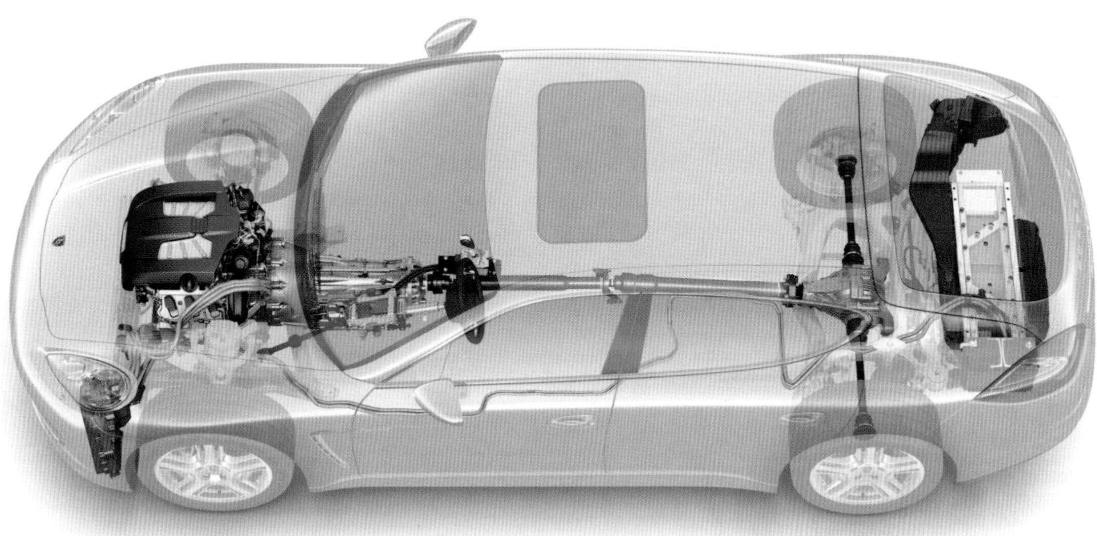

The new look Imperia promises supercar performance and supermini running costs.

In 1905, Porsche was awarded the Potting Prize as Austria's most outstanding automotive engineer in recognition of his groundbreaking efforts. Sadly for the Lohner company, Porsche's growing reputation had brought him to the attention of other car manufacturers, and the following year he departed for Daimler–Benz. A disappointed Jacob Lohner said prophetically: 'He is very young, but is a man with a big career before him. You will hear of him again.'

Today, Ferdinand Porsche's spirit lives on at the company that bears his name. In 2011, Porsche's first production hybrid, the Cayenne S SUV, went on sale across the world. Its power comes primarily from a supercharged 3.0V6 with direct fuel injection boosted by a 53bhp electric motor. However, the Cayenne can also drive in full electric mode and in the so-called 'sailing' mode the combustion engine is switched off and disengaged at high speeds. Maximum combined output is 374bhp and peak torque of 405lb ft (550Nm) at 1,500rpm, yet it consumes less than 9ltr/100km – equal to CO_2 emissions of less than 210g/km. The same parallel full hybrid system has also been adapted for use in the Panamera grand touring car and Porsche engineers are busy developing a 911 GT3 hybrid race car for competition, as well as the 918 Spyder plug-in supercar first shown at the Geneva Auto Show in 2010.

The Imperia GP can run on its internal combustion engine or electricity. A full battery charge takes four-and-a-half hours from an ordinary household plug.

Other Hybrids

Several manufacturers followed Lohner's lead by developing their own hybrid drive systems. The Krieger Hybrid, made by the Paris Electric Car Company in 1903, was almost identical to Porsche's car.

More interesting was the Auto-Mixte, which was made in Belgium from 1906 and used a 24bhp combustion engine, which drove a dynamo via a magnetic disc clutch that was connected to a transmission, which drove the rear wheels via a chain. Regenerative braking helped charge twenty-eight batteries in series, which, under heavy load, could be switched to assist the engine. The car could operate on electric power alone – a mode selected via a hand controller that operated a series of mechanical switches and relays. The dynamo could also be spun backward, acting as a crude electric reverse gear.

This innovative system was licensed from inventor and gunmaker Henri Pieper who had taken the hybrid concept to a new level.

Pieper's patent application, submitted on 23 November 1905 and granted on 2 March 1909, reveals advanced thinking on parallel-hybrid design that would be dusted down and used in cars like the Toyota Prius a century later. In particular, Pieper realized it was possible to use both electric and combustion power at the same time, as a means of increasing performance. The patent says:

> *The invention comprises an internal combustion or similar engine, a dynamo motor direct connected... and a storage battery in circuit with the dynamo, these elements being cooperatively related so that the dynamo motor may be run as a motor by the electrical energy stored in the [battery] to start the engine or to furnish a portion of the power delivered by the set. [It] may be run as a generator by the engine, when the power of the latter is in excess of that demanded, and caused to store energy in the [battery]. As long as the amount of power required falls short of that developed by the engine, the excess is utilized in charging the secondary battery. As soon, however, as an increase in propulsion power is required, as will happen, for example, whenever the car encounters an up-grade, the slackening of the speed causes the dynamo to work as a motor, thus supplying the engine with the additional power which it requires to keep an approximately uniform speed.*

Pieper's drivetrain was very sophisticated for the time. The driver selected various engine modes via a hand-lever. The first used the dynamo to start the engine, another used the battery to supplement the engine and a third charged the battery. In each case the spark timing and fuel/air mixture were adjusted according to the mode – Pieper had created the world's first engine-management system.

Sadly for Pieper, his brilliant invention was largely ignored by car manufacturers of the day. If his design had been taken up by a major manufacturer, the parallel-hybrid could easily have become the de facto worldwide automobile standard.

Pieper may have been a genius but the only luck he had was bad luck. By the time the patent was granted, the first Model T Ford had already delivered a decisive blow in the battle for market supremacy between electric and internal combustion engines. Only a handful of Auto-Mixte vehicles were built in Liege between 1906 and 1913. The Peiper factory was taken over by another Belgian vehicle manufacturer, Imperia, in 1907 and used for the production of gasoline-powered cars. In a strange case of history coming full circle, in 2009 the Imperia name was revived for a new roadster – to be powered by a parallel-hybrid

At the same time as Pieper was trying to get his ideas off the ground, Daimler–Benz – anxious to capitalize on the ideas of its new chief engineer Ferdinand Porsche – was preparing a hybrid of its own. The Mercedes Mixte, which was built by the group's Austrian affiliate, used various gasoline engines, which were permanently coupled to a six-pole dynamo by means of a drive shaft. The dynamo's electricity was transmitted to a pair of Porsche wheel hub motors. The Mercedes vehicle used rear-wheel drive (although a few fire engines were apparently built using front-mounted motors similar to the original Lohner–Porsche design) and, although Porsche had refined the concept to make them slimmer, several reporters at the Vienna motor show in 1907 were less than impressed. One wag dubbed them 'dumplings' and wrote that they spoiled the aesthetic beauty of the car.

Possibly stung by this criticism, Porsche soon had a Mixte race car up and running. The generator was powered by a 55bhp combustion engine and uprated wheel hub motors transmitted the power to the track. Sadly, the Mixte racer skidded off the track during tests and was badly damaged. Porsche quit Austro-Daimler in 1923 after a bitter row over the company's future direction.

Although the Imperia GP is distantly related to the early days of the electric car, it uses the very latest battery technology for stunning performance.

Another publicity shot of the Imperia GP.

Beyond Europe, other manufacturers were exploring the benefits of hybrid power. In Canada, the Galt Motor Company of Ontario, used a simple two-stroke engine to drive a 90A Westinghouse generator. Chicago-based Woods – the company formed by MIT grad Clinton Edgar Woods – introduced a 'dual power' car in 1916. This used a 4-cylinder Continental engine coupled to an electric motor and cost $2,700. The top speed was 35mph (56km/h).

Even as late as 1921, Owen Magnetic's Model 60 Touring was still banging the drum for petro-electric drive, with its innovative electromagnetic transmission (the work of George Westinghouse). The Model 60 was powered by an in-line 6-cylinder gasoline engine, which drove a flywheel that had six coils spinning inside an iron housing connected to the driveshaft. Amazingly, there was no direct connection between the engine and the wheels. Instead, the coils created a magnetic field that turned a generator. By all accounts, the transmission seems to have been rather like the Chevrolet Volt when in petrol assist mode – the engine note would stay the same as the speed rose. The lack of a mechanical connection gave a smoother drive, too. It may sound simple but, with so many fragile parts that could go wrong, the electro-magnetic transmission was hugely expensive to manufacture. Its fiendish complexity and high price meant only the very wealthy could afford the benefits of an Owen Magnetic hybrid driveline. Such knowledge was scant consolation in the event of a magnetic drivetrain breakdown.

Edison–Ford: What Might Have Been

Despite Thomas Edison's exhortations to a young Henry Ford that internal combustion was 'the thing', the brilliant inventor hadn't given up on the idea of the electric car. His first effort, built in 1895, was a single-seat three-wheeler – two at the front and one at the back – powered by two electric motors that produced 5bhp. The design never caught on, not least because the car had to be steered like a boat – a tiller arrangement moved the rear wheel – rather than the easier-to-master front-wheel steering.

Regardless of the design drawbacks, Edison was convinced only a breakthrough in battery technology could make electric vehicles viable. Nevertheless, he was convinced such a breakthrough was achievable and, as he beavered away in West Orange, New Jersey, he forecast: 'In 15 years, more electricity will be sold for electric vehicles than for light'. To prove the point, Edison's wife Mina was often seen taking her electric car for a spin running errands and socializing.[16]

By 1903, Edison had created a nickel-iron battery for automotive applications and retro-fitted them to four large touring cars. No doubt mindful of the commercial potential if electric cars were to be successful, Edison became a voluble proponent of electric propulsion. He rightly pointed out how easy they were to drive ('There are no whirring and grinding gears with their numerous levers to confuse,' he said) and how refined the powertrain would seem (although his reference to the 'terrifying uncertain throb and whirr of the powerful combustion engine' seemed like hyperbole even back then).

Edison and Henry Ford had become firm friends since their meeting at the Old Manhattan Beach Hotel a few years earlier and the famous inventor still had the motor magnet's ear. In 1901, The Atlanta Constitution, published an intriguing article about Edison's plans to collaborate with Ford on an electric vehicle. The inventor told the paper he hoped owners would be able to recharge their cars at plug-in battery stations alongside trolley bus lines. Rather more fancifully, he also hoped batteries could be recharged at home via a small windmill coupled to a generator.

On 16 October 1910, a report in *The New York Times* by J. R. Anderson Junior revealed:

> *Two electromobiles equipped with Thomas Edison's new storage battery have completed their thousand-mile endurance run over the well known 'ideal tour'. Not only this, but as a side issue they have made seven of the eight mile climbs up Mount Washington, being prevented from continuing to the very top by rain, hail and heavy winds.*

The cars 'of Bailey and Detroit manufacture' were driven by a two-man crew and carried a selection of tools should the 2.5bhp motor give trouble and extra tyres. They started their proving run from the Touring Club of America, on Broadway and 76th Street, in New York City. One car took the shore route and the other drove inland.

On the third night, the Bailey reached Manchester, Vermont, where it was confronted with the Peru Mountain, part of the Green mountain range in southern Vermont.

The article said:

> *The owners of large gasoline cars laughed at the little car when informed by the crew what they were about to attempt, saying that it was an impossible feat to accomplish. Nevertheless they went over in fine shape and arrived in Sprinfield, Vt, the next evening.*

In the meantime, the Detroit car was sprinting along the Massachusetts and Maine coasts, from Boston through Lynn to Portsmouth. Both cars eventually met up at the Mount Washington Hotel slightly behind schedule due to delays caused by recharging their batteries because they couldn't find a plug. By way of explanation, *The New York Times* offered:

> *As one must realize, on this maiden trip through these parts, the electric being practically an unknown type, all conveniences were not at hand for recharging.*

Flushed by their success, and the schedule having gone out the window, at Bretton Woods it was decided to depart from the original plan and try for the summit of Mount Washington – the so-called 'climb to the clouds'. The cars were taken to Jackson, the nearest town capable of charging their batteries, fully charged and taken to Glen, at the foot of the summit. By this time the weather was closing in, so the crews decided to stay in a local hotel and make their attempt the following morning.

As the two vehicles pushed up the following morning, J. R. Anderson Junior described how it felt:

> *Fancy climbing 6,000 feet into the air, the clouds billowing beneath one the entire time, great banks like ocean breakers rolling in from every direction. The effect was weird in the extreme.*

Word had spread about the electric ascent. The manager of the Mount Washington Hotel kept in touch with the summit via phone and posted regular bulletins for excited guests.

If the ascent had started in beautiful weather, their luck was not to hold. Both cars had to contend with driving rain and strong winds as a storm swept over the mountain, forcing them to abandon their attempt to reach the very summit and return to the hotel. The cars had proved a point, however, and were able to complete the round trip to New York in triumph.

Certainly, J. R. Anderson Jnr was convinced that cars using Edison's new batteries were the future. He wrote:

> *This trip can safely be said to be merely a forerunner of greater achievements the electromobile is bound to make.... Her big sister, the gasoline car, is always more or less noisy, 'smelly', and, as she grows older, inclined to show a great deal of vibration. Not so with the little electric, no cranking, no odour or noise, no thrashing of a reciprocating engine, merely the steady rotary pull of her little motor which, small as it seems, does the work at hand.*
>
> *This trip... goes to prove that the long-talked-of Edison battery is no longer a myth, but an accomplished fact, not to be scoffed at, but to be regarded with awe and serious interest.*

Edison's battery breakthrough was a development of the nickel-iron cell invented by Waldemar Junger, the Swedish designer who also created the nickel-cadmium battery. Junger had abandoned nickel-iron due to its low efficiency and poor charge retention, but Edison persevered. In 1901, he described nickel-iron as 'far superior to batteries using lead plates and acid'. He was right, too. The nickel-iron battery he created specifically for transport applications had greater energy density than the lead-acid batteries that were in widespread use at the time. They could also be recharged in half the time and were far more robust – lasting for longer before the charge–recharge cycle took its toll. However, they performed poorly in cold weather (the report of the ascent of Mount Washington briefly mentions the cars' inability to achieve Edison's claims of a 100-mile (160km) range, which were put down to the poor climatic conditions) and, initially at least, were more expensive.

Edison spent $1.7m developing his new batteries and building a 200,000ft2 (18,000m2) factory to make them. Although take-up for cars was slow, the new cells were embraced by commercial manufacturers looking for a robust battery that didn't give trouble. They were used in battery-operated trams, trucks and for lighting railroad cars. Later, they were widely used in the US Navy's submarines because they gave off no toxic fumes – something for which Edison received the Distinguished Service Medal.

One of the first cars to use the Edison battery was the Detroit Electric, built by the Anderson Carriage Compa-

The Detroit Electric car was among the most elegant of its type with custom touches like curved window glass, which was both expensive and difficult to manufacture. AMERICA ON WHEELS MUSEUM, ALLENTOWN, PA

A Detroit Electric car from 1914. Customers included Thomas Edison, John D. Rockerfeller Jnr and Clara Ford (wife of Henry). AMERICA ON WHEELS MUSEUM, ALLENTOWN, PA

ny, which was owned by a consortium of rich businessmen. As an amusing aside, the Detroit Electric is said to have given Walt Disney the inspiration for Grandma Duck's car.

The Edison nickel-iron battery was a costly upgrade over the standard lead-acid battery and only the wealthiest customers could afford it. The batteries did, however, have longevity on their side. The durability rating of nickel-iron batteries is between 30 and 50 years. Reports of the vehicle's range vary from 45 miles (72km) to a review that claimed to have extracted a highly improbable 211 miles (340km) out of one.

Intrigued by the possibilities of electric cars, Ford bought a Detroit Electric for his wife, Clara, who complained she couldn't start a Model T engine using its hand crank. By all accounts Clara was delighted. She used her electric car for commuting and visiting the family farm in Dearborn. Although Edison's batteries were supposed to offer the holy grail of electrics – the 100-mile (160km) range – Ford played safe and installed a charger for his wife's car at the farm, despite it being a mere 10 miles (16km) from the main Ford home in Highland Park.

Ford also bought Edison a Detroit Electric car as a Christmas present. (This presented the Anderson Carriage Company with a PR windfall it couldn't ignore and within months it was advertising the Detroit Electric as the car of choice for both Ford and Edison.) Ford believed Edison's batteries would be the ideal choice for the Model T and is said to have loaned the inventor $1.2m – a down payment on the 100,000 batteries he would need for his new car. Ford and Edison also agreed to work on an electric starter system, similar to the one Carles F. Kettering had already created for the Cadillac company in 1912.

By 1914, *The Wall Street Journal* reported that Ford was sufficiently interested in Edison's ideas to be examining the possibility of building a low-cost electric vehicle. He had even drawn up plans for a battery factory in Detroit and told reporters it would be managed by his 21-year-old son, Edsel.

On 14 January, *The New York Times* carried more details of the plan and quoted Ford as saying:

> *Mr Edison and I have been working for some years on electric automobiles which would be cheap and practicable. Cars have been built for experimental purposes, and we are satisfied now that the way is clear to success. The problem so far has been to build a storage battery of light weight which would operate for long distances without recharging. Mr Edison has been experimenting with such a battery for some time.*

According to Ford Richardson Bryan in his book, Friends, Families and Forays: Scenes from the Life and Times of Henry Ford, the cars would be powered by Edison-designed batteries, which would weigh around 405lb (183.7kg). The entire car would weigh around 1,100lb (495kg) – around 100lb (45kg) less than the famous Model T – and, unsurprisingly, would have a range of approximately 100 miles (161km) on a single charge and a top speed of 25mph (40km/h). The asking price would be $600 (only $50 more than the Model T) – or the equivalent of four months pay for the average Ford assembly line worker.

At Ford's bidding, a test bed design – little more than a basic chassis, a battery storage compartment, a rear mounted motor, a seat and a steering mechanism – had been built the year before by Alexander Churchward, who was Vice President of Gray & Davis Inc., of Boston, and a keen advocate of electric transportation. The motor was the product of Detroit electrical engineer Fred Allinson who also did most of the proving work. Despite Edison's high hopes, the batteries proved problematic, not least in how to accommodate their weight. Churchward's design placed the 400lb (181kg) batteries beneath the driver, thereby keeping the centre of gravity as close to the ground as possible.

A second experimental car was built the following year using the Model T's chassis, suspension, steering and a worm-drive rear axle. The main battery pack once again sat beneath the driver's seat. However, in a bid to reach the fabled 100-mile (160km) range, extra cells were fitted ahead of the driver, where an internal combustion engine would normally be sited.

The second car was largely the work of Eugene Farkas, Ford's Hungarian engineering partner who had developed the Model T's chassis. Indeed, the Model T was so versatile that it was often pressed into service as the basis for development hacks of all kinds. As well as the electric car, Ford used Model T components for early tractor designs.

Throughout 1914 rumours circulated that Ford's next big thing would be an electric car. Henry was said to be looking at buying an electricity-generating plant in Niagara Falls and scoping out potential sites in Detroit for a bespoke factory that would manufacture his new car. Edison, in an interview with *Automobile Topics* in May, added to the rumours when he confidently predicted: 'Mr Henry Ford is making plans for the tools, special machinery, factory buildings and equipment for the production of the new electric'. Although he was rather vague about the on sale date, outwardly at least, Edison remained confident. 'Mr Ford is working steadily on the details, and he knows his business, so it will not be long,' he said.

Behind the scenes, however, it appears the project was struggling. Although the car was a reality – although it may not have progressed to a production-ready state, as no photos exist of it fitted with bodywork – the engineers were frustrated by Edison's batteries. The 100-mile (160km) range was out of reach. Swapping the nickel-iron cells for lead-acid just left them with another headache: the car became too heavy. When Ford found out his engineers had junked Edison's batteries he was furious and laid down strict instructions that only Edison's batteries were to be used.

As time dragged on – and the internal combustion engine went from strength to strength – it became obvious the tide had turned against electrics.

Edison's hope, that electric cars and trucks would have the city streets to themselves, while the dirty, noisy internal combustion engine would be used for long-distance duties, began to look like a forlorn hope. The Kettering electric starter had made internal combustion engines as convenient as battery-powered motors. Worse, the discovery of large oil reserves in North America had helped create a dependable infrastructure of petrol filling stations. The widespread availability of petrol also made it cheap. Running an internal combustion engines hundreds of miles was a simple matter of stopping for fuel and filling up.

Outside of one or two cities, no such infrastructure existed for electric cars and, short of swapping out flat batteries for newly charged ones, it was still impossible to travel more than relatively modest distances in them. For all their smoothness and refinement, the electric car hadn't advanced much beyond the early Electrobats of Morris and Salom nearly 20 years earlier.

Ford's own Model T had opened people's eyes to the potential of the internal combustion engine – there would be no going back.

Despite not wishing to fall out with his great friend Edison, Ford reluctantly pulled the plug on the electric car project. Did the man who did so much to popularize the internal combustion engine really ever seriously think about an electric alternative? Or did he simply toy with the idea to please his friend Edison? If the electric project was a ruse it was an expensive one. Ford invested $1.5m in research and development before concluding that the electric car didn't have a future – a huge amount of money at the time.

The work wasn't entirely without merit, however, as it led to Ford's adoption of the self-starter and electric lighting. And anyway Henry Ford was now America's leading industrialist thanks to the runaway success of the Model T. By 1918, half of all the cars on American roads were Model Ts. This incredible success had driven down the price to less than half the price of even the cheapest electric.

The threat of the Model T had forced electric car manufacturers to reappraise their methods. Some were content to occupy an expensive (albeit rapidly shrinking) niche market but one or two tried to meet Ford head on – slashing prices to the bone.

Milburn

The Milburn Wagon Company knew a thing or two about large-scale production. George Milburn was born in Alston, Cumbria, in 1820. He emigrated to Canada before moving across the border to the United States of America in 1835. A successful businessman who owned hotels and property, George started the Milburn Wagon Company to manufacturer farm wagons. The Milburn factory, in Toledo, Ohio, was a marvel of modern technology, boasting a level of mechanized production previously unheard of and making the company the largest farm-wagon manufacturer in the world by 1875.

After George died in 1883, the company diversified into building car bodies, including some for the Ohio Electric car company, which mainly sold upmarket brougham carriages. When merger talks between the two companies fell through, Milburn decided to enter the fray as a manufacturer in its own right. However, it would do so with a cut-price electric vehicle aimed at would-be motorists of more modest means manufactured using know-how gained in the wagon building business.

The 1915 Milburn Light Electric (painted Milburn Blue unless made to special order) was based on a design by Karl Probst, the freelance engineer and automotive enthusiast who is best known for creating the iconic Jeep in 1940. It was lighter than the competition at 2,100lb (952kg) (the company's motto was 'weighs nearly a ton less' than the competition) and simpler. Many of the key

THE MILBURN LIGHT ELECTRIC

COUPE
ROADSTER
DELIVERY

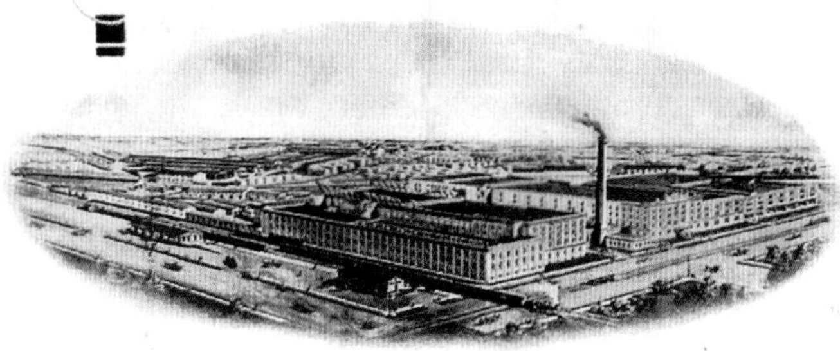

MANUFACTURED AND GUARANTEED BY
THE MILBURN WAGON COMPANY
TOLEDO OHIO, U.S.A.
ESTABLISHED 1848
MANUFACTURERS OF HIGH GRADE AUTOMOBILE BODIES

The Milburn Light Electric factory in Toledo, Ohio, was one of the largest of its type in the world.

Because we have the facilities—the experience—and the "know how" to apply them—

We can build better electrics—more of them—and price them lower than any other producer we know of.

For proof—we submit accomplishment.

Last season's Milburn was the most successful electric ever produced.

It cut the weight and the price of electric vehicles just about half.

Its success forced the reduction in weight and in price which is almost universal in electric cars shown this season.

But the Milburn is still by far the lightest electric.

And it is still much the lowest priced.

Milburn's Brougham cost $1,585.

The Milburn Light Electric was based on a design by Karl Probst, who is best known for his work on the iconic Jeep.

Milburn Light Electric Coupé (Model 15)

Body-style: closed coupé
Price: $1,485
Range: 50 miles (80km) (claimed]
Top speed: approx 15mph (24km/h)
40V battery
Worm drive
Four forward speeds and two reverse speeds.
Wheelbase: 100in (2,540mm)

components were manufactured by contractors (the motor and controller were both made by General Electric) with final assembly and testing taking place at the company's car plant. The first Milburn had a top speed of 15mph (24kmh), or 19mph (30km) as a roadster, and a claimed range of 50miles (80km). By the following year the roadster version was priced at $1,285, making it comfortably the cheapest electric car on the market, albeit still three times the price of a Model T.

Milburn continued to extend its range as other companies fell by the wayside. A Brougham arrived in 1916, a limousine the following year and in 1918 a sedan. The latter aped the design of its gasoline rivals. It had a 30mph (48kmh) top speed and claimed a range of 100 miles (160km) in 1918. The same year, Milburn sought to attract more buyers by redesigning many of the models in its range in the image of gasoline cars. More colour schemes were introduced but, according to electric vehicle historian Galen Handy, the redesigned cars failed to make much of an impact. The Milburn's rechargeable batteries were fitted in removable trays so that they could be swapped out for fresh ones at central power exchanges. Longer distances were feasible, provided you were in no particular hurry. The company also marketed a home-charging system that cost $145.

Such was the reputation of the Milburn electrics, that President Woodrow Wilson chose one to navigate the grounds of the White House. A fleet of similar special order vehicles was also supplied for the President's secret

The Milburn Charger

For those who wish to keep their car at home and do not have access to direct current, we recommend most highly the Milburn Charger, designed and manufactured especially for use in connection with the Milburn Light Electric.

This Charger is so designed that it is impossible to injure a battery while on charge. It automatically starts and tapers off at the proper rate. Any child can operate it—it being merely necessary to insert plug in charging receptacle and throw wall switch.

The use of this Charger will add to the life of the battery.

When wound for 110 or 220 Volt 60 Cycle Alternating Current the price of this Charger is $145.00 F. O. B. Toledo, Ohio.

For variations in voltage or cycle there will be a slight additional charge; prices quoted on application.

Milburn Dealers

Responsible dealers represent us in most large centers. They have our cars on hand to show and demonstrate.

If you do not know where to find the Milburn dealer in your locality, write to us and we will gladly supply his name and address.

With our increased production capacity we are prepared to extend our dealer organization. If we are not represented in your city we may find it advisable to establish a local dealer, and will be pleased to correspond with responsible parties to that end.

A home-charger made it possible to keep the Milburn's battery topped up, even if an owner had no access to direct current.

service detail – forerunners of 'The Beast', today's armoured presidential limo, perhaps.

The company suffered a major body blow in 1919 when its factory burned down. The blaze consumed thirty finished cars and many more bodies and spares. Total losses came to more than $900,000. Ever resourceful, the company switched production to a new site in the grounds of the University of Toledo and production began in January the following year.

Around this time Milburn began manufacturing taxicabs and electric trucks. It also built gasoline car bodies for other companies (mostly Buick) and, in 1923, General Motors bought the plant for $2m. Although Milburn retained the right to make electric vehicles – and a small team remained at the factory to finish up existing orders for several months after the GM buy out – the company had largely given up on large-scale manufacture. Cars and trucks were built to order at a smaller site, but production seems to have ceased in late 1923. During eight years

INSTRUCTIONS

for

Unboxing, Assembling and
Putting into Service

Milburn Light Electric

The Milburn Wagon Company
Toledo, Ohio, U. S. A.

The Milburn came with a comprehensive assembly/instruction book.

MILBURN LIGHT ELECTRIC *Brougham....22*

MILBURN WAGON COMPANY, Toledo, Ohio

Color, Body blue, Running Gear Black	Brake Systems, Contracting and expanding on rear wheels
Seating Capacity, Four Persons	Battery, 22 cells, 17 plates or 40 cells, 11 plate
Body, Length 137 inches, Width 61 inches	Speed, 25 miles per hour
Wheelbase, 105inches	No. Forward Speeds, Four
Gauge, 56 inches	No. Reverse Speeds, Two
Wheels, Wood	Control, Lever
Tires, 32 x 31/2 inches, pneumatic	Steering, Lever

Price, Coupe....................$1685 Town Car....................$1995

An advert for a Milburn Brougham. Prices start at $1,695 for the coupé and $1,995 for the Town Car.

of manufacture the company had built around 4,000 vehicles, making it the most successful electric car company of the period. That figure pales into insignificance, however, compared to the 15 million Model T Fords built during that car's lifetime.

By 1923 the game was well and truly up. Babcock, Buffalo, Chicago, Studebaker and Waverley had all given up on the electric car by 1918.

Of the big names, only Detroit Electric and Rauch and Lang soldiered on making cars for a rapidly shrinking market. Detroit sold its brougham electric until 1919, although by then the coach style must have seemed hopelessly old-fashioned compared to a Model T. When the company was divided into three separate parts in 1918, the electric vehicle division was left with no factory with which it could build car bodies. Although it still had unsold stock of the brougham to keep on satisfying orders, it contracted out construction of new bodies to HM Body Co., of Racine, Wisconsin, for a number of years. Production of new cars ground to a halt in the mid-1920s, although Detroit staggered on remanufacturing vehicles by installing electrical running gear in other manufacturer's bodies until 1939. Although it never made another car, the Detroit Electric Vehicle Manufacturing company remained a registered company until 1968, when it was finally expunged from automotive history. Despite being one of the most successful manufacturers of electric vehicles – and certainly the longest-lived – no one mourned its passing.[17]

CHAPTER FOUR

THE DARK AGES

By the 1920s, virtually every electric car manufacturer had gone out of business or thrown in the towel and moved on to making gasoline-powered cars. In the space of just two decades the electric car had gone from a technology that, in the words of *Electrical World* magazine, 'has no rival' to being utterly redundant.

Some of the big names, like Baker and Milburn, attempted to diversify into commercial vehicles, where there was still a market for light, electrically powered trucks, but demand for cars had all but dried up. By the mid-1920s the gasoline-engined motor car had the market in a vice-like grip. The battle for supremacy was over and electricity had lost. The victory was so overwhelming that, within a few years, the electric vehicle had been virtually erased from automotive history. The electric pioneers were overlooked or consigned to a footnote in history as mere technological curiosities.

How Did This Happen?

In simple terms, the success of the internal combustion engine is easily explained – 1 litre of petrol provides the same energy as a 50-kilo accumulator – but manufacturers of electric cars quickly recognized this drawback and refocused their marketing efforts on ease-of-use and in-town convenience. For a while, conventional wisdom held that gasoline cars would do the long-haul trips and electrics would dominate in the towns and cities. However, this theory only held good as long as automobiles were the playthings of the rich and famous, who could afford two vehicles. When Henry Ford introduced his keenly priced Model T, automobiles became an aspirational purchase decision for the middle classes. However, the average worker couldn't afford the luxury of buying a second vehicle solely for in-town use. A choice had to be made and the gasoline automobile required the least compromise. Ultimately, the gasoline engine served society's needs better than a battery-powered electric motor.

In some ways, the electric car companies were their own worst enemy. Firms like the EVC threw away a golden opportunity to create economies of scale by never really nailing down the specifications of their cars. Instead, vehicles were made in batches with whatever parts were available. This necessitated a considerable amount of hand finishing to ensure that everything fitted together properly. In some cases, this policy even extended to different batteries. Maintenance soon became a problem for harassed owners.

Industry efforts to publicize the advantages of electric technology were often lacklustre and, even in a market as potentially lucrative as North America, it took the interest of the electricity generating companies before a national association was set up to extol the virtues of going electric. And even then, the manufacturers and the central stations spent more time arguing amongst themselves than proselytizing the electric automobile.

More seriously, the technology did not advance fast enough. After all, the claims made for the first Electrobat, particularly in regard to the vehicle's range-to-empty, weren't so very different to the performance figures claimed for the Milburn Light Electric more than a decade later. Despite headline-grabbing initiatives like the 1,000-mile (1,600km) endurance run, by cars from the Samuel Robinson Bailey Company and Detroit, to publicize the efficiency of Edison batteries in 1910, electrics were always at a significant disadvantage to their arch rivals.

RIGHT: *Hybrids like the Semper Vivus were too expensive and too unreliable to prosper.*

BELOW: *Despite the innovative technology used by Porsche to create the world's first hybrid, sales were disappointing and by the 1920s hybrids had disappeared.*

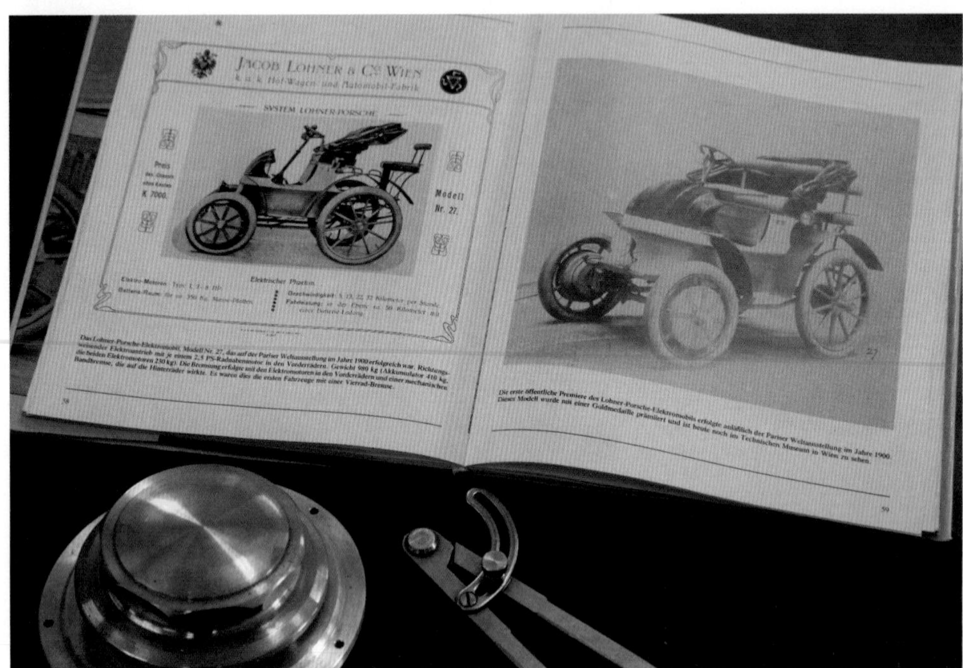

The widespread availability of gasoline and the invention of the electric starter were important developments. In the space of a few, short years vehicles like the Lohner–Porsche were consigned to the history books.

Attempts to ameliorate this by developing petrol–electric hybrids, like the Semper Vivus, were too expensive and too unreliable to provide a viable alternative.

However, it would be wrong to assume electric car technology wasn't refined during this period. In 1913, a review commissioned by the, admittedly biased, Electric Vehicle Association of America found that automobile transmissions, gears and ball bearings were anything up to 50 per cent lighter than they had been at the turn of the century. Closer manufacturing tolerances and better materials had improved their efficiency by the same amount, whereas their lifespan had more than doubled. Electric motors had evolved, too. They were smoother and easier to drive – but electric starters had made petrol engines just as straightforward. The design of electric automobiles also changed. Manufacturers eschewed the horseless carriage for a more functional shape that we would recognize as a modern motor car – bonnet, body and rear boot. In doing so, electrics aped the designs that had become the norm among gasoline-engined automobiles.

And then there was the battery. Although Thomas Edison's hopes of creating a super battery capable of trading blows with a gasoline engine didn't materialize, his nickel-iron design was still a huge improvement over the old lead battery. It was also designed with vehicle applications in mind, and thus less likely to fail in a hostile environment, and had a longer lifespan. Edison's invention still had its drawbacks, though. It was sensitive to cold and the voltage would drop precipitously when the battery was under severe load – making ascents of steeps hills a stressful affair. It was also expensive. Edison's battery advances did, however, provoke Exide into redoubling its efforts to develop the lead-acid battery. The response was a thinner plate design with greater energy density, a better range and more durable construction, known as the Ironclad.

However, then, as now, the battery remained the electric vehicle's Achilles' heel. Owners could not rely on an electric car to transport them more than a modest distance beyond urban limits and the problems of range were exacerbated by freezing weather, poor roads and steep hills. The technical drawbacks were frequently compounded by overcharging due to the inaccurate method of relying on an ammeter to indicate how much energy had been lost by the battery during a journey. This was a very crude method of calculating how long to charge a battery. Careless overcharging could easily boil a battery – leading to premature failure and even the risk of an explosion. Manufacturers tried to convince owners that the ammeter made battery charging child's play. On the contrary, poor ammeters (some weren't even connected correctly) were a major contributory factor in pre-

This photo – part of the backdrop to an electric car exhibit at the America On Wheels Museum, Allentown, PA – shows a woman preparing to recharge her car with a home-charger. The lack of on-street infrastructure was a serious drawback in the battle with the internal combustion engine.

mature battery failure. Even the central stations, which looked after customers' cars, cabs and trucks, often neglected battery maintenance.

Some critics have cited the failure to create an electric vehicle infrastructure as the main reason why electric vehicles failed to gain traction in the market. Recharging stations could only be found in big cities – and even then only for the wealthy élite – whereas gasoline was more easily available and at a far cheaper cost. Evidence for this theory can be found in America, where a comprehensive infrastructure in some cities led to increased interest in electric vehicles. When the local Edison central station set up the Boston Electric Garage Company in 1909 and built 'the largest electric garage in New England', the number of electric vehicles more than doubled in less than a year.[18] The efforts of the Electric Vehicle Company, which at its peak was the largest owner/operator of electric vehicles in the United States and, most probably, the world, came closest to creating the ideal charging infrastructure. However, the EVC suffered production problems, natural disasters, in-fighting and a predatory takeover by a syndicate more interested in stock options, complex finance deals and bogus patents than the development of a successful manufacturing/operating business. Although the EVC did establish a network of regional affiliates throughout America, they lacked the support and long-term financial stability they needed to prosper. By 1902, all of them had closed or declared bankruptcy. Although the New York operation soldiered on for a few more years, mainly based around the Central Park area, a downturn in the economy would see the EVC itself declared bankrupt in December 1907. With it went any realistic prospect of building a national infrastructure for cabs, commercials and private cars. In Europe, efforts to promote electrics, such as the creation of 700 charging stations in France in 1901, were less successful.

Infrastructure issues were less of a problem for cars that ran on gasoline. Although the world's first purpose-built petrol station, in St Louis, Missouri, didn't open until 1905, many pharmacies, hardware stores and even blacksmiths sold gasoline as a lucrative sideline long before then. Demand took off when Henry Ford revolutionized the motor industry by selling a cheap car that opened up the joys of ownership to the middle classes. By happy coincidence, America was enjoying an oil boom (sometimes called the gusher age due to the large number of wells being drilled at the time) following the discovery of vast reserves in Texas. The horse-drawn era quickly drew to a close. It was replaced by the horsepower era, which was fuelled by the availability of cheap oil and gasoline. In total contrast, outside the major cities, no serious effort was ever made to alleviate fears of electric vehicle range

The Model T Ford production line. Ford perfected mass production, while electric car manufacturers largely remained small-volume coach-builders.

Henry Ford with the car that killed off the electric vehicle – the famous Model T.

anxiety and to encourage widespread adoption of the battery-powered car. Anyone wishing to travel for a greater distance than 50 miles (80km) effectively found their progress limited by a public highway system devoid of a charging infrastructure.

Price was also an issue. Electric cars, with their expensive and often fragile batteries, were at a major cost disadvantage, to gasoline cars.

The final nail in the coffin was the arrival of the Model T Ford. Although it was an innovative design, with a single crankcase/cylinder block and unitary engine/gearbox construction, the major factor in the Model T's success was its incredible value. It made its world debut at the London Motor Show at Olympia in 1908 and went on sale in Britain a short while later priced at £225. Ford's endless quest for cost-reductions drove the price down relentlessly until it became impossible to achieve any more savings without changing the basic design of the car.

The idea of cheapening the design was anathema to Ford so, when a conveyor-belt manufacturing system helped reduce the assembly time of the flywheel magneto assembly from 20 to 13 minutes, he tried a simple experiment.

A bare chassis was pulled through the factory using a rope and windlass with workers adding key parts as it moved past. The results were startling. A static-build took Ford's best men more than 12 hours. Using the rope trick his workforce could do the same thing in a mere 5 hours 50 minutes. The assembly line – a method still used by every large car factory to this day – had been invented and soon output at Ford's factories soared to record levels.

By 1915, the cost of a Model T had been cut by almost 50 per cent to just $440 in its domestic market – still a lot of money but eminently affordable for a middle-class wage earner. Despite its enormous output (more than half-a-million cars by 1916) Ford could barely keep up with demand. By 1919 every other car in the world was a Model T, or 'Tin Lizzie' as it became affectionately known. Electric car manufacturers took a disastrously high-handed attitude to the increasing utilitarian role automobiles were playing. Although some tried to build a cheaper car, many felt there was no market for a cut-price electric (!) because at such a price point it would represent a buyer's first car, whereas, in their blinkered view, the electric was supposed to be a second car purchased for urban use only.

An electric automobile may have been quieter and easier to drive, but the massive price differential was a deal-breaker for many would-be motorists.

With the benefit of hindsight it seems strange that it was two decades before someone had the idea of mass-producing cars, especially in America, a country steeped in the advantages of large-scale manufacturing – having successfully applied it to firearms, watches, sewing machines and bicycles in the previous century.

Of course, some far-sighted entrepreneurs did foresee the demand a cheap electric car would create. Among them was Charles Proteus Steinmetz, the genius engineer who developed the world's first alternating current generators for General Electric and predicted (among others) the rise of television, power stations and solar energy.

Steinmetz hoped to build a relatively cheap electric car in co-operation with Harry Dey, an electrical engineer from New York. He had been converted to the benefits of electrical power in 1914 when he bought a model 48 Detroit Electric Brougham and was confident his car – co-developed alongside a truck – was capable of dethroning the gasoline car.

The Steinmetz Electric Motor Car Corporation's first vehicle went on sale in 1917 for the very reasonable price (for an electric car) of $985. But by then the sticker price of the Model T was less than $360 and the Steinmetz car never proved popular.[19] Worse, Steinmetz was sued by Patrick Hirsch who claimed that he had helped fund the company but hadn't seen a cent for his efforts. Hirsch claimed he was due 23 per cent of the company, with the bankers holding 51 per cent and Steinmetz 24 per cent.[20] The business closed soon after Steinmetz's death in 1923 amid recriminations over 'official' sales figures, which appeared to have been inflated.

High purchase cost, unreliable batteries, poor infrastructure and limited range – any one of these issues would have been damaging for an emerging new technology like electric cars, but taken together the drawbacks meant battery cars could never win the struggle with gasoline automobiles.

Even today, electric cars face many of the same issues. The difference between then and now is a general acceptance by governments, manufacturers and customers that the internal combustion engine is reaching the end of its useful life and a cleaner technology needs to be found.

Commercial Fight Back

If the electric car was doomed to failure 100 years ago, what of its commercial equivalent?

Initially, electric trucks did well in the market. Fleet managers preferred them over unreliable and noisy gasoline rivals and, to start with, their modest pace was acceptable to an industry where horse traction had been the norm. By 1905, almost two-thirds of America's heavy-duty commercial vehicle fleet was electric. According to historian Gijs Mom, in cities like New York, an electric vehicle was often the only alternative to the horse in many harbour-side warehousing districts because gasoline engines were banned due to the fire hazard they posed. As a result, fire insurance was far cheaper for a company using electric vehicles. Research undertaken by the Massachusetts Institute of Technology (MIT) also found that the electric truck was anywhere between 7 and 24 per cent cheaper than horses in an urban delivery environment. The lifespan of an electric truck was also considerably longer than its gasoline-powered rival.

Many of these trucks were built by the General Vehicle Company, established by General Electric in 1906, operating out of Long Island. Within the space of 5 years it manufactured 1,600 trucks, mainly for breweries, department stores and for bus companies. By 1920, New York had a 4,000 strong fleet of electric parcel delivery trucks.

Commercial manufacturers were supported by the electricity suppliers (the central stations) who saw power-hungry trucks as the perfect customers for their excess electricity. In September 1910, they set up the Electric Vehicle Association of America (EVAA), to help boost sales. Inaugurating the association, President William Blood stated the EVAA's principal aim was to inform the public that 'the perfected electric vehicle is an accomplished fact'. Despite that bold statement, most of the electric car manufacturers of the day considered the association to be largely concerned with trucks and not passenger vehicles.

In a bid to encourage wider adoption of electric vehicles, the EVAA put pressure on central station managers to purchase electric cars and trucks for local transport. It also offered cut-price deals for drivers who wanted to charge during off-peak hours. In one dazzling piece of clear thinking, the EVAA tried to adopt a common charging plug, so that different makes could be replenished at any of its stations. But, as seemed to be so common, these honourable intentions were thwarted by petty jealousies, short-sighted thinking and indifference.

Gijs Mom claims that garages outside the cosy central station élite found themselves placed at a deliberate commercial disadvantage – they did not receive the discount on parts enjoyed by their bigger rivals or a special rate for charging current. This was in marked contrast to garages selling and maintaining gasoline cars, which enjoyed substantial manufacturer support. In addition, the organization disapproved of dealers who sold both electric and gasoline vehicles.

Things soon turned sour. Electric vehicle manufacturers were unhappy with the central stations' efforts to monopolize service and supply. Proposals to set up a fairer infrastructure, circulated to 1,400 central stations across the United States, didn't even receive the courtesy of a reply. As for the publicity campaign, the New York branch did manage to publish a book for adventurous types with detailed route maps of scenic drives within a radius of 100 miles (160km), including crucial information about the nearest charging stations, and the EVAA published a map of the Lincoln Highway, which crossed the entire United States, in a bid to show that touring with an electric car was not out of the question. However, the longest distance between stations was 122 miles (195km) – a distance that would have left most batteries exhausted long before ever reaching it. Back-biting and open disagreements were ever-present during EVAA conventions. Instead of working for the common good, suppliers and manufacturers spent most of their time arguing. Eventually the EVAA's activities were folded into the more powerful National Electric Light Association (NELA), which set up an electric vehicle section.

By the mid-1920s, the central generating stations' brief love affair with the electric vehicle had come to an end. They were more interested in the possibilities of refrigeration, which consumed far more electricity than battery-powered cars, and, despite a scaled-down publicity campaign, support for electric vehicles was largely left to individual stations.

Would things have been different had the central stations supported the electric vehicle earlier? David Kirsch, whose book *The Electric Car and the Burden of History* discusses the issue at some length, wrote:

> *Had the association existed in the late 1890s, when [electricity, steam and gasoline] technologies were, in certain respects, equally 'weak', concerted intervention by a powerful industry might have been able to tip the scales towards a more robust separate sphere for the electric vehicle. Instead, a decade-long head start for internal combustion was too much for the central station industry to overcome.*[21]

In other words, by dragging its feet the electricity supply industry entered the fray too late to make a difference.

In one area, however, electric propulsion did succeed. Whereas electric cars proved only fleetingly popular, electric trolleybuses operated in towns and cities throughout the world for many decades – and some still do. Perhaps this was because they overcame the problem of battery storage by taking power direct from overhead cables, rather like an electric tram, although unlike a tram they had no need of tracks (and were, therefore, considerably cheaper to build). In Europe, some countries took the concept further, introducing trolly trucks. In Spain, these commercial vehicles used the trolleybus infrastructure; however, in Eastern Europe they had their own exclusive overhead lines. Some 800 trolleybus systems were built and operated. More than 300 still survive. However, apart from the fairground bumper car, no one has ever tried to design a trolley car as the technical hurdles would be almost insurmountable.

In Britain, the postal service had enjoyed a brief flirtation with electric delivery vans. When the adoption of a nationwide fleet of motorized vehicles was first examined it was felt electric trucks would be most suitable due, in part, to their silent running. The Royal Mail was using Daimler-built electric mail vans as early as 1899, but these early experiments proved inconclusive and the service refused to commit to a large order. However, in August 1920, it purchased a modest fleet of thirteen electric trucks for transporting sacks of mail between the main Birmingham sorting office and Birmingham New Street railway station. They proved so useful that soon small electric trucks, which resembled a basic version of the later electric golf cart, were plying their trade on railway station platforms across the UK. Electric trucks and mail vans were also used by the US mail service. In New York a battery-exchange system was even set up to keep them running. Outside the major American cities, however, the petrol truck was the delivery vehicle of choice.

By the end of the 1920s, the gasoline engine enjoyed total supremacy in America and Europe. Although a handful of electric cars were produced, or remanufactured, to special order, their numbers were tiny by comparison to the internal combustion competition. Between 1919 and 1925 production of electric cars in the US dwindled from a not-especially impressive 2,498 to just 22.

The year 1929, before the Great Depression, was a high watermark for the car industry. American manufacturers built 5.3m of them – 4.5m for the domestic market and 800,000 for export – a record-breaking production run that was not surpassed until 1949. Just 757 were electric cars. Three companies, General Motors, Ford and Chrysler, accounted for 80 per cent of the country's car manufacturing output and none of them built an electric car. The US had 26.7m registered vehicles, which covered an estimated 198 billion miles during the year. Worldwide there were more than 30 million cars in regular use but only a tiny proportion was electric.

Britain's Electric Workhorses

Of electric cars in America there was virtually nothing. However, on the other side of the Atlantic, the British had discovered a new use for electric vehicles: household deliveries. Battery-powered vans and light trucks often had a greater payload capacity than their internal combustion-engined rivals and were used to ferry milk, eggs, bread and coal to homes in towns and cities. The outbreak of war in 1939 led to the development of larger milk vans because the number of deliveries per day had to be cut from two to one.

As the war dragged on, both sides needed to preserve every precious gallon of gasoline for the Armed Forces. Germany developed electric vehicles as a cheap and efficient way of keeping its transport and delivery infrastructure running. It had more than 27,000 in service. The British Government responded with a marketing campaign similar to the one run by the Electric Vehicle Association of America three decades earlier. It stressed the advantages of an electric vehicle – simplicity, less maintenance and lower running costs (electricity was a quarter the price of petrol during the war years).

The world famous Harrods department store, in London's wealthy Knightsbridge district, had operated electric vehicles since 1919 when it invested in an American-made Walker electric van to speed up local deliveries. In 1936, the store splashed out on a fleet of sixty coach-built 1-ton vans. Their 60-mile (96km) range and 19mph (30km/h) top speed made them the perfect way to deliver bulky items to wealthy customers, and their silent running was entirely in keeping with Harrods' upper-class image. The batteries, which gave a total of 60V, were stored under the floor either side of the chassis in two boxes, and the motor was rated at 3.5bhp. Indeed, they were so successful that they remained in service for 30 years and one even features in the Beatles

The world famous Harrods department store, in London's exclusive Knightsbridge district, ran a fleet of electric delivery vans for 30 years.

film Help!. By the time they were taken out of service some had covered as many as 350,000 miles. Harrods recently restored one of the vans to pristine condition and presented it to the Science Museum, London.

Although the Co-op did its bit for the war effort by running large electric fleets across the country, electric vehicles failed to decisively break out of the delivery van niche they had made their own since the late 1920s. The country was locked in a life-or-death struggle, which was hardly conducive to the development of a new electric car industry with or without government support.

A shortage of petrol during World War II caused a brief period of interest in electric vehicles. More than a dozen companies built electrics during the war years, mostly in France, but also in Italy, where the famous Maserati factory gave up on race cars to build electric vehicles for the war effort.

One of the most striking French efforts was the CGE-Tudor. A joint project between the Tudor Accumulators Company and the General Company of Electricity, it was designed by the famous French engineer Jean-Albert Gregoire, who used an aluminium frame clothed by bolted-on sheet-metal pressings. Gregoire was familiar with the lightweight advantages of aluminium, having already used Alpax, an aluminium alloy, in the design of the Amilcar Compound B38. Indeed, when Gregoire started work on an electric vehicle in 1938 he toyed with the idea of creating a battery-powered version of the Amilcar Compound but eventually opted for a purpose-built design. However, the GCE-Tudor shared a number of

The CGE-Tudor was an electric car built in France during the Nazi occupation. As money was short, the company wasn't averse to a barter system – one was allegedly swapped for a large amount of biscuits.

The rather odd-looking Voiture Legere de Ville was Peugeot's answer to fuel shortages during the Second World War.

components in common with the Compound. In September 1942, Gregoire managed to drive from Paris to Tours – a distance of 158 miles (254km) – on a single charge at an average speed of 26.2mph (42.32km/h), which was no mean feat in occupied France. Presumably this was a special, however, as the standard range was 56 miles (90km). The forty-eight cells, split between the boot and under the long bonnet, weighed over 1,000lb (460kg). The motor was placed in the centre of the car for benign handling and drove the rear wheels.

The CGE-Tudor was strictly for two people, who sheltered beneath a canvas top. This allowed for a small luggage storage area behind the seats. The dashboard, fashioned from sheet metal and painted the same colour as the bodywork, featured a forward/reverse switch, lighting switch, rear-view mirror, an ammeter to keep an eye on charge reserves, a horn and turn signals. Rather confusingly, the car had three conventional-looking pedals: an accelerator, a brake and, in the place of a clutch, a decelerator. The CGE-Tudor was a revelation at the time but its price – the equivalent of three Citroëns – put it beyond the reach of any but the wealthiest.

Nevertheless, production ran at the modest rate of two vehicles per week – although none were ever exported beyond France. As money was short, the company was sometimes prepared to barter for a car. One was allegedly handed to the managing director of a biscuit factory in return for his weight in biscuits. A van appeared in 1944 and plans were laid down for a four-door saloon. After the war a pretty-looking coupé was shown at the Paris Salon in October 1946, but never went into production.

In 1942, one of France's biggest pre-war car manufacturers – Peugeot – wheeled out an electric microcar. The Nazis had taken over French factories to make arms and they imposed harsh petrol restrictions to preserve fuel supplies for the Wehrmacht. The little *Voiture Legere de Ville* (Light City Car) used four 12V batteries placed beneath the bonnet. It had three wheels – two at the front and one at the back – and Peugeot claimed it had a top speed of 22mph (36km/h) and a range of 50 miles (80km). The VLV weighed 771lb (350kg) of which 352lb (160kg) were the batteries. The VLV was used for distributing the post and dispensing medical supplies. It was very popular and Peugeot made 377 examples

Peugeot sold 377 VLVs before the Germans banned production.

The VLV's soft top was a simple fold-down canvas roof.

before the Germans banned all electric car production.

Peugeot would remain an enthusiastic supporter of electric cars into the 1980s and 1990s. In 2011, it was the first major manufacturer to bring a diesel-electric hybrid to the mass market but, to date, the 3008 Hybrid4 has failed to set the market alight, proving barely more frugal than a petrol–electric and considerably inferior to a much cheaper Peugeot turbo-diesel (see image on page 67).

The Second World War also forced two of France's most prolific electric car makers to join forces. Charles Milde had been building EVs since 1898, about the same time as electrical engineer Louis Krieger. Following the German occupation, the two men jointly designed an electric motor that was fitted to a 1939 6/7 CV La Licorne. They also converted a van. Around 150 examples of the Milde–Krieger were built between March 1941 and July 1942, before the German authorities called a premature halt.

This enforced interest in electric cars came to an end after the war when oil supplies returned to normal. Most of the Milde-Kriegers that survived suffered the ignominy of conversion to a petrol engine.

Japanese Rebirth: the Tama E4S-47-1

After the Second World War, Japan was in ruins. With the exception of Kyoto, all the large cities and towns were severely damaged. To the casual observer Tokyo looked indistinguishable from Hiroshima or Nagasaki – just mile upon mile of bombed and burnt-out buildings. The transport infrastructure and big factories had ceased to exist. Allied troops who arrived to occupy the country couldn't believe their eyes. Almost 9 million people were homeless.

The devastation caused by two atomic bombs meant gasoline and many of the raw materials needed to build a conventional car were in short supply. To answer the nation's need, a team of engineers from the Tachikawa Airplane company set to work developing a range of simple electric vehicles under the watchful eye of Allied administrators.

The Japanese were no strangers to electric vehicles. As early as 1917 Rauch and Lang sold ten electric taxicabs to Japan and, even in the misery of a post-war industrial landscape, they were quick to adapt what they knew. The

The Tama E4S-47-1 became popular with Tokyo taxi-cab drivers after the war.

Tama also built this interesting electric truck variant.

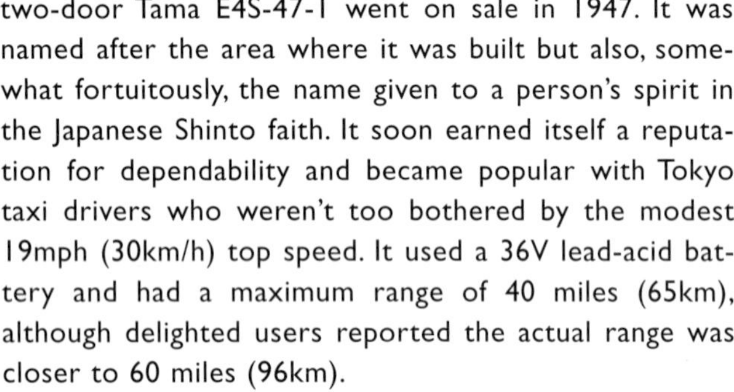

two-door Tama E4S-47-1 went on sale in 1947. It was named after the area where it was built but also, somewhat fortuitously, the name given to a person's spirit in the Japanese Shinto faith. It soon earned itself a reputation for dependability and became popular with Tokyo taxi drivers who weren't too bothered by the modest 19mph (30km/h) top speed. It used a 36V lead-acid battery and had a maximum range of 40 miles (65km), although delighted users reported the actual range was closer to 60 miles (96km).

The company also built a small two-seater pick-up truck, the rather more prosaically named EOT-47-2, which had a 1,100lb (500kg) load capacity and was available in both electric and gasoline variants.

The Tama incorporated a number of useful features, such as slide-out battery compartments built into the cabin floor on either side. The battery was placed in a special case that was fitted with rollers. Exchanging an exhausted pack was a simple matter of slotting in a freshly charged one – a far cry from the hydraulic ram system used by the Electric Vehicle Company in New York City 40 years earlier.

The following year, in March 1948, the Japanese Government introduced official performance tests for indigenous automobiles. In the first such tests, carried out by the Ministry of Commerce and Industry, the little Tama took the top honour. In June, Tachikawa Aircraft changed its name to the Tokyo Electric Cars Company. Work continued on the electric car and, in 1949, a radically improved model, called the Senior, was introduced. This had a claimed range of 124 miles (200km) on a full charge. With the advent of gasoline variants, however, the company changed its name again, to Tama Cars, in November 1951 and the following year it became the Prince Motor Co. (in honour of the Emperor of Japan, Crown Prince Hirohita). In April 1954, Prince became part of Fuji Precision Machinery's growing company portfolio.

Prince merged with Nissan in August 1968 and one of the last working examples of the Tama is now in the Nissan heritage collection. In 2011, the Tama was wheeled out into the sunshine for a spin round a Japanese test track as part of the build-up to the international launch of the Nissan Leaf.

Tama Electric Car

Date of manufacture: 1947
Overall length: 118in (3,035mm)
Width: 53in (1,230mm)
Height: 64in (1,630mm)
Curb weight: 2,425lb (1,100kg)
Seats: 4
Motor: 36V, DC-series wound, rated at 4.5bhp
Top speed: 19mph (35km/h)
Approx range: 40 miles (65km)

Pipe Dream: the French 'Atomic' EV

The French, too, were revisiting the electric car after the Second World War. The Symetric (also known as the Arbel or Symmetric-Paris) was a relatively sophisticated four-wheel drive hybrid design, which harked back to the country's glory days of the Krieger automobile. Lightweight, thanks to plastic bodywork, the car used a 4-cylinder gasoline engine to power four individual motors, rather like the Lohner–Porsche. It was unveiled at the Paris Motor Show in October 1953. Its futuristic lines and unusual powertrain prompted *Time* magazine to gush:

> *The most startling car on exhibit was a stubby, dome-shaped auto that runs on electricity. Built by two French brothers, Maurice and Casimir Loubiere, the Symetric-Paris has a 4-cylinder, 45bhp gasoline engine that turns a generator which, in turn, supplies current to four motors tiny enough to fit inside the wheels. If the cars were on sale to the public, the brothers estimate that the price might be about $1,000, but the French Ministry of National Defence has other plans. It is putting the car through exhaustive tests that may result in its being adopted as the French version of the Jeep.*[22]

The French men from the ministry must have known the Symetric didn't have a hope of becoming a new Jeep, at least in its Paris Motor Show guise. Apart from four-wheel drive, the two vehicles could not have been more different. The Symetric, which had a strange curved glasshouse with a wraparound front windscreen and all-enclosed bodywork, would not have lasted five minutes on a battlefield. However, the car got its name due to the interchangeability of its bodywork. Rather like a Smart fortwo city car 50 years later, the plastic panels could be chopped and changed as required, so a Jeep clone was not as ridiculous as it first appeared. The suspension travel and chances of damaging a motor, not to mention the complexity of the drivetrain, were major stumbling blocks though, and nothing came of the trials.

Nevertheless, development continued throughout the 1950s, and by 1959 the brothers unveiled plans to ditch the gasoline engine altogether. Instead they dreamt up a gas generator: diesel-oil burners heated a series of metal elements at one end, which were cooled at the other. The temperature difference produced an electric current with which the brothers believed they could power the four motors.

Even more in the realms of the fantastic was their final stab at revolutionizing the car industry: the Genestatom, which obtained a virtually limitless supply of power from 'atomic energy cartridges' filled with nuclear waste. The car's would-be creators admitted they had no way of getting the nuclear fuel without the authorization of the French Government. Undeterred, they drew up plans to produce a fleet of gas generator-powered electric taxis for Paris. Unsurprisingly, even the French Government stayed well clear of the whole dubious idea.

In Britain, the Royal Mail was re-examining its use of electric delivery vehicles, this time beyond the confines of railway stations and postal delivery offices. The Pedestrian-Controlled Electric Delivery Truck (PEDT) was supposed to reduce the average postie's workload by carrying bulky items and parcels. Basically a box on four wheels propelled by a battery-powered motor, they were initially used for parcel deliveries but were later introduced on urban letter delivery routes, too. Introduced in 1954, the PEDTs were highly successful and were quickly adopted by dairies for early morning milk rounds. The Co-Op Dairy operated a substantial fleet from the 1950s and the last weren't retired until the 1980s.

The PEDTs proved electric drive had its place, but a more determined attempt to recreate the electric vehicle's halcyon days was taking place in America – one that would use both US and European know-how to create a genuine modern mass production automobile.

Peugeot's 3008 was the world's first diesel–electric hybrid but proved something of a disappointment – being noisier and barely any more fuel-efficient than a petrol hybrid and considerably inferior to Peugeot's own diesel engines.

CHAPTER FIVE

THE SIXTIES AND SEVENTIES

The Henney Kilowatt

As the fifties drew to a close another company was preparing to launch an electric car on to the American market. Bankrolled by an ambitious would-be motor magnet, the Henney Kilowatt had a powertrain built by a vacuum cleaner company that was installed in the body of a Renault Dauphine. Quite why the Henney Motor Company, a respected limousine coach-builder best known for its funeral cars and work for the Packard Automobile Company, selected the quirky Renault as its donor chassis, when there were plenty of domestic alternatives, is unclear.

The Kilowatt was the idea of millionaire C. Russell Feldmann, who bought the Henney Motor Company in 1946 and harboured ambitions to become a major motor manufacturer. Indeed, Feldmann had a long association with the car industry having made his first fortune with the Automobile Radio Corporation, which he set up in 1927 to sell the Transitone, one of the very first in-car radios.

By 1946, Feldmann was a very wealthy individual thanks to his controlling interest in the Detrola Corporation, one of the largest manufacturers of domestic radios in the world. Henney, based in Freeport, Illinois, would become the object of Feldmann's new obsession: the creation of a new generation of electric vehicles.

In 1953, Henney bought Eureka Williams, one of the country's leading manufacturers of vacuum cleaners and a range of domestic waste-disposal units rejoicing in the wonderful name of the Dispos-O-Matic. Eureka had been waging a largely unsuccessful war with Hoover in a bid to

The Henney Kilowatt: an American car with a Renault body and an electric motor built by a company best known for its vacuum cleaners.

become America's number one vacuum cleaner brand. Feldmann, who paid $400,000 in cash for the company, merged the two. When the Henney limousine coach-building business fell victim to cheaper rivals and an attempt to create a truck came to nothing, Feldmann brought the two companies under the umbrella of his National Union Electric Company, a manufacturer of heating and air-conditioning equipment.

During one of Feldmann's acquisitive phases, Henney had inherited a factory that once manufactured school buses in Canastota and, in 1959, this would become the production facility for the Kilowatt.

Although Feldmann was rich he couldn't fund the development of a new kind of car entirely on his own, so he set about lining up some powerful partners. Union Electric was a major manufacturer of batteries for Exide and Feldmann convinced its chief executive, Morrison McMullan Junior, that a new electric car would be just the thing to drive sales. McMullan Jnr came on board as a developer. Eureka Williams would build the propulsion system and another company, Curtis Instruments, provided the speed controller to a design laid down by scientist Victor Wouk.

Feldmann approached Wouk, who would go on to play a leading role in the development of electric cars and hybrids during the sixties and seventies, for help in developing the drivetrain. He sold Wouk on the idea by telling him that the electric car would be a project for the good of mankind, and invited the scientist to his estate in Stamford, Connecticut, to let him try a couple of prototypes.

Getting Wouk on board was a major coup. After receiving his doctorate in electric engineering from the California Institute of Technology (Caltech), Wouk had developed an ionic centrifuge that was used to purify uranium used by the Manhattan Project during the Second World War. After the war, he set up a company to manufacture AC/DC convertors. By the time he received a call from Russell Feldmann, Wouk was an acknowledged world leader in his field.

The visit to Feldmann's Stamford estate couldn't have gone better. Indeed, the cars were so easy to drive that even Wouk's son, who was 12, could master the controls, but it was obvious that the propulsion system wasn't ready for the market. According to Wouk, Feldmann had chosen the Dauphine to be the donor car because it was considerably smaller and lighter than American cars of the time. Intrigued by the possibilities, Wouk, who was the brother of writer Herman Wouk (The Caine Mutiny, Winds of War), agreed to bring his expertise to the project.

Victor Wouk

The Kilowatt project wasn't the end of electric vehicles for Victor Wouk. He continued his research and came to the conclusion that batteries as a power source were not practical. Instead, he advocated a hybrid – electric motor and internal combustion engine – as the answer to America's pressing pollution problems.

Wouk's chance came in 1974 when the US Government promised him a $30,000 grant to design and build a prototype. He and colleague Charles Rosen purchased a Buick Skylark (chosen for its large engine bay) from General Motors. They ripped out the V8 engine and replaced it with a Mazda RX2 rotary, a 20kW DC electric motor and several batteries.

According to Wouk, the Skylark was a great success that easily passed all the requirements laid down by the government. For reasons that were never fully explained, the US Environmental Protection Agency didn't agree and pulled the plug on the prototype. Despite tentative expressions of interest from other car manufacturers, nothing came of the Skylark's potential, and a couple of years later a bitter Wouk gave up.

He never lost his belief in hybrid technology, however, and as time went on, and many of his predictions came true, he received long overdue recognition for his work. He never stopped lobbying officials to restart work on hybrid technology. Wouk lived long enough to see his ideas become reality, but it was Japan, and not America, that embraced hybrids. Nevertheless, he was one of the first owners of a Toyota Prius and used it every day to drive through Manhattan.

Wouk – known as the 'grandfather of the hybrid car in the US' – died of lung cancer in New York on 19 May 2005.

Jubilation at Wouk's involvement was short-lived, however, and his conclusions would come as a major blow to the Kilowatt project. After driving the car, measuring the performance and consulting with colleagues at Caltech, he concluded that the lead-acid batteries the Kilowatt was using simply weren't up to the job. Wouk believed the problem could be solved but the development cost was too much for even Feldmann's deep pockets, so the millionaire ignored his advice and pressed on regardless.

The Kilowatt was a serious attempt to offer an EV with the same convenience features as other mass production cars of the day.

In 1959, the Henney Kilowatt was launched. A proper four-door saloon with room inside for the driver and three passengers, it was advertised as the 'silent, dependable, simple, versatile, uncomplicated and undemanding' electric car of the future.

Available initially to electric utility companies, the first 'customer' was, somewhat unsurprisingly, Feldmann's own National Union Electric, which took delivery of twenty-four Kilowatts in 1959 and a further eight the following year. The first models ran on a 36V system of eighteen sequential 2V batteries and had a modest top speed of approximately 30–35mph (50–56km/h).

For the 1960 model year, engineers at Eureka Williams replaced the 36V system with a more powerful 72V drivetrain, which boosted the top speed to nearly 60mph (90km/h) and increased the range to 60 miles (90km).

Due to the weight of the batteries, the Kilowatt had a torsional stabilizer at the front, heavy duty coil springs and an 'air stabilizer' on the rear.

This second-generation Kilowatt was made available to the general public. Henney's advertising literature described its operation as 'light switch simple'. The six-step control was operated via a conventional accelerator pedal. Changing direction from forward to reverse was a simple matter of moving a switch on the dashboard from the forward position to the reverse position. With no gears to worry about, driving the Kilowatt was rather like driving a fairground dodgem car.

The Kilowatt used the standard Dauphine backlit speedometer, which still had gas and temperature scripts on the instrument faces, although the 'petrol gauge' was actually a charge indicator. A voltmeter and an ammeter were fitted to the dashboard to show the amount of power being consumed. The windscreen wipers, indicators and horn were all within fingertip reach from the steering wheel.

The company's advertising emphasized the reliability and smooth running offered by an electric vehicle. The Kilowatt, it said, 'draws dependability from failure-free electricity. The uncomplicated electric motor is inexhaustible; owners compute cost of its operation and upkeep in pennies. This is the car that redefines "new".' The reference to an 'inexhaustible' electric motor was somewhat disingenuous when the batteries had such a limited range. After a normal day's driving the battery could be recharged overnight with the 25ft (7.5m) electric cord that was found beneath the bonnet.

According to the sales literature, two models were available. Model A, for urban use, ran on the 72V system, which used twelve 6V batteries. It could be recharged in 8–10 hours and had a range of 40 miles (60km) of constant running or 50–60 miles (80–90km) if operated in

Henney Kilowatt

Years of manufacture: 1959–60
Body style: four-door saloon
Motor: Large frame-size traction electric motor with six-step control
Batteries: 12 x 6V heavy-duty batteries in two banks
Recharging time: approx. 8–10h from AC 110V outlet
Range: 40 miles (64km) on a constant run or 50–60 miles (80–96km) if operated with stops of 15min
Claimed power: 7.5bhp
Maximum speed: 30mph (40mph in short bursts) (48–64km/h)
Final drive: direct from motor to reduction gears and rear axle
Suspension (F/R): Coil springs and shock absorber/coil spring with air suspension units mounted between swing axles and frame
Steering: rack and pinion (24:1 ratio)
Brakes (F/R): Lockheed hydraulic 9in (22cm) drums; mechanical parking brake
Length: 155in (3,937mm)
Wheelbase: 89in (2,260mm)
Width: 60 in (1,524mm)
Height: 57in (1,447.8mm)

short bursts with stops of 15 minutes or longer to allow the batteries to recover. The asking price was $3,995. The Model B used an even more powerful 84V set-up consisting of fourteen 6V batteries, which could be recharged in as little as 4 hours using a 220V supply. Set against this extra performance and practicality was the eye-watering asking price of $5,995. Both models featured hydraulic drum brakes, a separate 12V battery for the lights, turn signals and windscreen wipers, a washable interior, a door-operated interior light and locking front doors. The heater was, however, a $400 optional extra and air-conditioning was not available at any price. They were covered by a 6-month warranty.[23]

Feldmann hoped that the Kilowatt would prove attractive to bored housewives who would appreciate its ease-of-use, but he was wrong. The car was a massive flop. Approximately 100 Kilowatts were manufactured during the 2-year production run but only a mere forty-seven were actually sold and most of them went to National Union Electric.

Having already taken delivery of the Dauphine bodies from Renault, Henney soldiered on into 1961 using whatever components were available to fulfil orders, but the public remained indifferent.

Feldmann was years ahead of his time. His dogged determination to build an electric car was partly a result of his fear that pollution, caused by the internal combustion engine, was becoming a major problem. But that view wasn't commonly held at the time. To the ordinary American, petrol was simply a cheap, plentiful source of fuel for cars. Once again, an electric car had failed to find favour with a largely disinterested public.

In 1968, the Mars II appeared. It used a Renault 10 body and ran on four 30V lead-cobalt batteries packed beneath the bonnet and in the boot. Its manufacturer, Electric Fuel Propulsion, claimed the batteries could attain an 80 per cent charge in just 46 minutes. The top speed was 60mph (100km/h) and the maximum range 120 miles (200km). The Mars fared no better than the Henney. Fewer than fifty were made – but not before it became the first electric car to drive on the famous Indianapolis race track.[24]

Commercial Developments

Meanwhile, in Britain something of a silent revolution was taking place. A major post-war reconstruction phase saw new towns and prefabricated housing estates springing up across the country. To serve these concrete towns and housing developments, fleets of mobile shops and delivery vans were required. The Trojan Electrojan was a small battery-powered commercial van designed to be used in areas poorly served by public transport. The Electrojan was widely adopted by private shopkeepers and large companies alike. Delivery companies embraced electric vehicles because they were more reliable, easier to drive and quieter. Companies like Ringtons Tea and Corona soft drinks used electric vehicles to distribute their products to customers across the country. Vehicles like the Shopmobile even had a refrigeration unit to keep meats and perishables cool. Commercial EVs were big enough to accommodate larger batteries and, therefore, overcame the range restrictions that hobbled electric cars. This was the major reason why battery-powered delivery vehicles continued to be produced when cars largely died out and

By the 1960s electric vans were hugely popular in Britain. Harbilt was the market leader and its general delivery vans were even exported to California.

why commercial vehicles led the way in the nineties when interest in electric vehicles was rekindled by pollution fears and the soaring cost of fossil fuels.

The UK led the market in another way, too. By 1960, the UK had the largest electric vehicle fleet in the world in the form of tens of thousands of milk floats, which glided silently up and down streets delivering pints of milk and cartons of cream to doorsteps while Britain slumbered.

Many of these were built by Harbilt Electric Trucks and Vehicles, which accounted for 80 per cent of the 50,000 electric vehicles on British roads by the mid-1970s.[25] The Dairyliner range of eight vehicles was designed to fulfil a wide delivery role and could travel up to 50 miles (80km) at a maximum of 22mph (35km/h). Beyond the milk float, Harbilt also manufactured vehicles for mail deliveries and these were widely used for house-to-house deliveries by the Swiss Post Office. The Harbilt 551, a pedestrian-controlled vehicle, was developed with Swiss winters in mind and engineered for extra traction in snow.

The Harbilt HSV3 was a general delivery utility designed to keep pace with urban traffic. Compared to a milk float, the extra weight of the batteries meant a reduced payload. However, the United States Post Office was sufficiently impressed to order thirty HSV3s. These were delivering letters in Cupertino, California, in the heart of Silicon Valley, about the same time as Steve Jobs and Steve Wozniak were setting up a small computer company they called Apple. The switch to electricity saved Cupertino Post Office 23,000 gallons (103,500ltr) of petrol a year.

Harbilt also sold a variety of other electric commercial vehicles, including carriers, platform trucks and even an electric refuse wagon (via a subsidiary company, Tri-Truk Ltd). The company harboured no ambitions to build cars. However, another big player in the electric delivery market – Smith Vehicles – did come tantalizingly close to creating a passenger car.

Founded in 1920, as Northern Coach-Builders in Newcastle, the company initially concentrated on making electric trolley buses and trams. It changed direction, and name, in 1949 to concentrate on road-going commercials when demand for milk floats took off. From a modest Nissen hut the firm moved into a 30,000ft2 (2,700m2) factory then expanded into four additional smaller units. This was consolidated into a new 140,000ft2 (12,600m2) factory that opened in 1961.

By 1959 Smith Delivery Vehicles had moved to larger premises in nearby Team Valley, Gateshead, and was a major manufacturer of electric commercial vehicles.

As well as milk floats and delivery trucks, the company had also won the UK rights to the American Mister Softee ice-cream brand, which led to a profitable side-line building ice-cream floats. Smith built the vehicles and Glacier Foods Ltd, an off-shoot of the famous J. Lyons Company, provided the ice-cream.

The group's American connections led to an ambitious partnership with Boyertown, a coach-builder that manufactured Mister Softee ice-cream floats for the US market at a factory in Eastern Pennsylvania, and the Exide battery company. Smith, which was by then one of the world's leading manufacturers of electric vehicles, approached Boyertown with plans for an electric route delivery truck. It was to be called the Battronic and powered by Exide batteries.

The partners set up the Battronic Truck Corporation. The truck was designed by Smith, built by Boyertown using its high-strength corrosion resistant Multalloy body panels and powered by Exide's heavy duty traction batteries. They had a top speed of 25mph (40km/h) and could haul an impressive 2,500lb (5,500kg) cargo load for more than 50 miles (80km) before the batteries needed a recharge. The first customer was the Potomac Edison Company, which took delivery in March 1964.

However, in 1966 Smith withdrew from the Battronics partnership. It was followed out of the door by Exide in 1969. Undeterred, Boyertown turned to General Electric for help and continued manufacturing a revamped Battronic range

The North-East factory of Smith Delivery Vehicles in Team Valley, Gateshead.

The Roundsman was an electric milk-float made by Smith Delivery Vehicles and popular in the late 1960s.

The Roundsman's battery modules sat below the load bay and can clearly be seen in this photo.

with a more efficient battery system that could be swapped out for a fully charged pack in less than 10 minutes. Sales peaked in 1973 when total annual production reached 107 vehicles. As well as delivery vans, the company also built a minivan and an electric bus (one of which was bought by the Canadian Department of National Defence). The last vehicles were completed in 1983. Altogether, the company built 175 delivery vans, a lone pickup and more than twenty buses.

British Revival

Because of its size and population density, the UK was one of the first countries in the world to appreciate the damage unfettered automobile ownership could do to a small country. These fears came to a head in 1963 with the publication of the infamous Traffic in Towns report compiled by Professor Sir Colin Buchanan for the UK Ministry of Transport. The report painted a bleak picture of a future Britain choked with traffic. Although there were less than 7 million cars on the roads at the time, the report predicted:

> *It is impossible to spend any time on the study of the future of traffic in towns without at once being appalled by the magnitude of the emergency that is coming upon us. We are nourishing at immense cost a monster of great potential destructiveness, and yet we love him dearly. To refuse to accept the challenge it presents would be an act of defeatism.*

The report was commissioned by the Transport Minister, Ernest Maples, who wanted to know how Britain could cope with an explosion in car ownership without turning its towns and cities into concrete jungles. It concluded that a ban on cars in city centres was inevitable, otherwise they would be overwhelmed by noise, fumes and street paraphernalia; a state of affairs that would alter shopping centres beyond recognition – and not for the better. To avoid this dystopian future the report demanded planning constraints on road building in urban areas, official recognition that more traffic was not necessarily a good thing and a set of standards for pollution, noise and safety.

In addition to this, action to control exhaust fumes could be taken under the provisions of the 1956 Clean Air Act and planners could design urban centres to discourage drivers. The Buchanan report would influence road planning for decades to come.

It also encouraged another look at the electric car concept.

A horrified Ernest Maples established a Cars for Cities study group to examine the possibilities for using electric commuter cars to reduce congestion before Buchanan's predictions came true. He envisaged a small microcar with a top speed of 35mph (56km/h), powered by four 12V batteries and driven by a simple motor that could be sold for £300. Government interest spurred on car manufacturers – big and small – to develop suitable vehicles in the hope that legislation, or generous subsidies, would force motorists to take electric microcars seriously.

In 1964, Lord Esher, architect and town planner, told the Royal Institute of British Architects that he foresaw a time when the cars of commuters and visitors would be banned from city centres. Even vehicle deliveries to shops might be banned for all but an hour or two either side of early morning and the late evening.

He proposed a two-tier transport system where drivers could use battery-powered 'rickshaws' for getting about historic cities like Oxford or York. Lord Esher described his idea as a 'slightly comic' price to pay for the development of 'a silent and smell-less, presumably battery driven, little rickshaw'.

The proposal was seized upon by H. W. Heyman, the Managing Director of Smith Delivery Vehicles, in Gateshead, who forecast:

> *Cars will be left on the fringe of the town and small electric cars will be used for the internal journeys instead of driving around in huge monsters. The limitation on the speed and range of an electric vehicle will be of no importance within the town.*

Heyman even forecast the rise of home-shopping, predicting that the problems of delivering bulk items to department stores would be negated by people buying white goods via the television. However, his idea of fitting CCTV cameras to silently scan the shelves of giant warehouses for an acquisitive TV audience seems slightly comical in retrospect. 'It will be unthinkable to go shopping,' he explained. 'You will have colour TV sets at home. There will be a shopping hour when you can see what there is in the warehouse. You will press the appropriate button for what you want and the quantity. The order will then be delivered, probably by an electric vehicle.' Mr Heyman's prediction that the supermarket was on its way out was also wide of the mark. 'The supermarket was very nice when it was new, but in the affluent society, housewives won't want to be pushing baskets around,' he predicted confidently.

The same year as Heyman was crystal-ball gazing, another British company – Scottish Aviation based at Prestwick – was already working on a concept for a small electric city car.

Originally a flying school, Scottish Aviation moved into aircraft maintenance and manufacture during the Second World War. By the early sixties, however, the British aircraft industry was in disarray after a series of setbacks, political backstabbing and poor decision-making. Management looked for a way to diversify and car manufacturing seemed to be a good fit. Concerns about pollution and congestion – spurred on by the Buchanan report – appeared to have created a niche in the market for a small electric city car.

The resultant two-seater was called the Scamp. The concept, which was overseen by Dr W. G. Watson and project leader J. Chalmers, owed more to the bubble cars that were popular in the fifties than the traditional saloon car as used by the Henney Kilowatt. However, there was sound thinking behind the Scamp's odd looks. Watson said he wanted a small electric car that was easy to drive and a doddle to park, which could be sold for £150 less than a Mini. Congestion worries forced the designers to keep the car's dimensions to a minimum. This also made it manoeuvrable. The body was fashioned from fibreglass as a way of avoiding the inevitable dents metal-bodied cars picked up during the cut and thrust of busy inner-city driving and the enormous windscreen (quite out of keeping with the otherwise diminutive proportions) gave a panoramic view of the road ahead and avoided the claustrophobic feeling that was a common complaint at the time.

Before the Scamp's specifications were laid down, the company investigated a wide range of concepts, including a Reliant-style three-wheeler and a body that had no doors. The final car was 7ft (2m) long and 3ft 10in (1m) wide. It had a remarkably tight turning circle of just 16ft 6in (5m) – almost half that of a standard Mk I Mini – which made it very manoeuvrable in tight spots. Unfortunately, it also looked like a poorly designed toy with its tiny wheels completely out of proportion to the tall windscreen and high roof.

Nevertheless, the Central Electricity Generating Board saw enough potential in the Scamp to begin tentative discussions about marketing the car via its national network of showrooms. Of course, the Scamp's small size also made it a challenge to give it a battery pack capable of decent performance. Just four 48V batteries powered two motors, one each driving the rear wheels via a motorcycle-style chain. This gave it a top speed of 35mph (56km/h) and a maximum range of 25 miles (40km) on a good day.

When the Central Electricity Generating Board saw the Scamp, they immediately drew up plans to sell it through a network of showrooms. Disastrous testing results soon put an end to the idea but the CEGB would continue to be an enthusiastic supporter of electric vehicles throughout the 1970s. LESLEY PEARSON

It seems that W. G. Watson recognized the Scamp's power-related drawbacks. Speaking to author Richard Carr for an article published in the *Design Journal* in 1966, he predicted the advent of a zinc air battery, with its lighter weight and higher energy density, would be the only practical solution to the Scamp's pitiful range. He is quoted as saying: 'Once the zinc air battery becomes available then I really will have created a town car.'

Nevertheless, early tests were faintly encouraging. After a brief drive, the motoring correspondent of the Press Association wrote:

> *I found it extraordinarily easy to handle. Because there are no gears, the acceleration, although slower than most petrol driven cars, seemed good. A deep screen and large back window gave excellent all-round visibility and there was plenty of room for two adults. There was some noise from the motors, but in production this could be reduced considerably as the prototype had a wooden body, whereas it is intended to use fibreglass in production.*

Unfortunately for Dr Watson, the puny output of the Lucas batteries was the least of the Scamp's problems. Testing of the early prototypes revealed all manner of chassis and suspension-related issues. The body leaked like a sieve in wet weather and puddles would build up in the footwells, making the pedals slippery – with potentially disastrous consequences. Taller drivers complained that the cramped cabin and reduced width meant their knees and elbows bashed against the doors and the steering felt rather like stirring a stick through a bowl of thick Scots porridge oats. At the UK Motor Industry Research Association testing ground, the limited suspension travel took such a pummelling that the whole assembly collapsed. Goodness knows what racing driver Stirling Moss thought when he agreed to drive one for a publicity stunt.

The July 1966 edition of Popular Science hailed the Scamp – and the Trident, another bizarre-looking battery-powered microcar built by Peel Engineering – as the answer to London's growing congestion problems. Incredibly, the Scamp was a full 12in (30cm) longer than the Trident, although it wasn't as fast and had an inferior range – the Trident was said to be good for 40 miles (64km). The journal concluded: 'Used by commuters, the little cars would reduce city traffic jams and eliminated fumes'.

However, by 1966 management at Scottish Aviation had come to the conclusion that the Scamp's problems were so fundamental that there was little point in continuing. The Central Electricity Generating Board had long since abandoned talks so, after just a dozen prototypes were built, the company cut its losses and returned to building planes.

Against all odds, however, the other microcar featured by *Popular Science*, the Peel Engineering Trident, which was built on the Isle of Man, survives to this very day.

Peel Engineering began life as a manufacturer of fibreglass boats and 'barn door' fairings for motorcycles. In 1962, the company unveiled the P50, a three-wheeled microcar, powered by a moped-style 49cc two-stroke engine. Equipped with only one headlight, seat, door (opening on the left) and a single windscreen wiper, it was actually classed as a scooter – making it cheap to tax and meaning it could be used by anyone with a motorcycle license without the need to sit a driving test. Peel's advertising boasted that the P50 was capable of carrying 'one adult and a shopping bag'. It still holds the Guinness World Record for the world's smallest production car.

The Trident was a larger version of the P50. It was available with the original 49cc powerplant and a 99cc 'high power' variant, which used the engine from a Triumph Tina scooter.

In addition, Peel offered an electric four-wheel version that used a 5bhp motor. The batteries were in a small compartment behind the driver and passenger seat backs and the whole bubble dome roof lifted up to give access to the cabin. The Press Association was less than enthusiastic: 'It felt more like a dodgem than a real car, gave a bumpy ride, was noisy and there was a pungent smell'. Ironically, Peel's vision of an electric microcar would finally come true in the twenty-first century.

When car enthusiast Gary Hillman bought an original Peel at auction he was so smitten that he also negotiated the rights to restart production. The new Peel Motor Company plans to manufacture both the P50 and the bubble-roof Trident as emissions-free electric vehicles. True to the original specification, the power output is said to be a modest 4bhp but, with 16.4lb ft (22.2Nm) of torque, the tiny Trident is claimed to be capable of reaching 50mph (80km/h) and has a range of 50 miles (80km). Sadly, European legislation means they will be limited to 28mph (45km/h) in the UK and EU. A 'fun' version, packing a far more modest 1.6bhp DC brushless motor, is also available and has a top speed of 8mph (13km/h).

The UK Electricity Council, which oversaw the regional Electricity Boards and the Central Electricity Generating Board in England and Wales, was also researching electric propulsion in the sixties and seventies. It converted two Mini Travellers to battery power as a way of evaluating the possibilities of battery power before committing to a purpose-built design. In a bid to extend the range, one of the two concepts was fitted with simple regenerative brakes. As was the case with previous regenerative systems the benefits were rather modest. Despite a boot filled with batteries, the best electric Traveller could only cover 35 miles (56km) if driven non-stop. Stop–start driving reduced this to a far less practical 16 miles (26km). The

The Peel P50 still holds the record for the world's smallest production car.

The Peel Trident – originally sold with a moped 49cc two-stoke engine – gave birth to an electric variant. The car is still in production.

Both the Trident and the P50 have been reborn as fun electric commuter cars.

Press Association's motoring correspondent described the performance as 'very fast on acceleration and absolutely noiseless' but concluded it was too heavy to be practical.

Mr A. N. Irens, Chairman of the Electricity Council's Research Committee, said the Council had no plans to start producing its own cars. 'Our intention is to see that the battery electric car is launched as a viable, popular commercial proposition in the not-too-distant future,' he said. As a way of stimulating development of new technologies, the Council offered generous subsidies to companies looking to market electric vehicles.

Initially, it championed the Scamp as the perfect electric urban commuter and even placed an order for nine vehicles to be used by regional Electricity Boards. But when the Scamp project ran into trouble the Council invited tenders for the supply of up to sixty more electric vehicles in three categories: a bicycle or tricycle with a speed of 20mph (30km/h) and a range of 40 miles (60km); a two-seater city car with a top speed of 40mph (60km/h) and a cruising range of 40 miles (60km); and, most ambitious of all, a four-seater family car with a similar range-to-empty as the others. Carter Engineering, a Tamworth firm that made car transporters incorporating electrical lifting gear, boldly took up the challenge for the family car.

Engineer Alistair Carter had been working on a radical design for a small electric four-seater, called the Coaster, since 1962. The prototype, which was said to weigh only 710lb (322kg), used a 6bhp motor driving the rear wheels via a conventional axle, but production plans called for two wheel-hub mounted motors. The car derived its name from Carter's plan to use a freewheeling regeneration system to boost the four 12V batteries. Using this method, he claimed the Coaster would have a range that was at least 25 per cent better than its rivals. Carter believed the Coaster's excellent acceleration made it the perfect commuter car and he forecast that by 1970 at least a quarter of a million would be on Britain's roads. By May 1967 the company was running a prototype on Staffordshire's roads.

The Coaster had a range of 60 miles (90km) and the batteries could be charged from any ordinary 13A plug. With an overnight charge costing a mere three shillings, Carter said his vehicle was capable of the equivalent of more than 100mpg (2.83ltr/100km). The Coaster's acceleration to 30mph (50km/h) was said to be in the region of 7sec and the maximum speed coincidentally met the Electricity Council's 40mph (60km/h) target exactly. Sadly for Alistair Carter, no-one took the claims of a small company from Tamworth very seriously and the Coaster ended up as another 'might have been' project.

The electric car wasn't the exclusive preserve of Britain's cottage industry motor manufacturers. Big companies were interested, too.

The British Motor Corporation displayed a woeful ignorance of the technical challenges it faced when in 1967 it announced plans for a two-seat EV that would have a range of 500 miles (800km). To be developed with a battery company, the BMC design staff at Longbridge were asked to come up with something in a mere two years. Sir Alec Issigonis, the genius who designed the Mini, sketched out an interesting three-wheeler for a British Pathé news report on electric vehicles, which looked somewhat like Lord Esher's rickshaw, but nothing ever came of his idea.

Also in 1967, Ford unveiled its vision of an electric shopping car – the first to be designed and developed by a major manufacturer for many years – at Ford of Britain's Research and Engineering Centre at Dunton, Essex.

The Ford Comuta showed what was possible when a major manufacturer put its mind to a small electric city car.

Sadly, Ford's management soon cooled on the Comuta.

Called the Comuta, the experimental car was just 6ft 8in (200cm) long – less than half the length of a Cortina – and had been designed so that three could be parked in the normal parking meter space. It had an 18ft (5.5m) turning circle – not as good as the Scamp but very impressive nevertheless – and could carry two adults and two children, in the same cramped manner a Mini could. If the kids stayed at home, the rear seats could pull double duty as a luggage storage area. The Comuta was a fully developed small car with independent suspension on all four wheels and rear-wheel drive (via two series-wound DC motors). It had all the usual items the average Ford buyer of 1967 would have expected, such as dipping headlights, anti-burst door locks and a heater.

Unveiling the Comuta, Leonard Crossland, Ford of Britain's Assistant Managing Director, said:

> *We expect electric cars to be commercially feasible within the next ten years, although we believe that their uses will be primarily as city-centre delivery vans and suburban shopping cars. The internal combustion engine will continue to be the most practical form of power for long distance and motorway driving, but we are sure that electric cars will have a part to play in meeting some future transportation needs.*

Crossland was realistic about the Comuta's capabilities. The car could cover 40 miles (64km) at a steady 25mph (40km/h), courtesy of four 12V 85A lead-acid batteries, but he said: 'With other – more expensive – batteries we can achieve more than 40mph (60km/h) and a greatly increased range. A great deal of effort is being put into more advanced battery technology.'

Explaining the thinking behind the prototype's development, Crossland added: 'We regard this as a step in our programme to develop a commercially practical electric car. We have not yet reached the stage where consideration of production is appropriate. This will depend upon performance improvements which we cannot tie to a time schedule at the moment.'

The second Comuta prototype was shipped off to Detroit, where the company was examining the possibilities offered by sodium sulphur batteries. Further work was undertaken on the powertrain with a view to possible commercial application. But, after its initial burst of enthusiasm, Ford went cold on the Commuta.

The problem, as ever, was the poor performance of the batteries. Despite pleas from drivers to put the car into production, Ford wasn't interested. Indeed, it seemed the company never missed a trick to put the little car down.

In 1971, when hopes were fading that the car would ever see the light of a showroom floor, Ford said its tests had shown the genuine real world range to be a mere 25 miles (40km). A Ford executive cruelly summed it up: 'The housewife would take the kids to school, then decide to go shopping and, in the afternoon, have a bridge party and then run a friend home. On the way back the vehicle would stop. We do not think the housewife would like that much.' Setting aside the rather condescending reference to 'the housewife' as the only buyer mad enough to want to own a Comuta, and her packed social diary, the unnamed executive's remarks ignored Leonard Crossland's description of the car as a suburban shopping vehicle – not a minibus for running friends backwards and forwards. Anyway, surely the solution to the hypothetical outline would have been for an enterprising Ford executive to sell the car-less friend her very own Comuta. Problem solved.

As if that wasn't bad enough, Ford went further in denigrating the car's potential. In snow (a not uncommon occurrence in the UK) the range could be as little as 15–20 miles (24–20km), it said. 'It would stop in the most embarrassing of conditions,' sniffed the anonymous assassin. No, Ford concluded that, although it would sell a few thousand on gimmick value alone, demand would not be high enough to justify full-scale production. The Comuta project was quietly shelved only to be dusted down and rehashed as the remarkably similar Ford Think city car 30 years later.

If the Comuta was the most rounded electric shopping car of the sixties, the Enfield 465 and 8000, made by Enfield Automotive of Wimbledon, were probably the most successful. Built under the direction of ex-racing driver, Sir Jon Samuel, the Enfield 465 made its debut at the first International Electric Vehicle Symposium in Phoenix, Arizona, in October 1969. It was the only British entry, but one of the few with genuine commercial prospects thanks to the Electricity Council's enthusiastic support.

For a start it didn't look like a toy. The fibreglass body was neat and contemporary with its recessed headlights, sliding windows, aerodynamic bumpers and integrated brake lights and indicators. Inside, there was space for two adults and two children (or a couple of well-acquainted adults). The motor was good for 4.65bhp and a 28mph (45km/h) top speed courtesy of batteries specially designed for automotive use by Oldham. Special features included an electric screen demister, heater, two-speed wipers, independent front suspension and hydraulic brakes. The target retail selling price was £550.

The Enfield was another brave attempt backed by the Electricity Council.

The Enfield 8000 was similar to the 465 but the body was more substantial thanks to a switch from fibreglass to aluminium. The Electricity Council's interest necessitated a change to a more powerful 8bhp motor which gave the 8000 a genuine top speed of 40mph (64km/h), although at that speed the car's short wheelbase made it feel like an accident looking to happen.

The suspension was derived from the Hillman Imp and the rear axle was a Reliant three-wheeler cast-off but the steel tube chassis was unique. Konstantine Adraktas, the company chairman and chief technician, brought the 465's body up-to-date, although the unusual squared-off wheel arches (which dwarfed the 10-inch wheels) remained.

Early cars were fitted with eight traction batteries (four in the front and four in the back) plus a single 12V battery for the various electric ancillaries. The main batteries were accessed via the bonnet and rear boot lid. The driver could also get to the rear batteries via the centre portion of the rear parcel shelf, which was a lift-off cover held in place by snap-in fasteners.

The accelerator was linked to a rotating cam, which operated microswitches connected to solenoids that controlled three voltage stages (12V, 24V and 48V) and for each there were two field stages, parallel and series, giving six progressive power stages. They were recharged via a plug in the car's boot. Sadly, the batteries were very heavy, and the car's weight (at 965kg it wasn't far off a ton) sapped their power. Although the company claimed the 8000's range was between 25 and 55 miles (44–88.5km) depending on the driving conditions, the former figure was a more realistic estimate.

According to Konstantine Adraktas, however, the later 8000s had a barely believable top speed of 70mph (110km/h) and a range of 50–90 miles (80–140km), due, he says, to the decision to use 12V batteries.

In January 1973, after tests at MIRA (including a full crash test) proved the car was rather more useful than the lamentable Scamp had been, the Electricity Council signed a contract with Enfield to buy sixty-one vehicles. The initial cars had a rather spartan specification – even a heater, pretty much essential if you wanted to run an Enfield all year round in the UK, was an optional extra. However, the company did offer an extensive options list, unusual for a small car at the time, which even extended to leather bucket seats. The paint shop was rather less

Enfield 8000

Years of manufacture: 1973–76
Body: two-door hatchback
Motor: 48V DC series 4-pole
Batteries: eight lead-acid batteries 12V 110Ah (also eight 6V batteries in a single series string) plus one auxiliary battery (12V 55Ah)
Recharging time: approximately 8h
Claimed power: 8bhp
Maximum speed: 40mph (64km/h)
Final drive: differential axle 3.55:1 ratio
Wheels and tyres: 4.5 J x 10in (250mm)
Tyres: radial 145 SR 10
Suspension: Independent coil over shocks with wishbone front/live axle twin trailing parallel radius arms
Brakes: Lockheed dual hydraulic drums/mechanical parking brake
Length: 112in (2,845mm)
Wheelbase: 68in (1,725mm)
Width: 56in (1,420mm)
Height: 55.6in (1,410mm)
Weight: 2,150lb (975kg)
Payload: 350lb (160kg)

generous. Just four colours were available: red, white, yellow and, that quintessential seventies hue, burnt orange.

Nevertheless, the Enfield, complete with 'experimental electric car' decals running from the door into the front wings, was rolled out to nonplussed electricity board officials across the country in 1975. Trevor Smith, transport superintendent at the Stockton depot of the North East Electricity Board (NEEB), commented: 'It is compact, high manoeuvrable, almost silent, completely fumeless and economical. But perhaps the most important aspect is the contribution they can make to the wise and efficient use of the nation's resources.'

Ron Patterson, NEEB's North Yorkshire energy marketing engineer, added enthusiastically: 'It's early days yet but we have fallen in love with the car. I am sure it is the answer to Britain's traffic problems: so clean, quiet, simple and, above all, economical. You just plug it in at the mains and an eight hour charges gives maximum range. What could

Emlyn Warderder, transport foreman at the Darlington electricity depot, with his Enfield company car in 1976.

Another Electricity Board employee demonstrates how to 'fill up' an Enfield.

be easier?' The NEEB even convinced *The Northern Echo*'s motoring correspondent Clive Birtwistle to have a go. After a quick drive, he wrote: 'I have tested several prototype electric vehicles in the past ten years and the Enfield 8000 is the most sophisticated and satisfying by far'.

The Electricity Council may have been convinced but ordinary motorists weren't. The hefty asking price didn't help, either. The saloon cost £2,808, a soft top was £2,106 and a van cost £2,214. For that kind of cash, you could buy a couple of Minis and have enough change for a decent holiday. Despite the enthusiastic backing of The Daily Mirror, which gave ten away in a competition, the public remained indifferent.

Enfield's Greek owners had already shifted production to their home country, possibly with one eye on Greece's thriving holiday car-rental market. They also developed an intriguing open-top variant called the Bikini. However, the company suffered a major setback when it failed to win government permission to market the Enfield or the Bikini in Greece. The plans came to nothing. Discussions to form a joint company with the Greek shipping magnate, Aristotle Onassis, founded on hopes of renting the Enfield at airports, also fizzled out. Production came to an end in 1977. In total, Enfield made somewhere between 108 and 150 cars.

The electricity boards used them for more than a decade before they were pensioned off – at least one, possibly a relic of the NEEB fleet, ended up in a scrap yard in Gateshead. An analysis after 3 years revealed that the fleet had covered an impressive total of 251,577 miles at an average of 3,700 miles per vehicle per year. However, the figures concealed wide variations in battery reliability and the survey suggested that, in future, several cars should be run from the same depot where they were likely to be better looked after.

Meanwhile, BMC's bold assertion that it could develop an electric car with a 500-mile (800km) range was quietly forgotten. When BMC was bundled up into British Leyland it continued to dabble.

In 1971, BL commissioned Michelotti to design an electric two-seater based on the Mini. The car was a joint effort between BL and Crompton–Leyland Electricars of Tredegar, Monmouth, which already had a track record in building small battery-powered vans and milk floats. It was displayed at the Geneva Show but BL had more pressing priorities at the time (such as impending bankruptcy). Shortly afterwards the partnership was dissolved.

Bedford, GM's UK commercial vehicle arm, formed an

This was British Leyland's idea of a future electric car. Michelotti did the design and Crompton–Leyland Electricars the engineering. At the time, BL had more pressing matters to attend to and the project was quickly shelved.

Throughout the seventies, designers focused on electric commuter cars.

CLOCKWISE, LEFT TO RIGHT: This city car design has a solar panel on the roof for trickle-charging the battery – but the benefits were debateable in Britain's dreary weather.

The French Government chose three electric vehicles – a Peugeot truck and van and a Renault 5 – to be put into production for use by public utilities.

Lucas sponsored an electric 'Grand Prix' at Donington Park circuit in 1979.

Not every entrant made it to the finish of the Lucas electric prototypes race.

electric van partnership with battery manufacturer Lucas. The alliance was moderately successful. In 1978, a Bedford design won its class in a major international competition organized by the French Government to determine the level of electric vehicle technology in Europe. As a result, the partners were invited to tender for the provision of a substantial number of 1,000kg payload electric vehicles to take part in extensive trials with French utilities around Paris.

The French Government had set up a committee to examine various electric vehicle proposals, which chose three – a Peugeot truck and van, and a battery-powered Renault 5 – to be put into production for eventual use with public agencies. The trio could cover 37–124 miles (60–200km) at speeds of up to 50mph (80km/h).

Lucas also put forward an innovative alternative to the traditional London 'black cab' taxi. It also sponsored a contest for inventors to build and race their own electric vehicles. The only stipulation was that the cars had to be powered by two Lucas car batteries. The contest was held at Donington Park race circuit, near Derby, on 2 September 1979, and the winner was 19-year-old William Yates, a television engineer, who finished first out of a field of fifty-two entries. Mr Yates, from Cannock, Staffordshire, drove to victory – and £1,225 in prize money – lying flat on his stomach in a low-slung, box-like electric car nicknamed the 'flying coffin'. The vehicle average 20.81mph (46.1km/h) – a speed that seemed very much faster to Mr Yates with his nose a mere three inches from the circuit.

America: California Dreaming

In 1967, the Governor of California, former actor turned politician Ronald Reagan, signed an act that established the California Air Resources Board, or CARB. The board's job was to improve the state's air quality by protecting the public from airborne contaminants. The automobile was directly in its sights.

CARB's other mandate was to examine and encourage innovative ways manufacturers could comply with impending clean air regulations. Ultimately, this would lead to the zero-emissions vehicle programme, which was responsible for the creation of the pioneering General Motors EV-1 in the nineties.

Back in the sixties, however, growing fears over air pollution and congestion prompted a flurry of interest in electric vehicle technology, led by GM, which initiated a $15m programme that resulted in a couple of interesting prototypes but little else.

The first GM electric car was based on the Corvair, selected because it was the lightest GM production car available at the time and its rear drive layout made it the ideal donor vehicle for an electric motor installation. The General's marketing men dubbed it the Electrovair. The Mark I concept used an early model 1964 Monza sedan with the engine and guts ripped out and replaced by a high-speed three-phase induction motor. The rear doors were welded closed in a rather crude bid to stiffen the body sufficiently so it could deal with the considerable weight of batteries slung beneath the bonnet and boot. The Electrovair II, unveiled in 1966, used the new four-door Corvair saloon body. Painted metallic blue, because it was the favourite colour of GM's Vice President of styling Bill Mitchell, the Electrovair II weighed 800lb (362kg) more than a regular Corvair, thanks to the huge battery packs in the front and back. GM chose silver-zinc batteries because they were able to develop high power.

Indeed, the Electrovair was the most powerful electric car produced by a major manufacturer up to that time thanks to a 115bhp AC-induction motor and a solid-state controller, which gave it comparable performance to a gasoline-powered Corvair.

However, the car's range was a maximum of 80 miles (128km) under ideal conditions. Its top speed was 80mph (128km/h) and it could do 0–60mph in 16sec. Once again, however, the batteries were the problem. Although the silver-zinc cells gave good power, they didn't respond well to

The Electrovair was a brave attempt to build an electric car in the mid-1960s.

The Electrovair boot was taken up by a huge battery module.

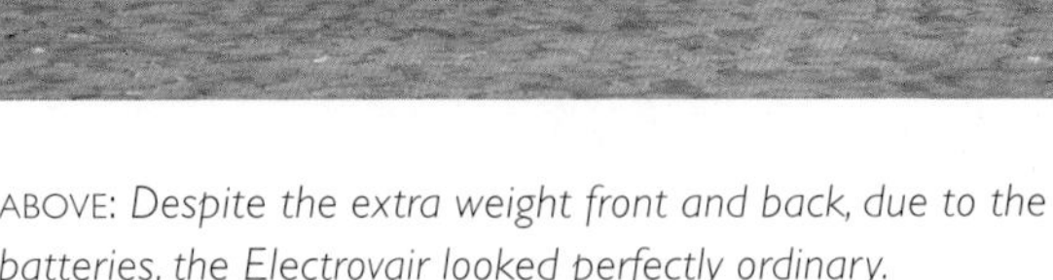

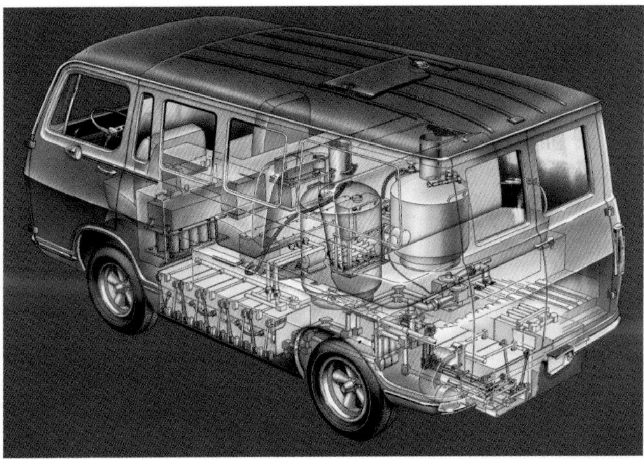

ABOVE: *Despite the extra weight front and back, due to the batteries, the Electrovair looked perfectly ordinary.*

The GM Electrovan was the world's first hydrogen fuel-cell vehicle. Much of the powertrain was carried over from the Electrovair II but the rear contained two large tanks of liquid cooled hydrogen and oxygen. The Electrovan had a range of 120 miles (192km) but was never sold due to (understandable) safety concerns.

BELOW: *GM's cutaway of the Electrovair.*

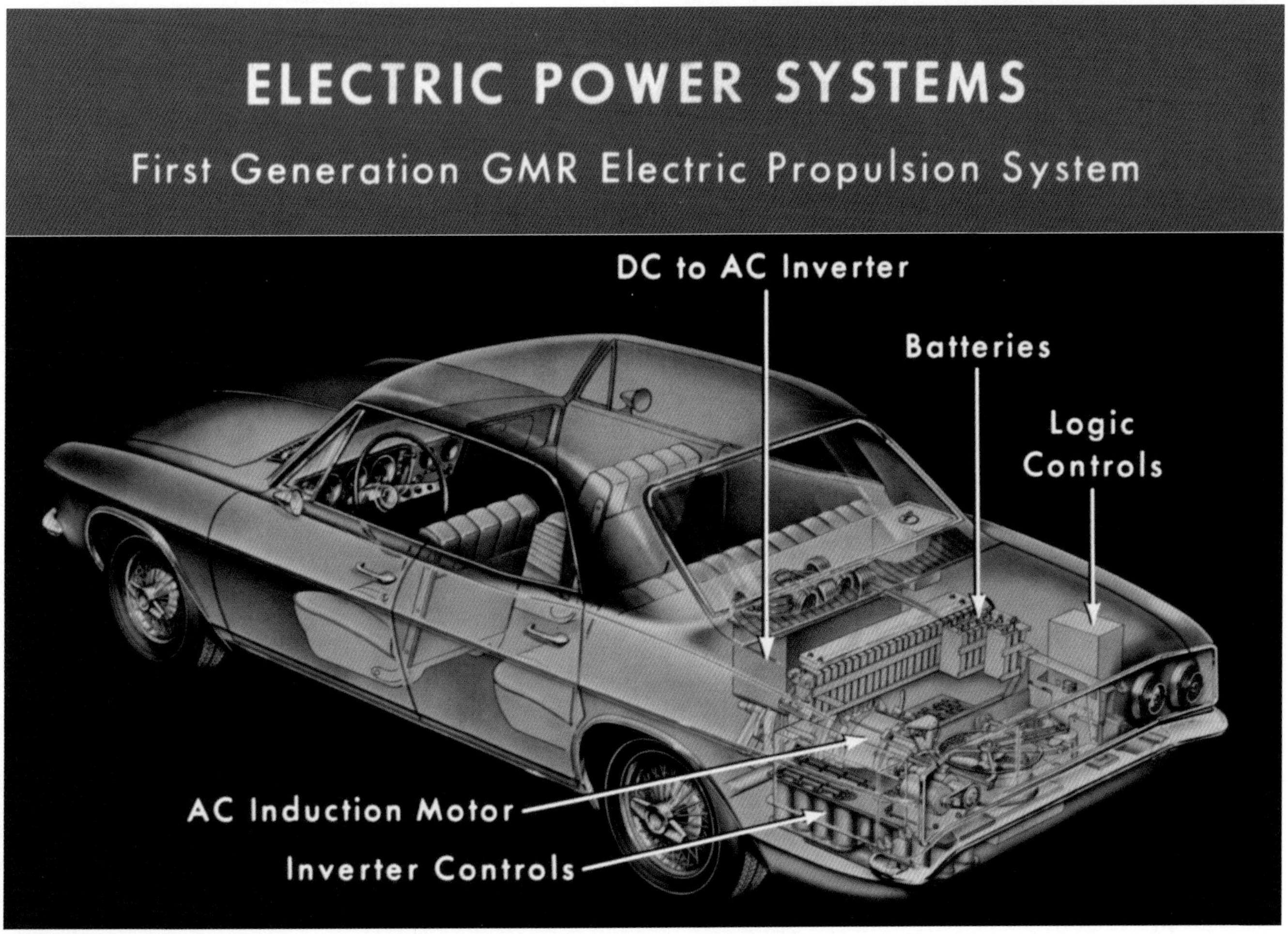

ELECTRIC POWER SYSTEMS

First Generation GMR Electric Propulsion System

DC to AC Inverter

Batteries

Logic Controls

AC Induction Motor

Inverter Controls

After the Electrovair failure, GM switched its attention to small commuter cars. The XP512E was supposed to be the perfect runabout for the wealthy girl about town.

recharging. Horrified GM engineers found they had to be replaced every 100 charges, making the Electrovair and the Electrovair II non-starters for production purposes.

GM also used the Electrovair II's innards for a van (the cunningly named Electrovan) but swapped out the silver-zinc batteries for a (even more expensive) cryogenic fuel cell.

The van was enormous – in part thanks to the need to carry liquid-cooled tanks of hydrogen and oxygen in the back – but could cover 120 miles (193km) before the fuel supply was exhausted. The design was a safety nightmare, and during testing several accidents occurred, including a serious explosion that scattered pieces of the Electrovan for a quarter of a mile. Not surprisingly, the dangers of driving a van with tanks of volatile gas in the boot meant the Electrovan was a non-starter for serious production but, as a technical demonstration of what was possible, GM's fuel cell van was important.

Bizarrely, however, when GM donated the van to the Smithsonian Institute, the world's largest museum politely declined the offer. The unwanted Electrovan sat gathering dust in a Pontiac warehouse for decades, forgotten about and unloved. The fact hardly anyone knew it was there probably saved it from the corporate crusher. It is now fully restored and on display at the GM Heritage Centre, in Sterling Heights, Detroit.

Having proved to its satisfaction that a large electric car (or van) was not commercially viable, GM changed tack and re-examined the microcar concept. The GM XP512E urban car was shown off in 1969 (alongside a hybrid, the XP512H, and a 300cc petrol-engined version) at the somewhat ironically named 'Parade of Power' event.

At least GM's accompanying press release was brutally realistic: 'The three cars, with their 30 to 40mph top speed and limited acceleration, would operate

The front cover of Mechanix Illustrated, October 1969, featured the GM XP512E and XP512H electric and gasoline/electric hybrid commuter concepts. The three-wheeler at the front is the earlier XP511, which used a 4-cylinder petrol engine.

either on a paved road system of their own or in reserved lanes of existing roads,' its said, 'because they could not mix safely with today's freeway of boulevard traffic'.

When *Mechanix Illustrated* tested all three versions, plus the earlier XP511, in October 1969, it wrote:

> *The all-electric (XP512E) has an 84V power battery plus a 12V unit for taking care of such things as the horn, windshield wipers and turn signals. As we had all [the] cars on the small handling course at the GM Technical Centre, before you could count to 16 in Chinese, Brooks Brender, editor Bob Beason and your... correspondent were racing. There was little difference in top speed and with the cars' roller-skate type wheels we had a ball.*

However, the magazine cautioned:

> *Whether you will ever get the chance to buy one of these four cars for your Aunt Harriet's botanical tours is questionable. They were fun to play with and ran very well, but I wouldn't advise holding your breath waiting for one to turn up at your neighbourhood Caddy dealer.*[26]

The year before GM's city cars appeared, General Electric demonstrated an experimental electric car called the Delta. A candidate for the ugliest car ever built, the Delta appeared to have been designed by an origami fanatic. The awkward body shape was fashioned almost entirely from flat panels and was so monumentally awful, even Noddy wouldn't have been seen dead driving around Toy Town in one. GE claimed the Delta had a top speed of 55mph (88.5km/h) and a range of 40 miles (64km) from its nickel-iron batteries. It could carry two adults and a couple of children. After this unprepossessing start, GE wisely gave up on cars and used the Delta's technology for an electric garden tractor instead.

The Lunar Rover

The world's biggest car company – General Motors – had tried to develop an electric car and concluded it couldn't be done. Others had fallen by the wayside. So it fell to NASA to prove that there was life in the electric car after all.

NASA started work on a lunar rover in the early sixties, when it became obvious a manned mission to the moon was the next logical step in man's exploration of space. The engineers who designed the moon buggy dusted down an old design – Dr Porsche's 60-year-old wheel hub electric motors – and hooked them up to standard truck batteries to prove they had the right stuff for the unique conditions on the moon.

Eventually, four lunar rovers were built, one each for Apollo missions 15, 16 and 17 plus an extra. The last vehicle was cannibalized for spare parts when Apollo 18 was cancelled.

They resembled four-wheeled bedsteads and had a motor in each wheel for maximum traction. Each DC series-wound motor produced just 0.25bhp, which was powered by two silver-zinc potassium hydroxide non-rechargeable batteries capable of 57 miles (91km). The batteries were also used to power the front and rear

Ferdinand Porsche's hub-motor design was used on the NASA lunar rover. Electricity was the only viable propulsion solution open to the moon-landing programme, and the vehicles are still there.

steering motors, the communications relay and a TV camera.

When they arrived on the moon, the lunar rovers greatly expanded the astronauts' ability to move around in their bulky space suits. However, the operational range was restricted to within walking distance of the moon lander (known as the 'walkback limit') in case of an equipment failure. The furthest they ever got from the lunar module was 4.7 miles (7.6km). The rover's 'official' top speed was 8mph (13km/h) but astronaut Eugene Cernan actually clocked 11.2mph (17.9km/h) and is thus the current holder of the unofficial lunar land-speed record.

The rovers were fitted with a front-mounted TV camera, which could be remote-controlled by mission control back on earth. This allowed the cameras to provide some of the most dramatic pictures of the entire moon mission programme when they filmed the lunar module blasting off back to earth.

For the lunar rovers a mission to the moon was a one-way trip. All three were abandoned on the lunar surface. They are still there – one was photographed by the lunar reconnaissance orbiter as recently as 2011 – standing as a monument to man's first visit to another planet and the usefulness of electric vehicle technology.

Millions around the world watched the lunar rover as NASA astronauts explored the moon's surface.

After the mission was finished, the lunar rovers were abandoned. They are still there and were photographed by a moon orbiter as recently as 2011.

1973: the Energy Crisis

Back on earth, the 1973 oil crisis gave governments around the world a wake-up call, none more so than in America, the country that had embraced the car more whole-heartedly than any other. An oil embargo by the Organization of Arab Petroleum Exporting Countries (OPEC), in retaliation against US support for Israel during the Yom Kippur War, produced a spike in oil prices that sent the cost of a barrel soaring by 70 per cent. Long queues became a common sight at gas stations and petrol prices hit record levels. American motor manufacturers had grown fat and lazy, preferring large-capacity inefficient 'gas guzzlers' to the small-capacity, more technologically advanced – and fuel efficient – engines used by European and Japanese car makers.

The transport sector was America's largest single consumer of petroleum – using more than 60 per cent of all gasoline and more oil than the country could produce. It also made transportation a major contributor to air pollution. America's legislators reasoned that car companies wouldn't do anything about this unless they were compelled to. Public Law 94-413, the Electric and Hybrid Vehicle Research, Development and Demonstration Act of 1976, authorized the Department of Energy (DOE) to 'encourage and support accelerated research into, and development of, electric and hybrid vehicle technologies'. If the car companies weren't prepared to come up with a viable alternative fuel vehicle – the US Government would force them.

However, the administration would face formidable obstacles. The 'Big Three' (Ford, GM and Chrysler) were adamant there was no demand for electric cars and, anyway, they couldn't make one cheap enough to sell it in big numbers. Worse still, electric vehicles had a serious image problem. Drivers thought of electric vehicles as toys not worthy of serious consideration. In many ways, they were.

The Electra King was typical. Built by the B&Z Electric Car Company, in Long Beach, California, it was an electric three-wheeler similar to the BMW Isetta.

Prior to 1972, it was propelled by a 1bhp DC electric motor (allegedly an army surplus tank turret motor). Given a long enough road and a following wind the Electra could reach a top speed of almost 20mph (30km/h) and had a range of 45 miles (72km). Continuous development eventually pushed the top speed up to 36mph (58km/h). B&Z also manufactured a four-wheel

The Electra King was another abortive attempt to sell America on the concept of an electricity commuter car. ROGER WILLIAMS

version and the little two-seater was used in airports and factories.

The CitiCar was built between 1974 and 1977 by a Florida company, SebringVanguard, which thought it saw an opportunity to sell a small two-seat electric vehicle in the aftermath of the oil crisis. Bob Beaumont, the New York car dealer behind the idea, had taken his inspiration from the lunar rovers. But the first CitiCar, the hilariously mis-named Vanguard Coupé, was nothing like as sophisticated as the lunar rovers. In fact, it was little more than a modified golf cart. The wedge-shaped nose left it looking like a piece of cheese sitting on four small wheels (the

New York car dealer Bob Beaumont was behind the launch of the CitiCar in 1974.

resemblance was especially clear on vehicles painted yellow). Still, the wedge was quite popular at the time (the Lamborghini Countach launched the same year as the CitiCar and the Triumph TR7 was only a year away) and the car was very cheap for an electric vehicle. At less than $3,000 it was half the price of a typical family saloon. It was available in two versions: 36 or 48V producing 2.5 or 3.5bhp via a GE electric motor. The 36V version had a top speed of 28mph (45km/h) and the 48V 'high-power' version topped out at 38mph (61km/h). Range-to-empty was a claimed 50 miles (80.5km).

As safety was always a major concern for American buyers, the company made much of the aluminium roll cage, impact-absorbing polyurethane bumpers and standard-fit safety belts. The zip-up plastic door windows did nothing for security, however. The bodywork was made from ABS plastic and the 'high-power' car weighed 1250lb (567kg).

Bob Beaumont must have been one heck of a salesman as he managed to sign up 240 dealerships to sell the CitiCar. Initially, the reaction was very positive. Beaumont told the Baltimore City Paper in 2008: 'Everybody heard what we were doing in Florida and they came flocking to us like we were the salvation of the world'.

In 3 years the company sold 2,200 examples. At one point, it could lay claim to being the sixth largest car manufacturer in the United States. Sebring Vanguard was also one of the first companies to sell cars in Bermuda, which had banned motor vehicles for many years.

But reservations over the little car's safety remained and Beaumont found himself constantly on the back foot from suspicious legislators who feared the CitiCar was an accident waiting to happen. During one episode, an angry Beaumont defended his vehicle against legislators in Michigan who were threatening to ban it. The feisty boss took a baseball bat and cracked it against the Citicar's ABS panels, which shrugged off the impacts without a scratch. Then he asked if he could try the same thing on the car of anyone who still wanted to outlaw his vehicle. However, a damning test in *Consumer Reports* magazine, which branded it 'dismal' and 'foolhardy to drive', delivered the kiss of death. Sales never recovered.

When the company failed, the Citicar rights were sold to Frank Flowers of New Jersey who redesigned it, added

The CitiCar's zero emissions' credentials enable Bob Beaumont to sell it in Bermuda, which had banned motor vehicles.

a better motor, glass side-windows and bigger bumpers and relaunched it as the ComutaCar. Flowers extended the range to include a coupé and a van (some of which were used by the US postal service). Several thousand more of these vehicles were built between 1978 and 1981. In 1986, Flowers placed a 'For Sale' ad in *The New York Times* offering the ComutaCar business to anyone who would take it on for $200,000. He died a couple of years later.

Bob Beaumont remained a keen advocate of electric cars. He never gave up trying to convince a sceptical American public and started another company, called Renaissance Cars, during the nineties to sell a battery-powered sports car called the Tropica. Sadly, Beaumont was a man ahead of his time and the Tropica had nothing but novelty value going for it. Only a couple of dozen were ever built.

Around the same time as the CitiCar was making headway, Roy Haynes, the man responsible for the original Ford Cortina, was designing a rather better looking line-up of microcars for the Electraction company in Essex. The company built four fibreglass-bodied vehicles: a two-door called the Precinct, an open-top sports car called the Tropicana, a beach buggy and a small van. There was also a prototype rickshaw, which used Vauxhall parts, aimed at the foreign holiday resort market. In 1977 the company was confident of success. 'Electraction's marketing director has the job of holding back the avalanche of potential customers until production gets underway,' it said in a press release. Sadly this was just wishful thinking and, despite much publicity, the vehicles failed to sell in big numbers. Electraction gave up in 1979.

Fearing a political backlash over pollution, GM never really gave up on electric cars. In the mid-1970s it returned with the Electrovette, a Kadett converted to DC drive using lead-acid and zinc-air batteries.

About the same time, GM showed off a clay model of an electric-car concept and said a similar vehicle could be on the road by 1985

The Electrovette was GM's 'plan B' solution developed in case gas prices rose to $2.50 a gallon. If that happened, GM reckoned one in ten cars sold by the middle of the eighties would be battery-powered. But the fuel crisis came and went, as did a smaller one in 1979 after the Iranian revolution, and the cost of a gallon never reached the $2.50 mark. The Electrovette was quietly shelved.

Nevertheless, in 1979 General Motors' GMC truck and coach division in the US built thirty-five electric vans for the American Telephone and Telegraph Company (better known as AT & T) under a US Department of Energy demonstration project. Twenty were delivered to Pacific

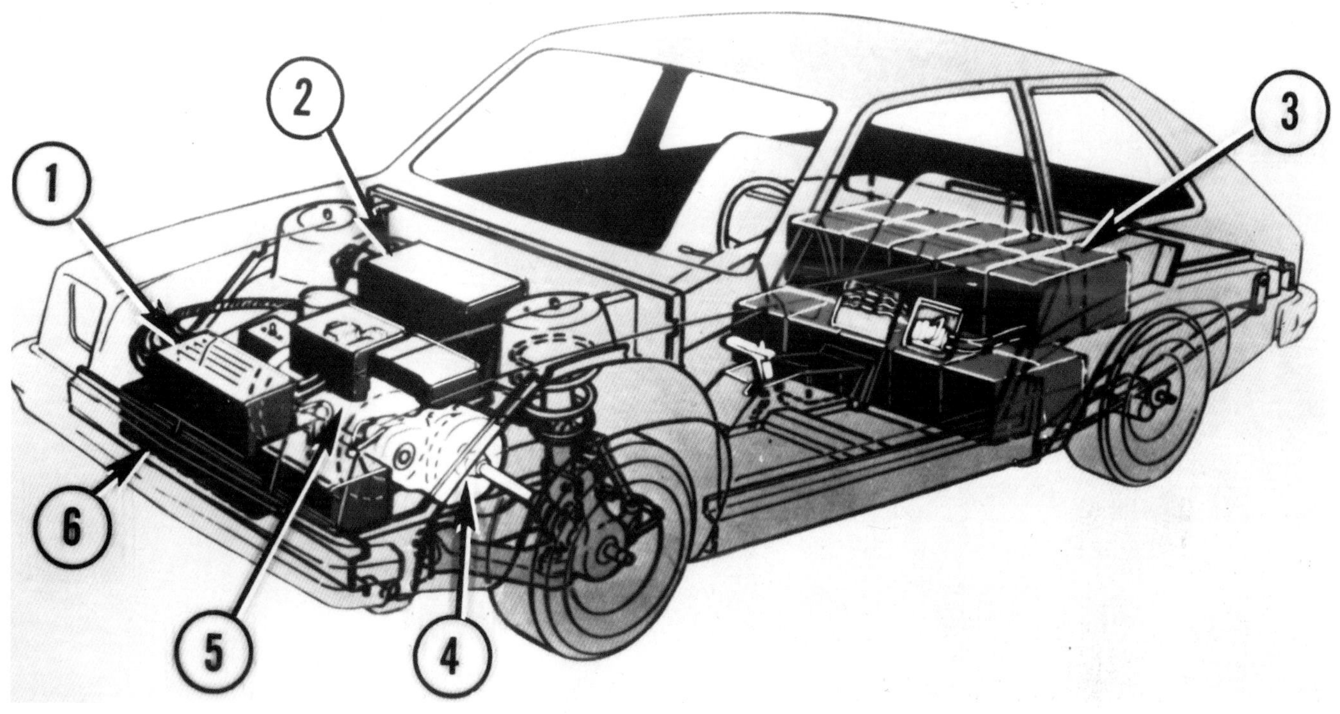

A cutaway of the GM Electrovette shows the placement of the battery modules behind the seats.

In the early 1980s, GM issued this artist's impression of what it thought an electric car might look like. Pop-up headlights and the wedge profile were popular at the time.

GM's fleet of electric vans ready for work in 1985.

Fiat showed this intriguing electric prototype in April 1977 but opted for the utterly conventional Panda instead.

Telephone Company in Culver City, near Los Angeles, California, for telephone installation and repair work.

George England, AT & T's Project Manager in Culver City judged them to be 'very satisfactory'. 'They fit in well with our short-range use,' he said, 'which averages fifteen to twenty miles per day'. The vans certainly stirred up interest among drivers and customers who wondered at their silent operation. AT & T talked about ordering as many as 40,000 to buzz about the entire country and GMC said the availability of zinc-nickel oxide batteries would substantially increase the vans' range.

In Europe, Fiat produced a series of electric prototypes including the interesting X1/23B two-seater in 1975. As a major manufacturer of small cars, Fiat could appreciate the potential of a compact electric city car. Its most advanced concept was unveiled in April 1977. The Electric Town Car was a micro-sized, front-wheel drive city car with seating for two people and a modest amount of luggage. Fiat claimed the zinc-nickel batteries had a capacity 1.75 times greater than the conventional lead-acid type – enough to give the car a top speed of 47mph (75km/h) – sufficient for inner-city use – and a range of 45 miles (72.4km) at a constant 30mph (48km/h) – although it was considerably less in the kind of stop–start traffic a city car would most likely encounter.

Unveiling the prototype for the first time, Fiat announced:

> *Its performance is compatible with normal city traffic speeds even over hilly routes. Characteristics of the new DC propulsion system used – which includes regenerative braking – are considered to be suitable for early application to cars for town use.*

Sadly for proponents of electric power, Fiat had a change of heart. Instead of the Electric Town Car, in 1980 it produced the utterly conventional Panda, which was to be Fiat's cheap, no-frills city car offering for the next 23 years. As for the electric two-seater, it sank without a trace.

The Japanese Government also showed renewed interest in electric vehicles during the seventies. In November 1970, Nissan showed off a striking two-seater prototype co-developed with Hitachi. The car was revealed at the Tokyo Motor Show and the batteries were said to weigh just 330lb (150kg). Advances in technology were making batteries more efficient and lighter.

In 1971, the Japanese Government announced a $20m 5-year programme to fund development of battery-powered cars. The same year, Subaru showed off the Electro-wagon XI, which was said to be capable of 55mph (88.5km/h). The batteries (a combination of nickel-cadmium and zinc air) and drivetrain were developed with help from Sony and the Shinko Electric Company.

However, despite sporadic interest from Toyota, Mazda and Mitsubishi in electric vehicles, it would be a couple of decades before the Japanese finally had their day.

As the seventies closed, the prospect of a breakthrough in electric cars looked as far away as ever. Despite advances in control systems, aerodynamics and packaging, the battery-powered car was still crippled by a poor range and pitiful performance. Beyond niche markets, like Britain's fleets of milk floats and for golf ranges the world over, electric vehicles just weren't a practical alternative to a gasoline-engined car.

However, something had to be done to tackle congestion, noise and air-quality concerns. In places like California, pollution had reached dangerous proportions. A dense cloud of choking petrochemical smog hung over major cities, respiratory problems, particularly asthma, were soaring and the health of children, senior citizens and people with breathing difficulties was a major concern.

Politicians, fed-up with slow progress gave automobile manufacturers and oil companies an ultimatum: come up with a way to reduce pollution or face legislation. Suddenly, battery-powered cars – as the only viable alternative – were back on the agenda. As the eighties dawned, car manufacturers were starting to take the electric car seriously once more.

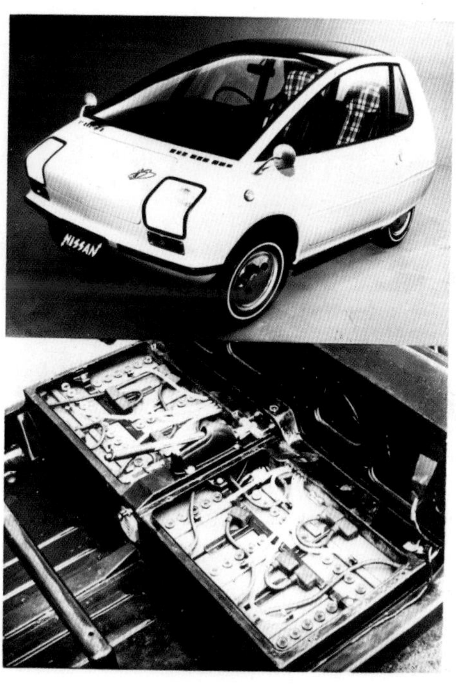

Decades before the LEAF, Datsun (Nissan) was working on electric vehicle prototypes. This was developed in conjunction with Hitachi.

The Japanese Government's interest in EVs spurred Subaru into building this 'Electro-wagon' concept in 1971.

CHAPTER SIX

THE EIGHTIES AND NINETIES

In 1979, the Middle East was thrown into chaos when Islamic revolution swept the Shah of Iran from power and replaced him with the Ayatollah Khomeini. Foreign oil-workers fled for their lives and Iran was forced to suspend oil exports, prompting a second oil crisis in less than ten years. Although Saudi Arabia and other OPEC members increased output to off-set the loss of production, the price of a barrel of oil more than doubled.

Panic-buying exacerbated the problems. In the United States, the world's biggest car market, it was estimated that drivers were actually wasting 150,000 barrels of oil a day simply sitting in gas station queues waiting to fill up.

The second oil crisis caught American car-makers by surprise. Despite the Corporate Average Fuel Economy (CAFE) regulations, which had come into force in 1978, Detroit's Big Three auto-makers were still peddling over-stuffed gas-guzzlers. Cars like the Ford LTD were physically smaller than their predecessors but they still relied on large-capacity V8 petrol engines. As another fuel crisis gripped the world, Japanese manufacturers cashed-in with cars that used smaller fuel-efficient multi-valve engines and front-wheel drive. Soaring pump prices also acted as a pretty big incentive for car makers to pursue alternatives to fossil fuels with renewed vigour.

One of the first concept cars out of the blocks was from an unusual source. Briggs & Stratton, best known for its lawn-mower engines, unveiled its vision of the future, a bizarre-looking six-wheeled gasoline/electric hybrid car, in 1980. The company had dabbled in automobile design (of a sort) 66 years earlier when, in 1914, it bought the rights to the Wall Auto Wheel, a strange go-kart lookalike that had been developed by Arthur Wall, in Birmingham, England. The company sold the patent to the Automotive Electric Service Company in 1923 when it became an EV – the small internal combustion engine was replaced by a motor and 12V batteries.

In 1980, Briggs & Stratton management decided to create a petrol–electric hybrid. However, as development funds were strictly limited, it did so using off-the-shelf parts. As a result, the twin-cylinder 694cc engine was 'borrowed' from a garden tractor and combined with an 8bhp motor removed from a treadmill drive. The batteries were originally intended for an electric motor boat. Unfortunately, the combined power of this parallel hybrid design was a mere 26bbhp – a severe limitation in a car that carried a 1,000lb (454kg) lead-acid battery pack and required twin rear axles. The car's fibreglass body was designed and styled by Brooks Stevens, who was better known for his work on Harley Davidson motorcycles, and another Milwaukee-based company, Johnson Controls, helped out with the powertrain controller. One innovative feature was a flip switch that enabled the car to run on batteries, gasoline or both.

Although the hybrid concept featured a racing bucket-seat, its performance was modest, to say the least. On a long enough stretch of road it could just about struggle to 70mph (112km/h) but a more realistic top speed was 50mph (80km/h). On battery power alone it could travel around 30 miles (48km) and recharged from a standard power outlet.

The company boasted that it had 'advanced the electric car a step closer to a practical reality' and described the six-wheeler as a 'sporty family sedan'. 'On short urban commutes, the electric power is ideal – economic and clean at speeds up to 40mph (64km/h),' it went on. 'For longer trips, where extra power is needed, the hybrid uses both motors to overpower hills or maintain cruising speeds up to 55mph (88.5km/h) for nearly 300 miles

Bill Latus, manager of advanced research at Briggs & Stratton, and Bob Mitchell, a former advanced-development manager, stand proud next to the hybrid car they helped develop almost 30 years ago. TOM LYNN, *MILWAUKEE JOURNAL SENTINEL*

A racing seat and interior didn't make up for the lack of performance on the Briggs & Stratton six-wheel hybrid. TOM LYNN, *MILWAUKEE JOURNAL SENTINEL*

(483km) between gas pumps. If electric power runs low, the gas engine alone can get the driver back home, where he can plug into the battery charger.'

Once it was finished, Briggs & Stratton maximized the company's investment by sending the hybrid out on the road. It was taken to Washington DC for an Earth Day event, driven in rush-hour traffic and sent to San Francisco, where it climbed the city's steepest hills (albeit rather slowly). American Indy Car and Formula One legend Mario Andretti even drove it on a parade lap at the Road America track in Elkhart Lake, and another race driver, Johnny Rutherford, used it to set a bunch of national speed records for hybrid vehicles. The project cost around $300,000 and the company certainly got its money's worth in terms of publicity, but its long-term hopes for the concept came to nothing.

According to Bob Mitchell, who was the company's manager of advanced research, Briggs & Stratton never had any intention to put the car into serious production. He told the Milwaukee-Wisconsin Journal Sentinel that it hoped instead to supply engines and motors to other companies already working on electric vehicles and hybrids.

'The idea was that cars really didn't need hundreds of horsepower to go down the road,' he explained. 'If you were willing to drive at a moderate speed, saying 40mph without a lot of acceleration, then perhaps 12 horsepower would be enough.'[27] The six-wheeler now lives out its retirement at the Briggs & Stratton museum in Milwaukee.

The Ford ETX-1: What Might Have Been

Bob King, of General Electric Global Research, had built his first battery car in 1972. Working with a Volkswagen chassis, a DC motor and lead-acid batteries, he built an electric car with a real-life range of 50 miles (80km). Since his daily commute to work was just 20 miles (32km) he could make it there and back with charge to spare.

In 1977, King helped create the wedge-shaped GE100, a four-passenger electric vehicle built as a technology showcase for the company's centennial anniversary. The following year GE revealed the Electric Test Vehicle-1 (ETV1) built in collaboration with Chrysler. GE provided the traction motor/drive and Chrysler donated the body – the US Government stumped up the development cash. The ETV1 was an impressive start but it was just a warm-up for an altogether more ambitious project.

In 1981, GE teamed up with Ford to work on an advanced electric vehicle powertrain that was subsequently presented to the US Department of Energy (DOE) as an unsolicited proposal. The concept used the best of both companies' technology and was based on the idea of a motor and transmission concentric with the drive-wheel axis. Officials at the DOE were impressed by the concept. They reasoned that the combined motor/transaxle combination would be smaller and lighter than the DC motors that were ubiquitous in electric vehicles at the time.

Beginning in 1982, DOE initiated an aggressive research effort with universities, the private sector and federal agencies, to develop technology to reduce EV maintenance costs. Subsequently, a contract for the development of a proof of concept electric vehicle was awarded to Ford on 15 April 1982, as part of the Government's Electric and Hybrid Vehicle Program (EHVP).[28]

The ETX-1 vehicle used a very advanced AC drive system co-developed by Ford, General Electric, Exxon Research and Engineering and Lucas Chloride EV Systems. A tubular lead-acid battery provided 200V, which drove a 50bhp two-pole induction motor.

Ford selected its most fuel-efficient car as a donor vehicle for this new drivetrain: the Mercury LN-7, a curious two-door coupé, which was somewhat loosely based on the European Mark III front-drive Escort. It removed the asthmatic 1.6-litre CVH 4-cylinder petrol engine and replaced it with the integrated motor/transaxle, which contained a two-speed automatic transmission with the oil-cooled AC motor mounted concentrically with the drive-axle axis. The power electronics and control system fitted beneath the bonnet and the battery modules sat, in a stepped arrangement, in the boot and beneath the seats.

According to the DOE, the ETX-1 was the first electric vehicle to demonstrate a useful range in excess of 100 miles (160km). A report on the project concluded:

> *In comparison to earlier electric vehicles, the ETX-1 demonstrates significant technological improvements such as a 50 per cent weight reduction, a 40 per cent reduction in size and a 25 per cent improvement in acceleration, without compromising efficiency. The ETX-1 program has demonstrated that EVs can effectively compete with conventional vehicles in certain market segments. The project validated the use of the integrated system design for effective use of resources in EV research and development.*

The ETX-1 advanced electric powertrain programme was officially completed in August 1985. Tests performed under the programme verified that the vehicle met its targets for energy consumption, acceleration and what the DOE called 'automotive-industry-acceptable driveability', although, as it was an offspring of the fairly unremarkable Escort, no one was hailing the EXT-1 as a great driver's car.

Encouraged by this success, the DOE had already placed a second contract in March 1985 for a second-generation, single-shaft, electric-propulsion system. However, the US Government had given up on the idea of convincing North Americans to forsake their gas-guzzlers in favour of EVs. The ETX-II project was for a small commercial van application. This was a shame as, by July 1988, Ford and GE had developed the AC drive system used in the ETX-1 into a very advanced powertrain indeed, using new UK-designed sodium-sulphur batteries.

The advanced AC electric drive system used a 70bhp motor, courtesy of GE Motors, that was claimed to be 96 per cent efficient. The maximum torque output was 81lb ft (110Nm), which made it perfect for commercial applications. Fitted to a Ford Aerostar minivan, the ETX-II had a range of 100 miles (160km) and a top speed of 60mph (96km/h).

Unlike the ETX-1 powertrain, which was designed to replace a front-wheel drive set up, the ETX-II was designed for rear-wheel drive applications. The major powertrain differences were:

- The ETX-II incorporated an AC interior permanent magnet traction motor, as compared to the AC induction motor used in the ETX-I.
- The motor/transaxle was arranged as a rigid rear-wheel drive axle, eliminating the need for the constant velocity joints that were needed for front-wheel drive.
- The ETX-II powerplant was also designed for much heavier applications, where higher power and torque were required.
- The ETX-II incorporated new gear ratios to satisfy the requirements for performance and energy efficiency.

Although the ETX-II powertrain had been developed with a small van in mind, had it been fitted to the ETX-1, it could have given that car the performance it so dearly needed.

Worse still, the oil fields of the Middle East were working again and no one felt the need to buy an electric vehicle. It was a bitter blow to Bob King. 'I thought that, in five years, maybe EVs would be commercially viable,' he

The ETXII took the best bits of the original ETX prototype – the drivetrain – added a new motor designed for heavier loads and fitted it to an Aerostar van.

Ford's early sketches of the ETXII reveal an interesting colour scheme.

remembered in 2010. 'But once the price of gas settled at a dollar a gallon, there was no shortage of gasoline. The energy crisis was over, and everyone went back to consuming gas.'[29]

King's hard work wasn't all for nothing, however. GE's research into reducing emissions paved the way for New York's first hybrid buses in 1996 and established the emissions requirements for a new generation of environmentally friendly public transportation.

The Sinclair C5

In the United Kingdom, electric vehicles were making headlines but, sadly, for all the wrong reasons. Although the much maligned Sinclair C5 is viewed as an object of derision in its home country, it was, until recently, one of the best-selling electric vehicles of all time. What is less well-known is that the C5 was only the start. Had the project gone well, the little plastic-bodied single-seater would have spawned a whole family of far-reaching electric cars. Sadly, plans for a new electric car dynasty were dashed by a combination of bad planning, mischief-making and public antipathy. The C5 was also the undoing of inventor Sir Clive Sinclair.

Although he made a fortune designing and selling gadgets such as the first electronic calculator slim enough to fit in a jacket pocket, the first affordable digital watch and

Clive Sinclair with the finished C5. Sadly, the public gave the plastic single-seater a resounding thumbs down. Although the C5 became a national joke, it is actually one of the most successful electric vehicles ever built.

the ZX81/Spectrum home computers that carried his name, Sinclair's real passion was electric vehicles.

He first aired his ideas while working for the Solartron Electronic Group as a teenager in the sixties. Sinclair espoused the usual reasons for using electricity: clean power, silent running and no pollution. But his employer did not share the same enthusiasm, citing the limited range of a battery-powered motor as a reason for not going ahead. It probably didn't help that the British motor industry – which was still a force to be reckoned with on the world stage – had just unveiled its own revolutionary response to fears of oil shortages called the Mini.

But Sinclair didn't give up easily. By the early seventies he was doing rather nicely, selling small transistor radios through his company Sinclair Radionics (an amalgamation of Sinclair Electronics, his original choice of name but one that had already been registered, and Sinclair Radio, which sounded too old-fashioned). Sinclair selected one of his brightest designers, Chris Curry, and asked him to look again at finding a solution to the electric vehicle's problems.

Sinclair reasoned that an electric car would only be effective if it were a clean-sheet design and not an existing car with batteries in the boot and an electric motor in the engine bay. He was convinced the solution lay in designing a new kind of motor that was more efficient than anything that had gone before.

Curry soon had a prototype engine up and running at St Ives Mill, the old steam flour-mill that was company's headquarters. It was mounted to a child's scooter and, provided the 'driver' gave it a good shove off with their foot, could power the two-wheeler quite successfully. Sinclair was excited but the unexpected success of his pocket calculator and problems with a digital wrist watch meant he had to put his pet project on ice.

By 1979, however, Sinclair's thoughts once again turned to the possibilities of an electric car. He approached designer Tony Wood Rogers, who had been the production director at Sinclair Radionics between 1972 and 1978, and asked if he would work on an electric car concept.

Wood Rogers remembers: 'I reluctantly agreed to do the job on a consultancy basis. I'd worked for Clive before and thought I'd moved on but the idea of an electric vehicle intrigued me.' The brief was for a lightweight vehicle designed to carry one person, or two at a squeeze, that would be a viable alternative to a moped. As it was to be primarily an urban runabout, the vehicle would have a maximum speed of 30mph (50km/h). However, it would be

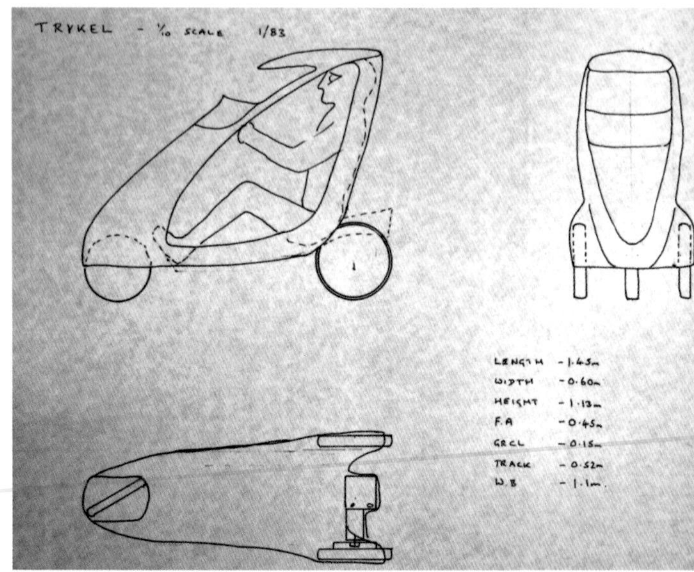

Designer Tony Wood Rogers' early sketches reveal a C5 with a roof – uncannily similar to the Renault Twizy, which didn't go on sale until 2012.

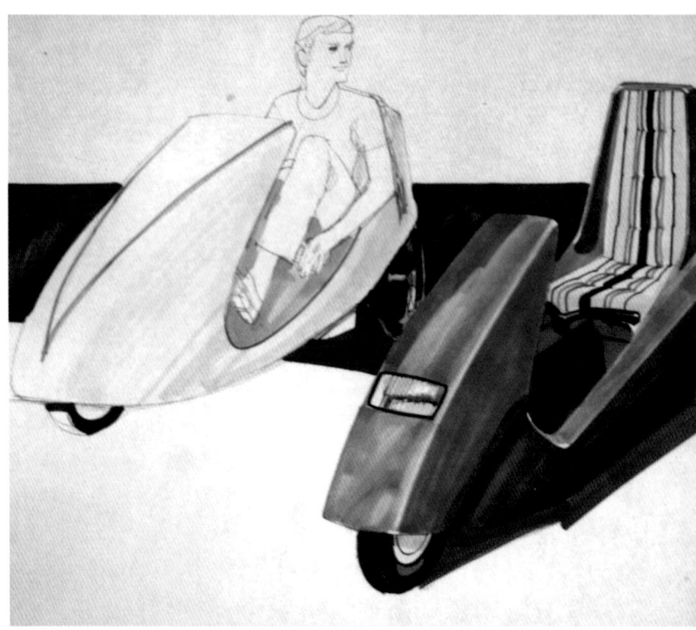

An early design sketch for the infamous Sinclair C5. Note the psychedelic seat covering.

cleaner, more comfortable and, crucially, a lot safer than a moped. Typical customers would be a housewife who hadn't passed her driving test and didn't fancy a moped, a teenager who could not afford a car and households looking for a cheap alternative to a second car. It would need a modest boot, a range of 30 miles (48.2km) on a fully charged battery, plus the option of an increased range with a second battery (more than enough given that the average moped trip back in 1980 was a mere 6 miles). Above all, it would have to be virtually maintenance-free – something of a novelty for hard-pressed drivers used to the vagaries of British Leyland's badly built domestic cars.

Sinclair's plan was to be no mere flight of fancy, however. There were signs that the British Government was now receptive to the idea of an electric vehicle. The Electricity Council, a UK quango, had already spent more than £5m funding research, including £2.3m to Lucas for the Lucas/GM delivery van, and a parliamentary working party had been set up to look at alternatives to petrol. On 26 March 1980, the government abolished motor tax on electric vehicles. According to Department of Transport figures, in 1978 there were 175,000 electric vehicles in Britain – a tiny percentage of the overall total of 17.6m registered vehicles. And of those 175,000, only 45,000 were actually in day-to-day use and 90 per cent were milk floats. Sinclair saw an opportunity and, just as he had with the calculator and was about to do again with the home computer, grabbed it with both hands. This was to be the moment he realized his dream.

The plan was for a launch in 1984. So convinced was Sinclair that the public would embrace his concept that he proposed annual production of 100,000 vehicles – an unprecedented figure for an electric car. Sinclair christened this car the C1 (the 'C' standing for Clive) and Wood Rogers built and tested several prototypes in a wind tunnel at Exeter University.

For someone with a dream about revolutionizing transport, Clive Sinclair took a very pragmatic view of the batteries that would power his forthcoming car. Although he had raised a considerable sum of money (believed to be around £12m) by selling some of his shares in Sinclair Research, the cost of designing and developing a totally new vehicle was still huge and Sinclair had to make every penny count. Spending millions chasing new battery technology would be a waste of money, he reasoned. Therefore, it would be a better idea to use existing batteries for the new car and, if it was a success, the battery industry would feel compelled to come up with something better.

However, the C1 would need a robust battery capable of at least 300 charge–discharge cycles. Wood Roger says: 'We were stuck with the standard technology of the time. A car battery was out of the question because it couldn't stand constant charge/discharge cycles, a traction battery, similar to the kind used in milk floats, could be recharged from flat and a semi-traction battery, often used by caravanners, offered a good compromise. Sadly, though, we had very little freedom of choice.' The search was ongoing when Wood Rogers received a letter from Joe Caine, a veteran of the Chloride battery company, asking to join the project. No doubt to his considerable surprise, Caine soon found himself established in a research lab in Bolton with thousands of pounds worth of testing equipment.

The C1 project was handed over to Ogle Design, the consultancy responsible for, among others, the Reliant Scimitar GTE, the Reliant Robin, the Bond Bug, the BSA Rocket 3 motorcycle and even Luke Skywalker's landspeeder in Star Wars.

Wood Rogers says Ogle Design were convinced the C1 would be a flop:

> *For 12 months all they did was come up with reasons why it wouldn't work. They said it wasn't fast enough, that people would get wet when it rained, that the battery wasn't good enough. They seemed to spend time proving it wouldn't work. Eventually, they killed it.*

However, things changed dramatically in 1983 when a new set of regulations became law, prompting a review of the Sinclair EV project that would have far-reaching implications. The Electrically Assisted Pedal Cycle Regulations introduced a new class of vehicle on Britain's roads. Although none existed at the time, the government laid down some basic guidelines for electrically assisted cycles. They could have two or three wheels, must weigh less than 132lb (60kg) including a battery, contain an electric motor rated at no more than 250W, be controlled via an on/off switch biased towards the off setting and meet the British standard pedal-cycle braking specifications. As with the moped laws, the electrically assisted part of the description meant they must also be fitted with pedals. If the Sinclair could meet these specifications, the car would be available to anyone over 14 years, who could drive one without the need of tiresome red tape like insurance, road tax, a crash helmet or even a driving license.

Sinclair and Wood Rogers decided to put the C1 on ice in favour of a much simpler electrically assisted bicycle, which would utilize a two-wheels-at-the-rear-one-at-the-front layout similar to the much-loved Bond Bug mini car. Sinclair still believed he could create a family of EVs and hoped the C5 (as it was now called) would presage more ambitious and technologically superior cars.

Wood Rogers had been hard at work making this dream a reality. As the C5 took shape, he sketched out a C10 city car and a C15 motorway car:

> *I'd bought an Isetta bubble car to study and, essentially, the C10 was a more modern interpretation of it. We built a full-scale mock up and it looked great. I specified open sides to keep the cost down and having no doors meant it escaped a lot of regulations, too.*

The C10 was capable of carrying two passengers and reaching 40mph (64.3km/h). The wide frontal area was carefully shaped in the wind tunnel to keep the rain off – even with open sides. The wide front track meant it was very stable, too. Seen today, the C10 bears an uncanny resemblance to the Renault Twizy, a fact of which Wood Rogers is very proud: 'It's nice to know we were so far ahead of the curve. You could put the C10 into production today and it would still look contemporary.'

The larger C15 was an even more ambitious project but Wood Rogers admits it could only have worked if a better battery solution had come along.

> *For a time we hoped sodium sulphur [batteries] would be the answers. They were supposed to be the holy grail of battery tech but thermal problems meant they never got off the ground. The only way we could have done a motorway car back in 1984 was with that kind of battery.*

In the meantime, Sinclair turned to Lotus cars to help him design and engineer the C5 ready for launch. Although he actually considered buying a share of Lotus, Sinclair finally settled on a standard contractual arrangement. Negotiations were helped by Barrie Wills, a motor industry veteran who had joined Sinclair after a spell at the ill-fated DeLorean factory.

Wills had a long-standing relationship with Lotus – it had done much of the design and engineering work on the DeLorean car before it went into production at the Dunmurry factory, south of Belfast, in Northern Ireland – and would become an effective link man between the two companies.

Work on the C5 had begun at Ogle Design. Ogle had also created the Bond Bug, which possibly explains why the C5 bore an uncanny resemblance to that car, but Lotus took the design to the next level, trimming weight and refining the pressed steel chassis.

Over a 19-month period, the C5 was extensively re-engineered by Lotus and tested at the Motor Industry Research Association proving ground, in Leicestershire, under conditions of utmost secrecy. One of the first on-

Tony Wood Rogers' sketch of the still-born Sinclair C10 illustrates Clive Sinclair's vision of building a larger electric vehicle.

The C15 would have been Sinclair's 'ultimate' electric car, capable of travelling at 70mph (112km/h) for more than 100 miles (160km).

the-road tests was conducted on 29 July 1981. The day had been deliberately chosen because it was the wedding day of Prince Charles to Lady Diana Spencer and millions of people would be indoors glued to their televisions. The C5 was also put through its paces at the Prescott hill climb, where both hill-climbing ability and braking performance were examined. Parts of the track were flooded and bad-weather performance-testing was done in sleet and snow.

Wood Rogers had decided at the outset that the C5 would use a handlebar arrangement to steer the front wheel. 'A steering wheel would have made it impossible to get in and out easily and that could have been dangerous in a crash,' he says. 'Putting the bars at the driver's sides made it easy to steer and felt very natural.' Building an adjustable set-up would have added too much cost.

The shape of the vehicle was revised by a 23-year-old graduate of the Royal College of Art called Gus Desbarats. Wood Rogers says the C5 design was almost completed when Desbarats arrived and all the key hard points were set in stone. In an interview with The Times to mark the twentieth anniversary of the C5, Desbarats remembered:

> *Clive was hoping that the design would need only minor changes but I had to advise him, on day one of my working life, that I thought we should start again. He stared at me, asked me how long I needed. I said four months and he gave me eight weeks.*

Desbarats added a small boot and extra cushioning to the seat. The designer didn't feel comfortable being so close to the ground, so he also added a vertical safety mast – but the shape essentially followed the form of the pressed metal chassis.

Meanwhile, Wood Rogers had found a suitable motor – designed originally to power a truck's cooling fan and not, as is often said, a washing machine – which delivered the required 250W output. Joe Caine had developed a suitable battery, which could be 80 per cent charged in 4h at a cost of less than 5p. It weighed 33lb (15kg), which meant a spare could be carried and the C5 would still not exceed the 132lb (60kg) maximum stipulated in the new regulations. With two batteries – the so-called touring configuration – the C5 had a range of 40 miles (64km).

At launch, Sinclair claimed the C5's body was the largest injection-moulded polypropylene shell in the world. The upper and lower pieces, which were supplied by ICI, were bonded by means of a tape that was heated up via an electric current – effectively fusing the two parts together. The same process had been used to make the front and rear bumper assemblies of the British Leyland Maestro. This simple process took a mere 70sec and was perfect for mass production. Each mould was capable of producing 4000 parts per week.[30]

Sinclair had briefly flirted with the idea of buying the defunct DeLorean plant in North Ireland. The factory, built on the site of a peat bog, would have been ideal for his dream of a family of electric cars (it had a notional capac-

All that remains of the Sinclair C15 is this small model owned by designer Tony Wood Rogers.

ity of 300,000 cars a year) but negotiations dragged on too long for the administrators of DeLorean's assets.

However, when word of Sinclair's ambition reached the Welsh Development Agency it brokered a deal with Hoover, which owned a modern facility in Merthyr Tydfil with space for the C5 production line. In April 1984, a hand-picked team was established to begin assembling pre-production C5s. They operated in conditions of great secrecy in a part of the factory that was sealed off from the rest of the Hoover facility. At the same time, Hoover began work on a much larger production line, capable of meeting Sinclair's ambitious production figure of 200,000 C5s per year, on the other side of the Cardiff–Merthyr road, which was linked to the existing factory by an underground tunnel. Twin production lines could produce 100 vehicles per hour and, with a shift pattern, the factory was capable of churning out up to 8,000 per week.

Production began on 1 November 1984, as the company began to build up stocks ahead of a launch early the following year. The C5 was assembled on a conventional production line, which finished with a rolling-road test that simulated the weight of a 12-stone (75.6kg) driver, to check for any vehicle defects prior to despatch. Once the vehicle was given the all-clear, it was packed in a cardboard box that travelled on a conveyor belt to the despatch area, where they were loaded into a lorry and sent on their way to one of the three regional distribution centres in Hayes, Preston and Oxford.

The C5 was launched to an expectant press at Alexandra Palace, in London, on 10 January 1985. Sir Clive announced that the vehicle was the first of what was to be a full range of electric cars. In a masterstroke of understatement, he said:

> *We are not announcing a conventional car. Sinclair Vehicles Limited is dedicated to the development and production of a full range of electric cars, but today we have an electric vehicle, the first stage on the road to the electric car.*

Barrie Wills went further, hailing the C5 as the first in a 'family of traffic-compatible, quiet, economic and pollution-free vehicles for the end of the nineties'.

Addressing what was to be one of the C5's biggest problems, Sinclair said:

> *We've gone to great lengths to make the vehicle very visible, both in daylight and at night, and to make it tough. We're very much of the view that, by encouraging people to be on three wheels rather than two, we will be adding considerably to safety on the road.*

The cars made a dramatic entrance – bursting forth from cardboard boxes driven by promotions girls dressed in grey outfits to match the C5's battleship grey plastic bodywork. The C5 press pack bought into the hyperbole, glossing over the 15mph (24km/h) top speed in favour of claims that the vehicle could 'run at the speed of an Olympic sprinter'.

Sinclair was ahead of the game in other areas, too. At launch, Sinclair showed off an extensive catalogue of customization options and spin-off merchandise, including pullovers, hats, mugs, bags, caps, key rings and even a C5 video game (playable on a Sinclair, naturally). On a more

The C5 was an object of curiosity everywhere. Here the car reposes in the window of a regional newspaper office. NORTHERN ECHO

practical note, the all-weather C5 owner couldn't be without the official clip-on side-panels, which cost £19.95 per pair, and tonneau cover, a snip at a mere £7.95. A more expensive option, at £34.95, was the Sinclair weather-cheater, a waterproof jacket, which, according to the official catalogue, was a 'fashionable piece of leisurewear in its own right'. Other extras in included an indicator kit, the high-visibility mast, seat cushions and a booster pad for younger drivers. A 'free' accessories catalogue was in the box with every C5 sold.

To launch the C5, Sinclair spent £3m on advertising, including full-page national press ads and a television commercial. The theme was that the C5 represented a 'new power in personal transport'. The price of this new power? A mere £399, plus a cheeky £29 postage and packing fee, with no need for road tax or driver's licence. Perhaps mindful of Desbarats' worries about driving a C5 in traffic, every one also came with a free copy of A Guide to Safer C5 Driving, written by the Royal Society for the Prevention of Accidents.

Initially, the vehicle was only available by mail order, while Sinclair tried to thrash out a distribution deal with the regional electricity boards. In the meantime, buyers could place their order at Comet electrical stores and hundreds did so. Export sales were planned to Italy, France, Germany and Holland.

The Mayor of Scarborough was so impressed that he gave up the use of his official Daimler for a C5. Councillor Michael Pitts said if everyone followed his example the North Yorkshire seaside resort's parking problems would be solved overnight. The first C5 'race' took place in the North-East where the mayors of Darlington and Barnard Castle pedalled a couple of C5s around a track for charity.

But the launch euphoria soon turned sour when concerns over the C5's safety emerged. Just 24h after the launch, Cleveland County Council called for the vehicle to be banned from public roads. The authority's highways and transportation committee said it was 'criminal' of the UK's Department of Transport to allow unregulated use of the machine. Committee chairman Paul Harford said: 'I fear what might happen if someone driving one of these comes upon heavy traffic. It's so low on the road that they could get choked by the exhaust fumes of a lorry...'.

Despite a glowing endorsement from the Greater London Council, which dubbed it 'a positive advance in road safety', anxious parents were horrified at the idea of letting a 14-year-old out on the road in a C5. The poor top-speed meant drivers were forced to the side of the road with cyclists – fine when the road in question was smooth but a big problem in towns where gully grates and assorted debris awaited the unwary.

Questions were asked in Parliament and Transport Minister Lynda Chalker was forced to defend the vehicle, declaring it to be 'no more dangerous than a pedal cycle'.

The vehicle's reputation was hardly enhanced when newspapers reported how some drivers had bought C5s to avoid serving drink-driving bans because they required no licence (although, judging by the ridicule C5 owners suffered, a bicycle or a stout pair of walking shoes would probably have been a better choice). Student Nicholas Botting had the dubious distinction of being the first C5 user to be charged with drink-driving after volunteering to drive a girl's C5 home from a St Valentine's Day Ball, in

The C5 left drivers feeling perilously exposed to rush-hour traffic. Even a high-visibility mast did little to make nervous owners feel comfortable.

Although Sinclair countered that the C5 was more visible than a bicycle, questions were soon being asked in the House of Commons, whether the vehicle was suitable for teenagers.

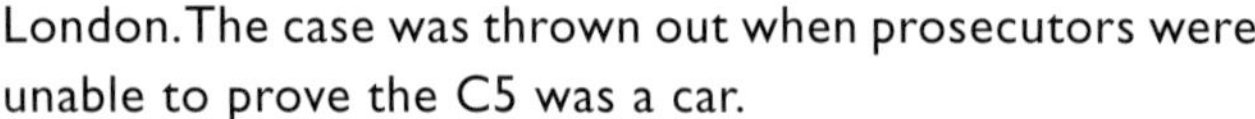

London. The case was thrown out when prosecutors were unable to prove the C5 was a car.

Soon Comet was discounting the vehicle – offering to waive the delivery cost, then slashing the asking price – as unsold stocks began to build up at the Hoover factory.

In June, the C5 was slated in a road test by the influential Consumers Association, which concluded it was 'of limited use and poor value for money'. The report, published in *Which?* magazine, examined the vehicle's braking, speed, acceleration, safety, durability and reliability. Testers found it hard to keep up with traffic due to a mere 13mph (21km/h) top speed on a fully charged battery. Other disadvantages were no speed control on the motor, the lack of suspension, which meant even shallow bumps were felt with bone-crunching force, the non-adjustable seat and pedals, and the poor boot space.

By the beginning of August the game was up. Hoover, alarmed at growing debts, called a halt to production and put the factory into mothballs. Creditors appointed liquidators after hearing the company was in the red to the tune of £6.4m. At the creditors' meeting, held in Coventry in November, Sir Clive was named as the biggest creditor being owed £5.9m. Some 4,800 C5s were unsold out of a production run of approximately 9,000. Overall, Sir Clive himself had lost £8.6m on the venture.

Although the C5 put the electric vehicle concept on the map in the UK, its failure did untold damage to the image

Another problem was the lack of any weather protection. An umbrella was impractical but Sinclair sold its own range of waterproof clothes.

Another design drawing of the ill-fated Sinclair C5.

of electric cars. Subsequent EVs became the butt of endless C5-related jokes and the stigma of owning and driving an EV in Britain was not overcome until the arrival of the Toyota Prius in the late nineties.

Undaunted by the C5's demise, Sir Clive carried on his work with electric vehicles, first with the Zike, an electric bicycle, in 1992 and 'son of C5' the X-1, an electric bicycle with an egg-shape acrylic bubble body in 2010. At the time of writing it has yet to be a success.

France in the 1980s

As Sinclair's dream was ending in crushing failure, motor manufacturers in Europe, spurred on by fears about exhaust pollution in big cities and the prospect of possible legislation to ban petrol cars from town centres, were taking a far more pragmatic attitude towards the electric car.

In France, Peugeot produced electric-powered versions of the 205 hatchback and a variety of Peugeot and Citroën van conversions, which it tested in everyday situations. The 205 Electric was by far the most sophisticated of these designs. Peugeot engineers stashed a dozen 6V nickel-cadmium batteries, weighing a total of 622lb (282kg), beneath the bonnet of a standard three-door 205. In finding a way to shoehorn the battery pack on top of the motor, the interior lost none of the 205's versatility and the boot space wasn't compromised. To cope with the considerable weight increase, the front suspension from the much larger 405 saloon was used. However, from the driver's seat, the 205 Electric was virtually identical to its petrol-powered cousin. The batteries were series wired to give 72V and 200Ah. They could be charged through either a 16 or 40A socket. Both types were fitted to the car. The controls were limited to an accelerator and a brake pedal. A pushbutton on the dash selected reverse.

Peugeot also came up with a novel regenerative braking solution: a hinged pedal that first activated the generator and then the brakes, depending on the degree of pressure applied. To charge the batteries, the driver pulled out a retractable cable, rather like a vacuum cleaner, and simply plugged it into a household socket. A full charge took 8h.

Jean Helmer, general manager of PSA's automobile division, told CAR magazine that the company had sought to keep the cost down by using standard 205 parts whenever possible. That way, the 205 Electric could be assembled on the same production line. 'We expect that we could reduce the extra cost of buying an electric car to a premium of £3,000 over an equivalent petrol car,' he said. 'If we could sell 50,000 a year, it would be possible to get the price to the same level, or even cheaper, than a petrol version.' Bold claims, especially taking into account the cost of nickel-cadmium batteries in the early eighties. If the price came down, Helmer said, he was confident sales of electric 205s would represent 2 per cent of PSA's total production by 1994–95.

Fifteen prototypes were handed over to utility companies in France and Belgium. Staff at PSA's electric power research centre, near Versailles, used them as daily drivers.

Sadly, the three-door 205 Electric was no GTi. Its motor was only rated at a modest 23.4bhp and it struggled to propel the car, which weighed in at 1,874lb (850kg), to more than 60mph (96.5km/h). However, *Autocar* magazine commented: 'Acceleration is modest, yet sufficient to keep up with most city traffic, and the car is virtually silent in operation'. The magazine also praised the regenerative braking for its effectiveness, but added the following caveat: 'Just as well, since the conventional hydraulic brakes are unservoed and need a fair amount of pedal pressure'. Despite Jean Helmer's unshakable confidence, the 205 was only produced for a single model year, in 1984. Approximately 500 were made and sold to customers – a far cry from the 50,000 envisaged.

Volkswagen and Audi

Volkswagen first experimented with electrification of its incredibly successful Golf range in the seventies, when it removed the internal combustion engine and replaced it with a battery-powered electric motor. These early tests gave rise to the 1985 CitySTROMer (strom is the German word for current), of which more than 100 were made. VW engineers retained the Golf bodyshell and fitted a 16bhp DC-motor in the engine bay. Powered by sixteen lead-acid gel batteries, the motor could produce 20.6bhp for 15 min or kick out 30.8bhp for a maximum of 5min.

To keep the batteries cool, the CitySTROMer used a single-point watering system. The car's front grille (a solid slab of plastic that was cut into the standard slatted grille) hinged down to give access to the on-board charger, which required between 8 and 12h to bring the batteries up to full capacity. For each hour of charge, VW claimed the car would cover 4 miles (6km) – giving a maximum range of around 50 miles (80km).

Top speed was around 60mph (96.5km/h) – something of a disappointment for anyone who believed the standard Golf 120mph (190km/h) speedo to be indicative of the CitySTROMer's performance potential. A small range indicator replaced the fuel gauge. A separate, small gas tank in the engine bay provided fuel for the heater.

In other respects, the CitySTROMer resembled nothing more unusual than a standard three-door Golf. It even retained that car's petrol cap (albeit blanked off with a warning sign that showed a petrol pump icon with a big red cross through it). The asking price was $30,000.

Although more than 100 left-hand drive examples were manufactured, only two right-hand drive cars are known to exist. They were both built for the UK utility company Southern Electric and remained on the company's fleet until they were sold to private buyers in the mid-1990s. One has since been purchased by VW UK and is in the process of being restored to full working order.

The same system was also lifted into the Golf's less glamorous sibling, the Jetta. Equipped with a conventional clutch and five-speed gearbox, the Jetta won praise from *Autocar* magazine, which praised its 'good speed range' and 'outstanding' refinement. Tester Tony Lewin added:

> *It kept up well with Birmingham urban freeway traffic right up to some 55mph (88.5km/h), and at no stage was I conscious of the milk-float syndrome. My worst problem was circumnavigating a pedestrian square: perhaps all electric cars should have powerful stereos as standard so people can hear them coming?*

VW's interest in the EV continued. As well as a Jetta CitySTROMer, there was a version that used the third-generation Golf bodyshell. Sadly, the CitySTROMer's usefulness continued to be hindered by a 60-mile (96km) range limitation.

In 1987, VW took the wraps off a diesel–electric hybrid drive Golf. The system was co-developed by VW and Bosch. It used a 1.6-litre VW catalyst diesel engine connected via a shaft to a 8bhp asynchronous motor/generator and a five-speed manual gearbox. Two automatic clutches sandwiched the electric motor; they were neatly integrated into the motor/generator assembly, helping to keep the hybrid drive relatively compact – it was only 2in (58mm) longer than the standard VW 1.6 diesel engine. The weight of the electric motor and the twin clutches added 64lb (29kg) to the car, however.

The motor/generator replaced the starter and the flywheel. VW also dumped the Golf's 12V alternator. VW reckoned the internal combustion engine would provide the acceleration and be used for speeds of more than 31mph (49.8km/h), with the electric motor helping out around town.

Despite the measly 8bhp output, VW reckoned the motor could push the Golf to 37mph (60km/h), given a long enough road. The diesel automatically cut in when speeds increased, and around town a computer determined the best power sources for any given circumstances. Interestingly, however, a drive-mode switch allowed the driver to select a full EV mode, although VW admitted: 'This, however, reduces acceleration performance'.

The Mark Two Golf's engine bay had no problem accommodating the extra equipment thanks, in part, to the elimination of the starter and alternator. The transmission was not relocated but the diesel was moved 2in (58mm) to the side.

The car's drive-mode selector switch, charge-level indicator and crude operation mode LEDs were installed in the standard Golf dashboard. There was no clutch pedal and the batteries for the electric motor were located beneath the boot (as they were in the CitySTROMers).

Thus equipped, VW made some startling claims for hybrid propulsion:

The Golf CitySTROMer sired a Jetta alternative and prompted further investigation by Audi.

The Jetta CitySTROMer.

Audi's Duo hybrid – note the solar panels on the roof.

> *The Golf Hybrid is designed to cut emissions by up to 60 per cent through a sophisticated engine-management system. Carbon dioxide emissions alone are cut by more than half. With optimum utilization of diesel and electric powertrains, the Golf Hybrid could achieve more than 100 miles per gallon of diesel fuel.*

Presciently, the company's publicity for the Golf hybrid correctly identified the huge potential offered by combining an internal combustion engine with an electric motor. It said:

> *Vehicles equipped with [hybrid] drive systems are far more flexible than electric vehicles; they are often just as flexible as vehicles with an internal combustion engine and, consequently, not confined from the outset to the 'second car' market.*
> *Hybrid drives thus have far more extensive potential applications than electric drives. Higher production rates could, in principle, therefore be achieved, leading to low manufacturing costs.*

More than fifty Elektro-Hybrid Golfs took part in a major field trial between Volkswagen AG, the Swiss Federal Technical University of Zurich and the Zurich authorities which ran until 1991. Sadly for VW, Toyota would become the company to demonstrate the benefits of hybrid powertrains on the mass market with the Prius 6 years later.

VW's sister company Audi also investigated hybrid propulsion and produced a series of cars based on popular models. It was concerned that growing environmental concerns may prompt towns and cities to ban petrol cars. A hybrid powertrain offered a possible solution: by allowing a petrol-powered car to avoid a ban by running on electricity. The company's first effort – called the Audi Duo – was built in 1989 and unveiled at the Geneva Motor Show the following March. It used the Audi 100 Avant body as a basis for a petrol–electric hybrid. Crowds at the show were impressed by the solar panels on the car's roof but the Duo's ambitions were modest, however, as the electric motor was barely more powerful than the Golf CitySTROMer at a mere 12.6bhp. It was powered by nickel-cadmium batteries that drove the rear wheels. The power pack, which had a service life of 10 years, used forty-nine nickle-cadmium batteries connected in series, delivering a total voltage of 58.8V. It weighed 399lb (181kg) and was sited beneath the boot in the spare wheel well. A space-saver spare was sited in a separate partition on the left of the luggage compartment. The extra weight of the motor and the batteries over the rear wheels forced Audi to fit uprated springs, dampers and wider 205/60 R15V tyres.

The system was designed by Pohlman, a German company based in Kulmbach, which had been awarded a grant from the Bavarian state authorities to develop an electric drive system.

In pure electric mode, which had to be selected via a button on the centre console when the car was at a standstill, the Audi Duo had a claimed top speed of 32mph (51.4km/h), 0–20mph acceleration in 8sec and a range of 'about 20 miles' (32km). Most of the time the Duo relied on a 5-cylinder, 2.3-litre petrol engine, which delivered 136bbhp to the front wheels.

However, the batteries were charged while the car was driven by the internal combustion engine and a full recharge took just 45min. A dashboard display informed the driver of the battery's state of charge. Turning the ignition key started either the internal combustion engine or activated the electric motor (after putting the gearbox in neutral and pressing a button marked 'E'). When running with electric drive, a small additional electric motor powered the hydraulics. All the controls worked normally and the car felt the same as any other automatic Audi. An auxiliary petrol-fed water-heater maintained the cabin temperature in cold weather and took the load off the electrical system.

A bullish Audi said:

> *In principle, the hybrid system can be installed in any Audi model with Quattro four-wheel drive... and is suitable for large-scale production. Extra complexity, compared with a car powered by a combustion engine only, is kept within acceptable limits, since the additional electric drive system merely requires modifications to an otherwise standard car.*

Just two years later, Audi developers returned with the second-generation Duo, once again in the guise of an Audi 100 Avant. The company had spent the intervening two years refining the concept. Whereas the first car had a primitive hybrid drive system – the engineers just disconnected the four-wheel drive, removed the prop shaft and directly coupled the 132lb (60kg) DC electric motor to the rear axle via an electrically operated clutch – the second generation

Audi even showed off a Duo taxi.

enjoyed the benefits of permanent four-wheel drive via the self-locking Torsen interaxle differential.

Using the Torsen diff allowed Audi to route extra power from the 115bhp, 2.0-litre, 4-cylinder internal combustion engine to the rear wheels. Once again, the second-generation Duo could be switched to an all-electric drive mode. Power came via a 28.6bhp water-cooled three-phase AC synchronous motor weighing 101.4lb (46kg) and directly flange-mounted on the rear axle. The motor's energy source was a lead-acid battery powerpack.

Although neither Duo was ever offered for sale, the Ingolstadt company maintained it was taking the technology seriously, adding:

> *At any given time, up to ten Audi Duos have been in operation, driven by selected end-users so as to gain everyday experience of the car 'in action' for the purpose of further refinement.*

At the Berlin Motor Show in October 1996, the company demonstrated just how seriously it had been researching hybrid technology when it revealed the third-generation Duo. Based on the A4 Avant, the duo (now spelt with a lower case 'd') incorporated two drive systems – the Volkswagen Group's well-known 1.9-litre TDI diesel engine and a water-cooled three-phase AC synchronous motor that developed the same 28.6bhp as its immediate predecessor.

Announcing that series production would begin the following year, Audi said:

> *With the Audi duo [Audi] is initiating a trend in the sphere of environmentally compatible technology which is certain to gain in significance in the years ahead. The duo's pioneering concept puts an end to the constant debate on how private transport can be used in car-free zones, or during smog alerts, to maintain deliveries to commercial enterprises, and the public at large, without exhaust emissions and without noise.*

The press briefing went on:

> *Seventy-five per cent of all journeys by road are of less than 50 kilometres. This makes the duo principle still more interesting to all those car owners who wish to avoid emissions entirely and to reduce noise to an absolute minimum when driving in inner-city areas and conurbations, but at the same time do not wish, or cannot afford, to sacrifice unlimited mobility over greater distances.*

Audi claimed the duo could travel 372 miles (600km) on its TDI engine, plus a further 31 miles (50km) powered by the electric motor. In the duo's 'hybrid' mode, a computer made the decision when to choose between the two methods. The electric motor was not used as a torque

The Audi e-Tron concept gives a clue as to where Audi plans to go next with hybrid technology.

The e-Tron drivetrain will almost certainly feature on the next TT.

booster and the weight of the batteries made the standard A4's stodgy handling even more ponderous. Nevertheless, the car had a top speed of 105mph (170km/h) and accelerated to 100km/h (62mph) in a not very impressive 16sec. On electric power, the car could do 50mph (80km/h) and could accelerate from 0 to 50km/h (31mph) in 9.5sec. In addition, the diesel engine was capable of running on plant-oil methyl ester.

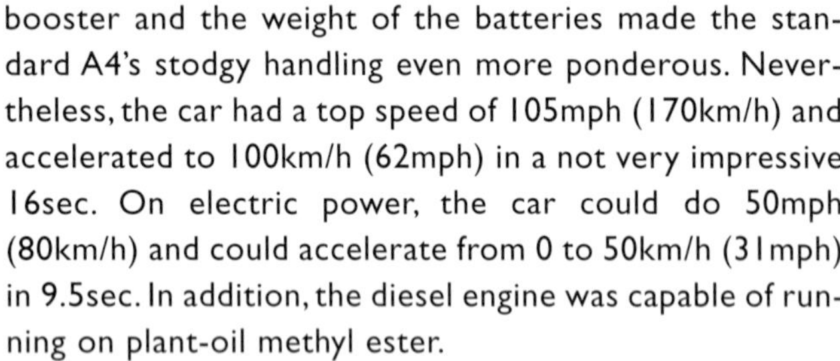

The advantages of electricity were clear, however. According to Audi's calculations, the fuel costs for inner-city driving on the electric motor were 2.86 Deutsche Marks (DM) per 62 miles (100km), with diesel consumption under the same conditions costing DM 8.40 per 62 miles (100km). After presenting those figures, the company stated the obvious:

> *Since the performance characteristics of the electric motor are perfectly adequate for inner-city travel, it makes sense to drive the Audi duo exclusively in electric mode in towns.*

Although the third-generation duo did make production, sales were modest. However, the duo did allow Audi to claim it had been first to market with a hybrid (if you ignored the Lohner–Porsche Mixte almost 100 years earlier) and the company continued to refine the technology. The lead engineer on the duo III project, Marius Lehna, was responsible for the early designs of the Q5 Hybrid.[31]

Audi returned with an even more exciting electric hybrid concept in 2009.

The e-tron high-performance electric sports car concept used four motors, one per wheel, just like Ferdinand Porsche's design, but its claimed power of 308bhp and the unbelievable torque figure of 3,319lb ft (4,500Nm) showed how far technology had come in a century. Audi said the e-tron was capable of 0–62mph (100km/h) of 4.8sec and its top speed was limited to 124mph (200km/h).

Unfortunately for Audi, the word e-tron sounded very similar to the French word etron, which means turd. This unfortunate coincidence didn't prevent the Germans introducing more e-tron concepts, including a Spyder high-performance sports car, and an electric variant of the A1 (which used an unusual 254cc Wankel engine as a range extender) and the A3 hatchback.

The R8 supercar is set to be the first volume Audi to use the e-tron technology in 2013. Engineers say the two-seater provides the perfect test bed for a hybrid powertrain that will undoubtedly trickle down to other models in the range. The car will make use of four electric motors, two each at the front and rear axles, driving all four wheels. Audi is aiming for a power output of at least 308bhp and the lithium-ion battery pack can be charged through an ordinary household outlet.

Having famously won the Le Mans 24h race with a diesel-powered race car in 2006, Audi entered a diesel–electric

The e-TRON Spyder was another hybrid concept.

The need to accommodate extra batteries didn't spoil the Spyder's lines.

Audi believes an electric motor will help make performance cars even more exciting to drive by improving low-range torque.

The Audi e-tron quattro at Le Mans 2012.

Audi made history when it became the first manufacturer to win the Le Mans 24-hour race with a hybrid.

hybrid (the R18 e-tron quattro) in the famous endurance event in 2012. The two Audi R18 e-tron quattros finished first and second after leading almost the entire way – becoming the first hybrids to win the prestigious race.

Audi motorsport boss Dr Wolfgang Ullrich said:

> *It was a very big challenge to develop a hybrid car in such a short time that is quick and able to hold up for 24 hours. We have always been pushing through the years to bring new technologies to Le Mans in race cars. To push them to the limit and bring this technology into our road cars and make it available to our customers is why we go racing.*

Dr Porsche would surely have approved.

The Zoom was Renault's interpretation of an electric commuter with a unique 'folding' body.

Renault's Folding Electric Car Concept: the Zoom

In August 1992, Renault unveiled a radical interpretation of an electric commuter car: a tiny two-seat city car with a body that contracted for parking. Called the Zoom, it was Renault's response to growing concerns over chronic urban congestion. The company claimed that every lunchtime in Paris, a third of all cars in the city were looking for a parking space. According to *Autocar*, equipped with a Zoom, the average Frenchman stood a better chance of enjoying his déjeuner thanks to the car's variable wheelbase.

In parking mode, the wheelbase moved by tilting the body upwards; this reduced the Zoom's overall length by almost 14in (350mm). During normal driving, electric motors lowered the body again, thereby extending the car's length to 103in (2,650mm), which still made it a remarkable 16in (400mm) shorter than a Mini.

The engine was an auto-synchronous electric AC motor transversely mounted and driving the front wheels. Power was said to be 33.5bhp. Thanks to a low weight of just 1,763lb (800kg), the Zoom was capable of 75mph (120km/h). More importantly, it could reach 30mph (48.2km/h) in less than 6sec – essential if a driver wasn't to be left standing in the cut and thrust of urban driving in a busy city like Paris. The range was said to be 90 miles (145km) and the batteries could be recharged to 80 per cent capacity in 2h.

Renault specified a bump-resistant body made from plastic colour-impregnated panels. The lower half of the body

The Zoom's body was fashioned from impact-resistant, colour-impregnated plastic, which also helped keep the weight down to just 1,760lb (800kg).

The Zoom's cabin included a hands-free phone and satellite navigation.

was protected by grey plastic cladding, similar to the enormous bumpers Ford would fit to the KA some years later.

Zoom was fitted with an airbag, anti-lock brakes, side-impact bars in the doors and a new design of seatbelt said to be more comfortable and safer in a crash. Convenience features included a hands-free phone and Carminat satellite navigation – both housed in a impressive-sounding 'communications centre' between the seats.

The car, which was developed by Renault's Matra division, was conceived as part of a £50m French Government plan to introduce fleets of electric cars into ten French cities. But the scheme depended on the country's electricity board creating the recharging infrastructure needed to allow recharging in public, as well as at home.

French ministers hoped commuters would be able to rent electric cars by slotting in a credit card and driving away. The idea was that when they were no longer needed, the cars could be parked at designated parking stations, where they would recharge ready for the next renter. The French scheme was ambitious and Renault – as the national car manufacturer – embraced the challenge.

As well as the Zoom, Renault also partnered with Siemens to develop an electric version of the popular Clio supermini. Called the Elektro Clio, it would use the same running gear as the Zoom, but with cheaper batteries. It was also a good deal heavier because the Clio was a conventional steel monocoque chassis, whereas the Zoom was built on a weight-saving aluminium frame with plastic body panels.

Autocar confidentially predicted the Zoom 'is likely to go into production within three years' but, in reality, it was nothing but a marketing exercise to test market acceptance for a variety of novel ideas.

Not to be outdone by its great French rival, Citroën unveiled its own radical EV concept, the Citela, at the Universal Exposition, held in Seville, in 1992. It, too, had a modular body that allowed it to transform from a bizarre-looking coupé to a mini-estate and a saloon. Citroën claimed the car had a top speed of 62mph (110km/h) and could travel 130.4 miles (210 km) before requiring a recharge. Citroën claimed the Citela was more than a mere flight of fancy and that the prototype had covered more than a million kilometres in development testing.

A far more serious stab at electrification was the 106 Electric built by Citroën's sister company, Peugeot. Launched in 1995, to coincide with a highly ambitious electrification project in the French city of La Rochelle, the 106 Electric was a modest success finding favour among local authorities and other urban business buyers in France and Great Britain. More than 2,000 were sold in France alone and several hundred in the UK.

To drum up publicity in England, Peugeot donated a couple of electric-powered 106s to Coventry's Chace Avenue police station, the nearest station to the company's UK headquarters, to provide additional transport for bobbies working in the local community. Peugeot UK lauded the vehicles' environmental credentials, as well as their excep-

The Citroën Citela, unveiled at the Universal Exposition, in Spain, in 1992.

The Citela in urban city car guise.

Modular body panels transformed the Citela into a useful pick-up/estate.

The Citroën Citela's interior was something of a let-down after the dramatic exterior.

tional quiet – perfect for the stealthy police officer looking to catch a criminal red-handed.

The electric 106 had a top speed of 56mph (90km/h) and could accelerate from 0 to 31mph (50km/h) in 8.3sec. The range was said, variously, to be somewhere between 40 and 50 miles (64–80km) per charge, with a full recharge taking 6h.

The officers of Chace Avenue police station certainly saw the electric hatchback as a step up from walking the beat. Inspector Mark Robinson said at the time:

> *They are fabulous and are already in daily use. Our officers enjoy driving them and recharging is simplicity itself. And because the cars are so quiet, they have created a lot of interest in and around the local community.*

Robert Browett, Peugeot UK's public affairs manager, added:

> *The electric 106 is ideal for making house-to-house calls; it's environmentally friendly, can comfortably accommodate four people, and is extremely cost-effective to run.*

At the time, 253 electric 106s were in daily use across the UK; one of the greatest concentrations being in Nottinghamshire, where a fleet of thirty-eight was used to promote green transport solutions. The Nottinghamshire Millennium Project was a joint partnership between the County Council, Nottingham City Council, energy company PowerGen and the Energy Saving Trust.

In April 1999, the 106 also made a little piece of electric car history when it gave rise to the UK's first on-street electric-charging point. Owner Simon Roberts had been campaigning for 4 years to have a plug-in point at the kerbside of his home. Nearly a century after electric motors failed to oust the internal combustion engine, due in part to the lack of a dependable charging infrastructure, the political landscape had finally changed for the better.

The same year, in France, car-hire company Europcar launched an electric vehicles programme in Paris to give drivers a chance to test drive the 106 EV and discover the benefits of electric power. Europcar officials were surprised by the demand.

But it was the city of La Rochelle that truly embraced the EV. The city's technical services – the post office and EDF electricity – had used electric vehicles from 1986 and in 1993 an ambitious scheme was unveiled for private users. From December 1993 to December 1995, a fleet of electric Peugeot 106s and Citroën AXs cruised the streets in the world's most forward-thinking EV initiative designed to test electric car performance in an urban environment.

In 1995, the Township Committee introduced a hire scheme for cars and electric scooters. At the same time, the city introduced free parking for electric vehicles and

The Peugeot 106 electric was a far more conventional stab at an EV.

Rob Browett, Peugeot's UK PR manager, hands over the keys of an electric 106 as part of a partnership with the police in Coventry.

introduced parking facilities with recharging units. A 106 could be recharged from flat in 6h and each unit could service three vehicles at a time. Fast-charging stations were also installed at three Total petrol stations.

The vehicles were available on a self-service basis from seven pick-up points in the city. Users borrowed them via a swipe card system, which unlocked the doors. The user tapped in a keycode on a dashboard-mounted pad and the car was good to go.

In addition to cheap transport, the scheme offered other benefits such as free parking anywhere in the La Rochelle area and easy availability. This innovative service cost 5.5 Euros per month. By the end of April 2002, the scheme had 485 users with six new subscriptions every week.

In Britain, the British Government stumped up £400,000 for an electric car trial in Coventry. Under the terms of the scheme Peugeot handed over electric cars to Coventry City Council, East Midlands Electricity, PowerGen and Royal Mail Coventry. Each had a battery-recharging point installed on their premises and the council added others in key points around the city. At the launch in 1996, the Transport Secretary, George Young, pointed to the La Rochelle project as a blueprint for the Coventry trial but, sadly, the UK experiment was on a smaller, less ambitious, scale.

CHAPTER SEVEN

A FALSE DAWN: THE GENERAL MOTORS EV1

The General Motors EV1 marked a step change in the public's perception of the electric car. It was the first mass-produced and purpose-designed electric vehicle of the modern era from a major car manufacturer. More than that, though, it was the first modern car designed, quite literally, from the tyres up to run on electricity.

It was developed with the full resources of the world's biggest car manufacturer, lauded (initially, at least) by the critics, and loved by those who drove it but ultimately it would be judged a failure. After it was controversially withdrawn, the EV1's creator branded it a flop and Time magazine named it as one of the fifty worst cars ever made.

But history has been kind to the EV1. More than a decade after it was unceremoniously pulled from production and, quite literally, scrapped, GM's chief executive Rick Wagoner admitted that killing the EV1 was the biggest mistake he ever made. Withdrawing the car in 2002 had, he said, squandered GM's lead in electric car technology and handed the initiative to the Japanese.

Sunraycer

The EV1 traced its roots back to 1987 when General Motors and AeroVironment, an electric car specialist, combined forces to design a single-seat concept called the Sunraycer in a bid to win the inaugural World Solar Challenge – a trans-Australian race for solar vehicles.

The Sunraycer project came about after GM's Australian division pitched a plan to enter the race. GM's Chairman, Roger Smith, was intrigued by the possibilities of a solar-powered car and gave the plan his blessing – but the timescale was incredibly tight. Smith said he would only back the idea if the team could design and build a credible solar challenger within 10 months.

To kick-start the project, Smith hired AeroVironment, a Californian technology company that specialized in electrical energy systems. Four weeks later, an excited team of engineers, designers and specialists concluded it could be done.

What started out as a fun project became deadly serious when Ford Australia announced it would enter the

The Sunraycer started out as a fun project but things got serious when Ford entered the race.

The Sunraycer's success prompted other manufacturers to seek solar success. Honda won with its Dream car in 1996.

race as well. The two rivals would go head-to-head. Teams from GM, GM Hughes Electronics, AeroVironment and more than a dozen other GM divisions and suppliers were seconded to work on the Sunraycer programme.

From the outset the team agreed that, if the car was to stand a chance of covering the length of Australia, it had to be lightweight and aerodynamically efficient. So the Sunraycer's body was dictated by the wind tunnel. Hours and hours of aerodynamic refinement led to a flat shape reminiscent of a manta ray. It tipped the scales at a featherweight 585lb (265kg) and had a very low coefficient of drag (just 0.125) giving it a top speed of 68mph (109km/h).

The experts at GM Hughes Electronics brought their knowledge of satellite solar panels to the team. They fitted 8,800 photovoltaic cells to the Sunraycer's sleek bodywork. In the unrelenting heat of the midday Australian sun, that was enough to generate 1,500W of power. To make the most of this, GM's physics department came up with a new engine utilizing state-of-the-art magnets and capable, according to its manufacturer, of 92 per cent efficiency. Power was stored in a silver oxide battery pack, so the vehicle could keep going even in cloudy weather. The bodywork was fashioned from Kevlar over a simple frame that weighed a mere 14lb (6.3kg). In fact, by far the heaviest element of the Sunraycer was the driver.

When the Sunraycer was wheeled out to do battle, it quickly became painfully obvious that the opposition didn't stand a chance. Sunraycer was so far ahead of anything else in the field, it was almost embarrassing. It won the 1,950-mile (3,138km) race from Darwin, in the north of Australia, to Adelaide, in the South, by a huge margin, finishing more than 620 miles (998km) ahead of its nearest competitor, the Ford Australia Sunchaser. Indeed, the well-beaten Ford team entrant trailed in a whole 2 days after Roger Smith had watched his victorious Sunraycer cross the finishing line.

And that was it. After setting a solar-powered world speed record the following year, starring in a promotional film and going on a trans-continental publicity tour, the Sunraycer was put out to grass. For all its mastery, solar power was a technological dead end.

However, keen not to see the company's $2 million investment and effort go to waste, Smith gave AeroVironment the go-ahead to build an electric concept car.

John Zwerner, executive director of GM advanced product engineering, explained the thinking that led to the concept:

> *The fact that we won the race in Australia in 1987 by some two-and-a-half days gave us a strong feeling that we had a pretty good lock on some technology. It looked like a good evolution [of the project) to examine a pure electric car. We wanted to drive a stake in the ground as to what a contemporary thinking, but producible, electric*

> *vehicle would look like and [how it would) perform, if we were to build it.*

Mules – conventional cars with experimental drivetrains – were soon up and running. GM used several different vehicles to evaluate various electrical power systems, including a Geo Storm and a Lumina APV minivan. The company invited several journalists to test the Lumina at its desert proving grounds in Arizona. Dual front-drive electric motors were examined but rejected in favour of a single, powerful AC induction motor.

The Impact Concept

A prototype – called the Impact – was unveiled at the Los Angeles Auto Show, in January 1990. Unveiling the car, Smith said the project 'keeps GM on the cutting edge of technology. It's an exciting new electric car that can go further and faster than any previous production-oriented electric vehicle. It can go from 0 to 60mph in eight seconds and it has all the comfort and convenience features of the modern automobile.'

To prove the performance claim, GM later organized a race between the Impact, a Mazda Miata (MX5) and a Nissan 300ZX. Up to 60mph (96km/h), the Impact walked away from the two sports cars. Zwerner said:

> *As we did that, it really moved the electric vehicle from the golf cart kind of mentality to 'this is a viable candidate for merging with traffic and fitting in with the kind of requirements we have on today's road systems'.*

The critics agreed. According to Brian Hatano, of *Car Craft* magazine, the Impact demonstrated that 'there's a definite future for the electronic (sic) car'. Kim Reynolds, of *Road & Track*, went even further, declaring the Impact 'would be competitive with most performance cars available today.' *Motor Trend* believed the car was 'one of those occasions where GM proves beyond any doubt that it knows how to build fantastic automobiles. This is the world's only electric vehicle that drives like a real car.'

When it was unveiled, the Impact looked like something from a Buck Rogers comic strip.

Gary Witzenberg and his handpicked team of engineers, known as the GM Advanced Technology Vehicles Test and Development Team.

GM claimed the Impact had a greater range than any previous EV, too. Under ideal conditions, at the company's Mesa desert proving ground, the car had covered 125 miles (201km) before its batteries became exhausted.

The almost universally positive public reaction was even more encouraging than the critical acclaim. At its Los Angeles unveiling, four out of five people surveyed said they would definitely consider buying an electric car. More impressive still, 95 per cent of people quizzed saw the Impact as sophisticated and high tech. The project was given added impetus when the Californian Air Resources Board (CARB) – impressed by the Impact's potential – passed a mandate, which decreed that by 1998, 2 per cent of all cars sold should be emissions-free. Since electric cars were the only zero-emissions game in town, the CARB mandate provided a massive incentive for auto manufacturers to produce workable electric vehicles.

On 22 April 1990 (Earth Day), Smith told members of the National Press Club that he was going ahead with an electric car. He said:

> *I'm very pleased to announce today that we are taking a major step toward helping our country meet its transportation needs and environmental goals. We are proceeding with our plan to produce and sell the Impact.*

In giving the green light, he over-ruled objections from GM North America President Bob Stempel, who would soon succeed Smith as company CEO. 'After the reaction at the LA Show he felt we needed to follow through with it,' Stempel remembers. 'He said, "I want General Motors to showcase its technology, and I want people to understand we are in the lead on this".'

The huge job of bringing the car to market was handed to Ken Baker, who had been chief engineer on another GM electric car, the Electrovette, 10 years earlier. Having got his hands burned on that project, Baker was understandably reluctant. He didn't want to get involved but was convinced after Stempel, GM President-elect Lloyd Reuss and Vice Chairman Bob Schultz launched a three-way charm offensive.

With Baker on board, the project took on a new impetus. Engineer Gary Witzenburg, who had been working in public relations for Buick, was recruited to be the vehicle's test and development manager. He remembers:

> *It was a very select team. The project had been given a high priority (by Bob Stempel) and we were empowered to work outside the General Motors structure so the car could be developed as quickly as possible. We knew the costs would be high, because we were doing something that had never been tried before, and the company wanted to invest as little as possible to get it done.*

Witzenburg hand-picked his own team of engineers to oversee the car. They were led by Clive Roberts, an engineer at Lotus – GM's British sports car satellite – who was fresh from work on the front-wheel drive Elan sports car.

Roberts was assigned to the project. 'I would do the boring management stuff, like sitting in meetings and Clive would do the seat-of-the-pants testing at the track,' remembers Witzenburg. 'I was a bit jealous of him but Clive was brilliant at what he did. The EV 1's handling was a testament to his work.'

It would be several years before the car was ready. To maintain interest in the project, Roberts suggested taking one of the development mules and trying to set a new speed record. 'It was fairly low at the time,' says Witzenburg. 'We

The EV1 would never be sold – vehicles were leased to eager users who bought into the project without realizing the car could be taken away from them.

knew it was within reach because the bar was pretty low and the publicity spin-off would be huge. So we changed the tyres and lowered the body a bit. With Clive driving, the car was fast but it would only do three laps before the batteries were exhausted.' Nevertheless, on 11 March 1994, a lightly modified Impact fitted with six additional batteries set a new land-speed record for electric vehicles by powering through a set of timing lights at 183.822mph (295.8km/h) at a test track near Fort Stockton, in Texas.

Led by Baker, the team knew from the outset that they had to work around the limitations of current battery technology. Rather than chase a new breakthrough in battery storage capacity, they elected to create the world's most efficient car to make the most of what they had. Then, if a better battery came along, the car could only get better. According to Witzenburg:

> *Battery technology hadn't kept pace with other areas of car development. The first car had twenty-seven lead-acid batteries, twenty-six for the motor and one for the ancillaries that held the equivalent of half a gallon of gas. That's why the rest of the car had to be so energy efficient. The next technology that was coming through was nickel metal hydride, which we put into the second-generation cars, although not without difficulty because we needed a cooling system to keep the temperature down, but they gave us double the energy for more or less the same weight.*

The project had a troubled gestation and came close to being cancelled more than once. Baker, who was promoted to vice president of GM research and development, managed to keep a core team of 100 engineers working on the car at an off-site facility in Troy, Michigan.

In 1993, desperate to convince GM the car had a bright future, Witzenburg arranged a risky test drive for eager journalists.

> *We had a handling car, a noise, vibration and harshness car and a bodywork car that was good for photos. What we didn't have was one car with all those qualities but I reasoned the writers would understand why. So we invited a select bunch of writers and entertained two a day – with presentations before and after lunch. Each product development team leader gave a presentation before we let them have a drive at the proving ground. We knew the cars would perform well and that we would exceed their expectations. After all, most of them were expecting a two-seat golf cart. Thankfully, it turned out to be right.*

Writers who got their hands on the car were impressed. *Popular Science* dubbed the car, 'the world's best electric car', although, at the time, the competition was scarce. *Popular Mechanics* said it was a 'masterstroke of engineering'.[32]

The positive critical reaction played a key roll in convincing GM's management to green light a limited public roll-out. Fifty hand-built Impacts were manufactured as part of a 2-year ride-and-drive evaluation programme run in a dozen cities across the United States. Each one was carefully turned and all the electrical systems given a 'burn-in' period to ensure they worked at peak efficiency before they were handed over. The test vehicles were essentially production-ready. They were fitted with twin airbags, cruise control, anti-lock brakes and air-conditioning – one of the reasons why they weighed 2,970lb (1,374kg) – more than 400lb (181kg) heavier than the original prototype.

The cars were to be loaned for a couple of weeks to drivers who were prepared to log their thoughts and experiences. Volunteers had to own a garage where a high-current charging point could be installed. With this in place, the Impact's lead-acid battery pack could be recharged in 3h. GM believed a 'real world' evaluation programme was the best way to gauge the project's viability for mass production.

However, it was unprepared for the intense public interest. Manning the phones in Los Angeles, Impact programme supervisor, Sean McNamara, was stunned when more than 10,000 people called to say they would like to be involved in evaluating the car. He had expected fewer than 100 callers. Eventually, so many would-be testers rang, he was forced to close the switchboard. It was the same story in New York.

The reaction from people who drove the car was equally positive. Of those drivers who used the Impact for a week or more, 83 per cent agreed that the car would meet their needs. They had quickly learned how to live with the Impact's limitations and were generally happy with the overall performance.

GM reasoned that the huge investment it had made in the Impact's technology could be recouped quickly – provided it lost no time in pressing ahead with a production version. If the car was a hit, GM would reap far more than its original commitment by licensing the technology to other car manufacturers unwilling (or unable) to develop their own EVs.

It was vital to maintain the project's momentum, so the project team was sub-divided and run in parallel, working not just on the first-generation car, but the second generation too. That way GM could build and sustain an unassailable lead in EV technology.

There was another reason for the breakneck pace. By refining the technology, GM planned to reduce its component and build costs as quickly as possible, because the first cars would be hugely expensive and it would lose money on each one. The batteries alone cost $25,000.

Meanwhile, work continued on refining the concept ready for production. As is common with concept cars, some of the prototype's more radical features were toned down. The slit-like projector headlamps and tail lamps were replaced by larger, and cheaper, units. The prototype used a front splitter air dam to channel air under the smooth body, but such a complex item would have been too expensive for production, so it was replaced by a more conventional front end. The Impact's most controversial feature, its teardrop bodywork, was too distinctive – and important – to change, however.

By 1996 everything was ready.

The EV1: the Future Arrives

In the days running up to the Impact's launch, GM bosses began to have second thoughts about the car's name. The word 'Impact' had negative connotations with accidents and the company feared its world-beating electric car might become the butt of talk show jokes. 'The name Impact was supposed to signify the impact we expected the car to have on the world but, as time went on, GM became concerned that talk show hosts like Jay Leno would mock it. I don't think we ever expected it to reach market as the Impact,' says Witzenburg.

So Impact became the rather more prosaic, EV1. Despite the dreary monicker, GM hailed the EV1's arrival as: 'The car of the future... today.'

The company's marketing material proudly boasted:

> *With twenty-three new patents that are being applied to future electric, hybrid and gasoline-powered cars, the EV1, like American cars that came before it, is sure to change the lives of not only those who drive it, but of everyone who drives.*

As with the Impact, EV1 was only available on a lease agreement, initially to people living in Los Angeles, in Southern California, and Phoenix and Tucson, Arizona. The first cars were delivered on 5 December 1996.[33]

In another parallel with the Impact, GM bosses grandly

claimed that EV1's early adopters were simply participants in a 'real-world engineering evaluation' into the feasibility of mass producing an electric car. Although the car was the first to carry the General Motors brand, it was leased through GM's Saturn division. Payments for the car ranged from $399 to a hefty $549 a month and they could only be serviced at approved dealerships. Drivers couldn't even change a tyre because they were a bespoke design, created by Michelin especially for the EV1.

Saturn employed a group of EV specialists who worked with lessees. It was their job to explain how to adapt to an electric car. They took care of everything from getting a charger installed, to arranging the lease, and even filing for tax credits. GM saw the EV specialist as 'the link between the customer, the EV1, the charger distributor, Saturn and General Motors'.

GM backed the car with a 3-year/36,000 mile (57,600km) warranty, which covered all routine maintenance and servicing. This included everything from the batteries to the tyres. Every EV1 also came with a cast-iron 24h roadside assistance package. GM knew the EV1 had to be completely worry-free if it were to be accepted.

Although it was similar in size to the petrol-powered Saturn SC2, the EV1 was heavier due to the weight of its lead-acid battery pack. Other similarities included the extensive use of corrosion-resistant, non-metal exterior panels fitted to an aluminium spaceframe chassis, which weighed just 290lb (131.5kg). The 162 pieces were bonded together into a unit using aerospace adhesive, spot welds and rivets. The composite exterior body panels were created using two forming processes known as Sheet Molding Compound (SMC) and Reinforced Reaction Injection Molding (RRIM). GM claimed they were dent and corrosion resistant.

The heart of the EV1 was its electric propulsion system. Twenty-six lead-acid batteries produced 137bhp – good enough to accelerate the car to 60mph (96.5km/h) in around 8sec. The system consisted of two major components: the power inverter module and the three-phase AC motor. The inverter was responsible for taking the AC current and changing it to DC power for the battery pack, then the current was converted back to AC for the drive motor. The inverter kept the batteries topped up at the same time as providing power for the AC motor, which used reduction gears to power the front wheels. Americans, always suspicious of the manual gearbox, were delighted to learn the EV1 had no visible transmission to worry about.

Its top speed was electronically limited to 80mph (129km/h). Of course, the Impact had clocked 183mph (294.5km/h) on the Bonneville Salt Flats (a land-speed record for an electric production car) but, just in case anyone was tempted to try and remove the governor, GM warned: 'Higher speeds will adversely affect the range of the vehicle'. Most of the EV1's owners were more than happy with the performance, however.

Darell Dickey was sold on the car from his very first drive:

> *The EV1 was one of the most enjoyable driving experiences I've ever had. There were faster cars, better handling cars and cheaper cars. But there were no cars that were more fun to drive. Who would have thought that an American car company would produce the world's most advanced vehicle? I was proud to own an American vehicle that was technologically so far ahead of all other cars on the market.*
>
> *The EV1 was a blast to drive. Mostly because nobody would suspect that it could beat everybody else off the line. Being able to beat loud muscle cars onto the freeway was a hoot.*
>
> *Laying on the throttle with an unsuspecting passenger was just a thing of rare beauty. The acceleration numbers don't do the car justice – the torque in the low end was astonishing.*

Initially, the charge pack consisted of twenty-six 12V lead-acid batteries wired in series. The batteries, which were 98 per cent recyclable and were made from recycled lead, were unusual in that the acid was held in a special 'mat' wrapped within each module and designed to prevent any acid spill in the event of a crash The pack was also able to disable itself in the event of an accident. A separate, single 12V battery under the bonnet powered the on-board electronics, indicators and power door locks.

GM's designers were conscious that the EV1's new technology had to be user-friendly. Charging was via an inductive paddle, which used a magnetic field to conduct electricity and was safer to use than the standard metal-to-metal plug and socket arrangement. GM claimed inductive charging overcame the problem of how to charge the car in wet weather. The paddle just slotted into a port built into the bonnet between the headlights. The battery pack could be charged in two ways: via a 6.6kW system that required 220V or a portable 1.2kW convenience

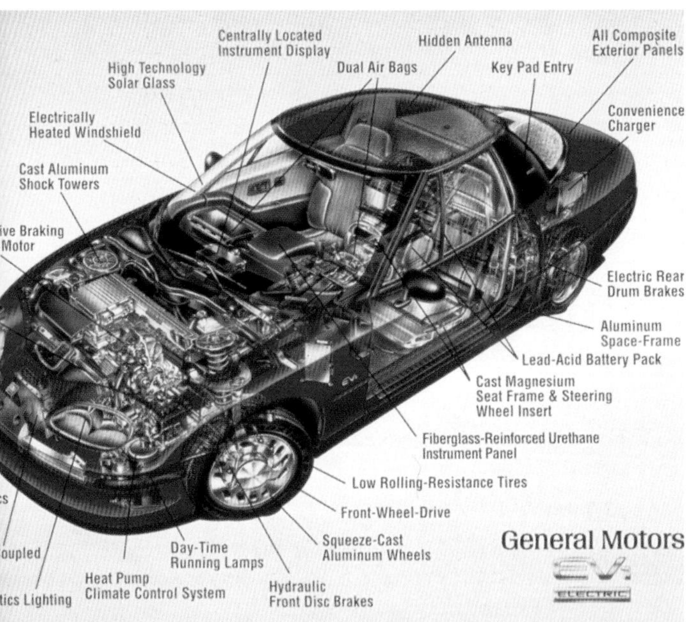

This cutaway illustrates the technology packed into the EV1.

GM placed the batteries down the spine of the EV1 – a method still applied today.

The proud EV1 team.

The EV1 was tightly packaged. Home mechanics were under strict instructions not to touch. Even the tyres had to be inflated by a dealer service centre.

The charger port used an inductive paddle to juice the battery module.

The paddle just slotted into the port without the need for a fiddly plug. This would become commonplace on EVs in the twenty-first century.

charger that could be plugged into any 110V domestic plug. The portable charger was about the size and shape of a pressure washer with a small carry handle on the top. When not in use it was designed to fit in the EV1's boot. The 6.6kW charger had to be permanently installed at home or the office.

The 6.6kW charger could bring the batteries up to 80 per cent of capacity in just 3h. The convenience charger took a rather less impressive 15h.

As for the EV1's range, GM hedged its bets. The official EV1 launch film cautioned:

> *The range, or how far the EV1 can go, will depend on many factors including the use of air conditioning, the heating, road conditions, outside air temperature and driving style. For example, on a seventy-two degree day, with the air conditioner turned off, on relatively flat terrain, using 85 per cent of the total battery charge, the range could be 90 miles at a constant 55mph. Assuming the same driving conditions, but in stop-and-go traffic, the range could be as high as 60 miles.*[34]

GM said the battery pack produced the equivalent energy of a gallon of gasoline, allowing it to claim the EV1 was good for 100mpg (2.83ltr/100km). The reality was rather different. For all the car's futuristic looks and innovative technology, the lead-acid batteries were already outdated and the real world range was more like 50–60 miles (80–96.5km) at best.

So why go with lead-acid batteries? Alec Brooks, AeroVironment's director of vehicle systems engineering, explained:

> *Rather than wait for a breakthrough (in battery technology) we thought let's take the batteries we've got today and see if we can make a viable electric car that can go*

The finished EV1 had a record-breaking drag co-efficient made possible by the teardrop shape and the semi-enclosed rear wheel arches.

one hundred miles. That we've done. A breakthrough in batteries will just make a car like this better. Maybe we will see a 300-mile (483km) range in the future.

Brooks' optimism a battery breakthrough was just around the corner would prove to be misplaced, but GM was already hard at work on an improved battery set that would allow the Gen II EV1 to hit the 100-mile (161km) range mark.

In 1997, GM introduced an electric pickup truck. The Chevrolet S-10 Electric used a lead-acid battery pack similar to the EV1, which powered an 114bhp three-phase liquid-cooled AC induction motor. The motor was in a lower state of tune to the EV1, so as not to drain the batteries too quickly. As it borrowed much of the EV's technology, the S-10 was front-wheel drive. The standard petrol-engined S-10 pickup remained stubbornly rear-wheel drive.

Unlike the EV1, a small number of S-10 Electrics were sold to fleet customers rather than leased. The majority, however, remained the property of GM and, when their leases were up, they suffered the same fate as the EV1s.

The Second Generation

Development continued on the EV1. GM unveiled the second-generation vehicle in time for the 1999 model year. Initially, the company kept faith with a lead-acid battery solution, albeit a more efficient 60Ah pack made by Panasonic, which offered a marginal improvement over the first model. Other changes, including a weight-reduction programme, helped improve the car's range. However, GM also offered an optional Ovonics nickel-metal hydride (NiMH) battery rated at a far more impressive 77Ah. These cars were the first to truly meet GM's claims for a 100-mile range in all conditions and, given a fair wind, could even travel up to 140 miles (224km) on a single charge. Official range figures for the Gen II were 55–95 miles (88–152km) for the higher capacity lead-acid power pack and 75–120 miles (120–190km) for the NiMH batteries. Charge time for the lead-acid batteries was 5.5–6h, the NiMH batteries taking between 6 and 8h.

Between 1999 and 2001, approximately one-third of the 660 Gen I cars were retro-fitted to run on the NiMH batteries and re-issued to their original lessees. Interestingly, the optional NiMH upgrade was not offered to customers in Arizona because the powerpack performed poorly in very hot weather.

To make the most of the original battery pack's meagre output, the EV1 had striking aerodynamic 'tear drop' lines, partly enclosed rear wheels and a narrow rear track. A great deal of aero work went on beneath the car, where a specially designed floorpan helped smooth turbulent air flow.

John Zwerner said the company set challenging targets for the car's performance that led to the unusual shape:

We set standards for each one of the systems in the car from an efficiency standpoint. For instance, the aerody-

The front charger port can be seen in this picture.

> *namic drag co-efficient is about half what current vehicles are. Some of the things that allowed us to do that with an electric drive, there's no drive shaft down the centre of the car that you have in a rear-wheel drive car, there's no exhaust system, so the underneath of the car can be very clean and smooth. In fact, it has a complete bellypan that makes it aerodynamically (efficient). The car is also 9.5-inches narrower at the back and so it has a tear-drop shape to it.*
>
> *Each thing you put on the vehicle that consumes power reduces the range of the vehicle. So every system has to be optimised because this car is not forgiving. When you use up the power it reduces the range and the range is a large concern to us from a customer acceptance standpoint.*

The EV1's drag coefficient was the lowest of any production vehicle at 0.19Cd. No-one ever proved GM's claim that this was about the same as an F-16 fighter aircraft 'with its landing gear down' but it sure sounded impressive. Drivers found that on a flat stretch of highway they could coast for miles. Lessee Darrell Dickey could not believe how far the EV1 would travel:

> *The thing would coast for days. On hills where other cars reached a terminal velocity of about 50mph, the EV1 would go over 80mph (129km/h) – this was due to the world's best aero numbers as well as the weight of the lead batteries.*

The EV1's luggage capacity was 9.7ft2 (2.7m2), although the 'convenience' charger, which was designed to be kept in the trunk, tended to get in the way. Many owners simply removed the device and left it at home. GM reckoned the boot could accommodate two golf bags. A cargo net helped secure delicate items.

In order to minimize the weight of the car – and shave a few dollars off the build price – the spare tyre and jack were junked. Instead, the EV1 ran on self-sealing tyres backed up by a tyre pressure-monitoring system. However, due mainly to the batteries, the car still tipped the scales at a hefty 3,000lb (1,361kg).

The sense of theatre began before you even sat inside the EV1. To open the door, a driver had to enter a numeric identification code into a keypad on the B-pillar. A simple key was an option.

It was the same deal inside. To start the electric motor, a driver entered their identification code on a pad next to the joy-stick style drive selector and pressed a button marked 'run'. A press of the adjacent 'Lock' button turned it off.

As the powerplant was virtually silent, especially at walking pace, the EV1 had a pedestrian-alert alarm designed to wake up dozy pedestrians unaware of the silent electric car about to run them down. There was also a faintly embarrassing audible reversing bleeper.

Not surprisingly, the EV1's instrument pack was an all-LCD display. Running the full width of the car, as well as the usual speedometer, odometer and gear selection indicators there were a number of more unusual displays. A battery 'capacity gauge' gave an at-a-glance indication of the power pack's status. Each bar represented 9 per cent of the pack's capacity. There was also a range-remaining indicator. This displayed a real-time estimate computed from the last 1.5 miles (2.5km) of driving and the remaining battery capacity. Pressing another button gave an instant readout of the EV1's power consumption.

Luxuries included a CD and cassette player with four-speakers, electric windows, heated front and rear windows and air-conditioning. GM defended the decision to go with a heated front windscreen claiming it was more efficient than a standard heater blower and thus likely to be used for shorter periods of time. Witzenburg says the equipment provoked a great deal of debate, particularly the sound system:

> *CDs were still fairly new and most cars only had a cassette player. We kept being asked why were we wasting precious electrical energy on a device when most people only had a couple of CDs but I was convinced a premium sound system was appropriate for the car. After all, it was supposed to be for commuting so you may as well make the journey as pleasant as possible. Some folk wanted a simple AM/FM radio but the CD argument won out and we went with the same unit as was in the Oldsmobile Aurora.*

A unique feature was the EV1's preconditioning buttons, which allowed the air-conditioning or heater to be pre-programmed while the car was connected to the charger.

Other features that were way ahead of the time were the regenerative brakes and the coast-down feature. The latter could be operated from the gear stick. It slowed the EV1 like an internal combustion engine going down through the gears but actually turned the motor into a generator to recharge the battery. The regenerative brakes worked on the same principal.

GM stressed the EV1's environmental credentials:

> *The EV1 is the car of the future. Not only for its performance, convenience and affordability, but for its environmentally friendly attitude. The EV1's electric motor requires no emission testing because it is a zero-emission vehicle – it doesn't even have a tail pipe. It requires no tune-ups. And no gasoline or oil changes, which means cleaner air and less dependency on foreign oil. The EV1 helps contribute to a cleaner environment. In California, for instance, there are 97 per cent fewer emissions with the EV1 than a conventional gasoline engine – this includes the electricity-generating emissions from the power plant. Also, when you use electricity at night to charge the EV1, it actually helps power plants operate more efficiently because of power plant load levelling.*

GM packed the interior with technology, too. Centrally mounted LCD instruments were popular at the time.

GM concluded: 'The EV1 is a thrill to drive – which makes cleaning the air more fun than ever'.

Just as the Toyota Prius would a decade later, the EV1 caught the public's imagination. Within a year of the car's launch, the lease programme was extended to San Francisco and Sacramento, in California, as well as the state of Georgia.

In the early days, GM appeared to be full-square behind the EV1. The car's launch was a media spectacular, accompanied by an $8m advertising campaign and prime-time TV ads created by Industrial Light and Magic, the special effects studio behind *Star Wars*. The EV1 was a special guest

General Motors EV1

Type: two-door coupé
Motor: three-phase AC induction with IGBT power inverter
Power: 137bhp @ 7,000rpm
Torque: 110lb ft (149Nm) @ 0–7000rpm
Transmission: single-speed reduction integrated with motor and differential
0–60mph: 8sec
Dimensions:
Length: 169.7in (4,310mm)
Width: 69.5in (1,765mm)
Height: 50.5in (1,283mm)
Wheelbase: 98.9in (2,512mm)
Curb weight: 3,086lb (1,400kg) with lead-acid batteries, 2,908lb (1,319kg) with NiMH batteries

star at the Hollywood premiere of the Sylvester Stallone action movie *Daylight* and GM even acquired air time – at great expense – to advertise it during the Super Bowl.

Subsequent TV ads were less successful. One featured a disembodied voice asking: 'How does it go without gas and air? How does it go without sparks and explosions? How does it go without wheels or transmissions? How does it go you will ask yourself.' The answer came back: 'How did we go so long without it? The electric car. It isn't coming, it's here', as the camera pulled back to reveal the EV1 in all its futuristic splendour. Critics said the ad did nothing to sell the EV1 and, with its slightly spooky voice and mournful music, may have actually frightened prospective customers away.

Whatever their merits, all the ads stressed the EV1's low-maintenance requirements. It never needed an oil change, spark plugs or belts. And the radiator was only required to keep the batteries, motor and electronics cool.

The EV1 was built at GM's Lansing Craft Centre, in Lansing, Michigan, a factory that specialized in low-volume production. Prior to the EV1, it had been responsible for production of the two-seater Buick Reatta coupé.

The unconventional EV1 quickly became the darling of image-conscious Hollywood stars and Disney executives. Among the celebrities who took delivery were Mel Gibson, Ed Begley Junior, Peter Horton and Alexandra Paul. Politicians, too, embraced the EV1. Ralph Nader, Frank Gaffney, David Freeman and Alan Lowenthal were all confirmed fans. Even the former director of the CIA, James Woolsey, leased one (presumably he was a fan of the EV1's stealth abilities). GM also provided Congressman Earl Blumenauer with an EV1 during the 2000 Democratic National Convention in Los Angeles.[35]

However, while customer reaction was extremely positive, GM was beginning to waiver. The customers may have been 'maniacally loyal', according to EV1 brand manager Ken Stewart, but there just weren't enough of them. A total of forty EV1 leases were signed off in the first week, but after a promising start 'sales' tailed off rapidly. Only 248 more leases were signed in the first year – a meagre return on GM's $1 billion development spend. Management began to ask if people really did want an electric vehicle after all. Fans of the car hit back, accusing GM of deliberately setting the EV1 up to fail in order to protect the internal combustion engine cash cow.

Storm clouds were gathering over the EV1 project.

GM Pulls the Plug

In January 2000, only one month after the Gen II models began to ship, GM said it was mothballing the EV1 production facility. The production line would be dismantled and placed in storage while existing inventories were run down. Jeff Kuhlman, GM's director of energy and environmental communications told local newspapers: 'GM can, and will, crank out another batch of EV1s if the market wants them'.

On 2 March 2000, GM issued a recall notice for 450 Gen I EV1s and a similar number of Chevrolet Electric S-10 pickup trucks. A faulty charge port cable could accidentally catch fire if it built up enough heat. The company admitted to sixteen 'thermal incidents' and one car was totally destroyed when it caught fire while charging. Lessees who lost their EV1s were warned that, although the S-10 pick-up trucks could be repaired, there was no known repair for the EV1 vehicles. Angry drivers asked how this could be, pointing out that, as the Gen II cars already had a modified charger port, a 'fix' had been found.

On 23 March, GM issued a press release to say a solution had been found. But it wasn't all good news. The release went on:

The lease arrangement included full servicing facilities at selected dealerships.

GM hoped a charging infrastructure would make the EV1 viable on longer trips.

The finished car looks a handsome beast in this publicity shot. The EV1 shape was very similar to the later Honda Insight Mk 1.

> *Although GM engineers now have developed a repair, the EV1 vehicles are not expected to be available until the first quarter of 2001. The delay is unavoidable, because it will take time to identify a supplier, validate, prepare for production, produce and finally install the replacement system in the vehicles and then inspect each vehicle for proper operation.*

Kenneth Stewart, brand manager for GM Advanced Vehicles (GMAC), said that the lengthy delay would require GM to settle leases with each customer, since the delay would prevent GMAC from fulfilling its obligations.

To the horror of EV1 drivers he said that, because the EV1 cars would have to be out of service until some time next year, GM's remedy in their recall would be to refund lease payments and terminate the leases.

In the event, the company softened its position and a trickle of cars began to be returned the following December. GM said it was only going to return those cars whose lessees had indicated they wanted them. The others would not be fixed. GM said this was as a result of a parts shortage.

Worse was to come. On 7 February 2002, Ken Stewart dropped a bombshell. In a letter to drivers leasing EV1s, he said GM would be taking their cars back when current agreements came to an end.

It was no surprise when GM's CEO Rick Wagoner officially cancelled the EV1 programme the following year. The company said there weren't enough customers to make the car viable. The whole project had become a financial disaster. In 2005, GN spokesman, Dave Barthmuss, told *The San Francisco Chronicle*:

> *After spending over $1 billion over a four-year time frame, we were only able to lease 800 EV1s. That does not a business make. As great as the vehicle is and as much passion, enthusiasm and loyalty as there is, there simply wasn't enough at any given time to make a viable long-term business proposition for General Motors.*
>
> *If we're really going to make a difference in environmental auto issues, we have to be able to see vehicles in the hundreds of thousands of units, instead of hundreds.*[36]

Barthmuss said there was no way GM could sell the cars to outraged lessees. He blamed lack of parts and added that, although some buyers said they would waive the right to sue GM over any design or production defects, 'in today's litigious society, there is no such thing as no liability'.

Witzenburg blames the inability of battery technology to keep up for the EV 1's demise:

> *The success of the project hinged on a new battery technology called lithium polymer coming to market. These batteries were supposed to be smaller, energy dense and easily shaped so they could be fitted into a car more easily, around the axles for instance.*

Lithium polymer batteries did reach the market but only in small electrical devices like PDAs. And Witzenburg says it just wasn't as simple as scaling the technology up to fit a car:

> *We waited and waited but lithium polymer just never came through. When it was obvious it wasn't going to happen the EV 1 was dead in the water.*

So the cars were rounded up and returned to GM. A few found their way to museums, albeit without the electric powertrain, but most were simply hauled out into the Arizona desert and crushed. A sad end for a truly innovative car.

Toyota's RAV4 EV

The threat from the California Air Resources Board galvanized several other car manufacturers to re-examine the potential for electric vehicles. The RAV4 EV – which looked outwardly identical to its conventional cousin apart from the exhaust pipe – was a winner even before it was launched. Designed and developed in record time, Toyota's engineers entered – and won – the Scandinavian Electric Car Rally with a pre-production prototype in 1995, a year before sales began in Japan. Toyota's decision to stick with a conventional-looking car meant customers felt comfortable with the idea of driving the RAV4 EV (unlike the EV1, which sometimes looked too futuristic for its own good).

The first cars were built using the three-door RAV4 body, but Toyota extended the range to include a five-door model. Using the larger body meant the nickel-metal hydride battery could be secreted beneath the cabin floor without restricting the boot space or rear passenger room.

Toyota's EV looked utterly conventional compared to the EV1.

To compensate for the extra weight, the five-door RAV4 EV had a more powerful motor (it produced 50kW as opposed to the 45Kw motor used in the three-door variant).

The top speed of both was limited to 77mph (124 km/h) – although, given the modest output and barn-door aerodynamics, they probably couldn't have gone much faster – and they had a theoretical range of 124 miles (200km). It took a slothful eighteen seconds to reach 60mph (96km/h), even on a full charge, which was a far cry from the speedy EV1.

Despite their SUV ancestry, both versions were strictly front-wheel drive only. Presumably, the addition of motors front-and-back would have had a deleterious impact on the vehicle's weight, cost and packaging. The posher five-door model also had a timer-operated heating and air conditioning system.

The first RAV4 EV evaluation scheme outside of Japan took place in spring 1997 on Jersey. Five three-door models were based at five hotels on the island and could be hired for £30 per day. The Jersey Government, Jersey Elec-

Toyota RAV4 EV

Type: 4-door SUV
Motor: Permanent magnet electric motor driving the front wheels
Power: 61hp (45kW)/68hp (50kW)
Top speed: 77mph (124km/h)

Dimensions:
length: 156.7in (3980mm)
width: 66.7in (1694mm)
height: 64.4in (1636mm)
wheelbase: 94.9in (2410mm)

Toyota tried again with an all-electric RAV 4 in 2010.

The second generation RAV4 EV was developed with help from US electric car specialist Tesla.

tric Company, British Airways and the five hotels sponsored the project. Despite this, the RAV4-EV was never offered for sale in the UK.

It did reach New York and California in 1997 but sales to the public didn't begin until early 2002 (until this point it had only been available on a three-year lease plan similar to the EV1). However, with a retail price of $42,000 it was more than double the cost of an ordinary RAV4 and buyers had to be both wealthy and dedicated to the idea of electric cars. Not surprisingly, although it leased more than 1,000, only 328 examples were actually sold outright. The final few were almost hand-built from whatever spares inventory Toyota had left. This meant the specification chopped and changed constantly. Some came with luxuries like heated seats and electric aerials; others didn't.

Just like the EV1, the Toyota had its celebrity supporters. Tom Hanks evangelized the car on a US talk show. Legend has it that he was talking about the EV1 but he was, in fact, praising the RAV4 EV.

In a lousy piece of timing, Toyota discontinued the car just one day after the California Air Resources Board passed a new mandate that absolved manufacturers of the need to build and sell EVs. Unlike GM, however, Toyota kept faith with owners and the car can still be serviced at its dealerships. Many are still on the road and have clocked up impressive mileages.

The affection owners had for their cars prompted Toyota to try again in 2010 when it unveiled a new RAV4 EV. Jointly developed with Tesla, the RAV4 EV was pulled together very quickly. To save time it used a modified Tesla powertrain rather than a bespoke set up, and Tesla also supplied the battery. The asking price was $49,800 – not much more than the first generation RAV4 EV had cost ten years earlier – before US government incentives. Tesla's involvement meant the second-generation RAV4 EV had greater performance – in sport mode the top speed was 100mph (160km/h) – and a switch to a Li-Ion battery gave it a similar range.

Ford's EV Pick-Up

About the same time as Toyota was preparing its first electric SUV, Ford was hard at work on an electric sport utility built around its Ranger light truck chassis.

The Ranger EV was made available, again on a lease basis, in 1998. It was strictly rear-wheel drive, power coming from a three-phase alternating current electric motor operating through a single speed three-to-one reduction transmission and differential. Ford reckoned the motor, which was manufactured by Siemens, was good for 90bhp and could operate at a maximum speed of 13,000rpm. The drivetrain – motor, transmission and differential – were contained in a single unit mounted high between the frame rails, transversely between the rear wheels. The half shafts had to be angled downward to drive the wheels.

The ford Ranger EV was surprisingly successful.

Note the green leaf side decal alerting pedestrians to the Ranger's green credentials.

The Ranger's battery charger.

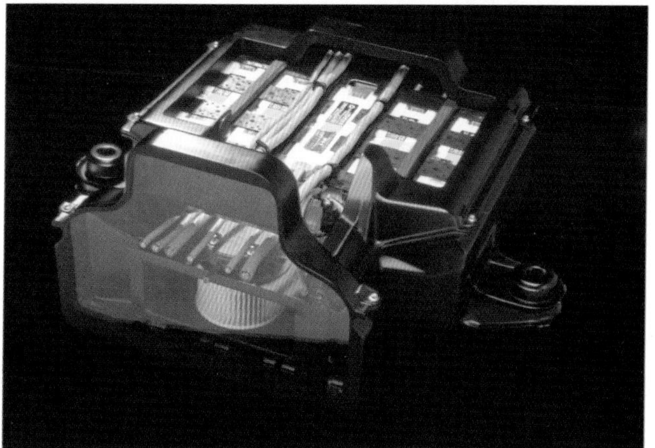

The 1998 Ranger EV battery module.

A modest 'electric' script alerted motorists to the Ranger's unusual power source.

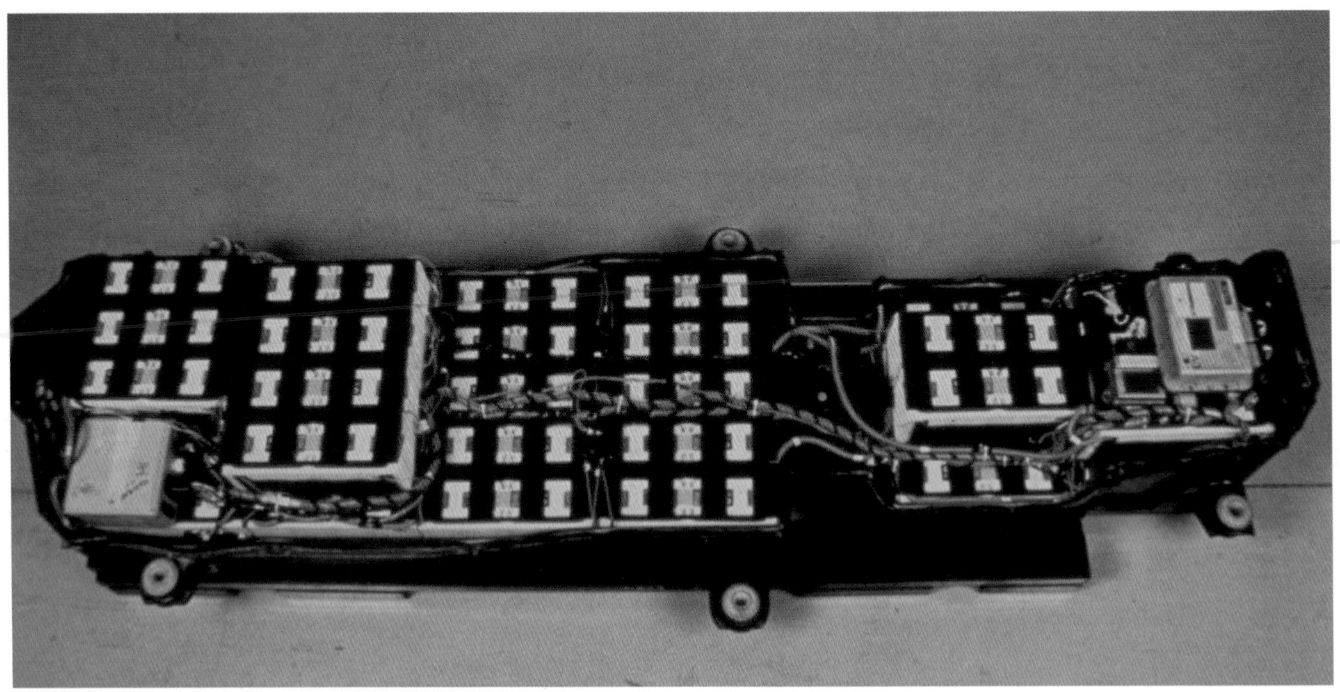

The original 1998 Ranger EV involved a traditional lead-acid battery pack powering Ford's best-selling Ranger compact pickup.

The largest order for electrical vehicles ever was placed by the US Postal Service, which ordered 500 delivery vehicles based on the Ford Ranger EV pickup. The postal vehicles used the Ranger EV battery pack and electrical drive system. But instead of the compact pickup Ranger body, they were outfitted with a cargo van body and right hand drive.

Between 1998 and 2002 Ford built approximately 1500 Ranger EVs. By far the biggest customer was the US postal service, which ordered 500 custom-built delivery vans based on the Ranger chassis. They were fitted with a cargo van body and converted to right-hand drive.

And, unlike the EV1, when production came to an end, Ford didn't take the Ranger back. Spokesman Neil Golightly said the company recognized the strong feeling about the car. 'People were very keen to keep them,' he told *The San Francisco Chronicle*. 'We made a conscious decision we would risk liability and parts concerns (for the sake of) customer satisfaction.' Nevertheless, fewer than 400 electric Rangers are still on the road today.

Chrysler's Van

The Chrysler TEVan, built from 1993 to 1995, was sold primarily to electric utilities in the US. The strange name was an amalgamation of company's internal T-115 code name for the minivan and the 'EV' for electric vehicle. Lacking the development resources of GM, Ford and Toyota, Chrysler partnered with the US Electric Power Research Institute to develop the TEVan.

No one quite knows how many TEVans were sold. In 1992, chairman Lee Iacocca said Chrysler would build 'at least' 50 TEVans for 'controlled fleet use' and, officially, fifty-six were completed. What is certain is that some used nickel-iron batteries and others nickel-cadmium. They sold for approximately $120,000 each.

The TEVan was virtually hand-built at Chrysler's minivan plant in Ontario, Canada. It had a top speed of 70mph (113km/h), seating for five adults and a hefty curb weight of 5,060lb (2,295 kg). The nickel-iron pack offered a pitiful 50-mile (80km) range. The nickel-cadimum cells added a further 10 miles (16km) or so. Both fell short of Chrysler's official range of 90 miles (hastily reduced from the original 120 mile boast).

According to Chrysler, the battery pack powered a 70bhp General Electric DC motor but, with continuous power rated at a mere 27bhp, it took a long time before the TEVan reached its 70mph (112km/h) top speed.

Chrysler returned to the market with a second EV, called the EPIC (Electric Powered Intra-urban Commuter Vehicle), in 1997. Although it used the TEVan powertrain, this futuristic people-carrier was a far more convincing stab at the EV market. The windscreen adopted an aggressive 'cab forward' look and the whole body was a one-box design, similar to European MPVs like the Renault Espace.

In a further nod to practicality, the EPIC had sliding doors on both sides and a hatchback. Inside, the rear seats folded into the floor when not required. The production version of the EPIC was introduced in July 1997, and leased to government and utility fleets. Available as a Dodge or a Plymouth, it was powered by a 336V (28 12V modules) nickel-metal hydride battery pack.

The California Air Resources Board had forced car manufacturers to take zero-emissions vehicles seriously and the EV1 showed what was possible with cutting-edge technology, but the law requiring car makers to offer such cars was relaxed after intense lobbying. Manufacturers argued that the failure of their cars demonstrated that the car-buying public would not accept electric cars. They claimed the vast majority of sales had been to public utilities mandated by law to use a percentage of zero-emissions vehicles. Reluctantly, legislators agreed to defer the electric car legislation pending a battery technology breakthrough. Instead of battery-powered EVs, hybrids and super-low emissions vehicles were chosen to help America clean up its act.

The electric car had lost again.

CHAPTER EIGHT

A NEW BEGINNING: THE TOYOTA PRIUS AND THE HONDA INSIGHT

Ironically just as electric vehicles pretty much reached rock bottom in America, developments were taking place in Japan that would lead to their rebirth as the environmentally acceptable facing of motoring in the twenty-first century.

In 1992, Toyota unveiled its Earth Charter, a new set of policy guidelines that would help make the company's future cars more efficient and kinder to the environment. The charter's stated aim was: 'To build clean, safe automobiles, while working for affluent societies and a green earth'. If cynics thought the Earth Charter was nothing but public relations hot air, they were wrong.

President Fujio Cho summed Toyota's philosophy up:

> *It bothers me when I'm told that, in 100 years of automobile development, Japan has not contributed anything. Toyota will make every effort so that we can hear that Japan's technology has contributed this much to the environment.*

The following year, in February 1993, the core Earth Charter policy was combined with a set of actions to create the Toyota Environmental Action Plan.

This initiative would influence Toyota's decision-making

The Prius marked a step change in the way buyers perceived petrol–electric hybrids. If the world's most successful car company had faith in the technology, what was there to fear?

and model planning well into the twenty-first century. In doing so it would enable the company to steal a march on its rivals to become the global standard-bearer for petrol–electric hybrid technology and, for a time, the world's biggest and most successful car maker.

Toyota's decision was no knee-jerk reaction to what was happening in North America. The company had been researching and developing hybrid drive systems for more than 30years. In the seventies, it designed and built hybrid versions of the S800 and Century models, which used a combination of gas turbine engines and electric motors. Research into electric vehicles commenced at the same time and, in a far-sighted move, an in-house electric motor development programme was given the green light in the early eighties.

Toyota's research into alternative powertrains took on more importance in the nineties, when concerns over the causes of global warming and CO_2 in exhaust gases reached new heights. Legislators in Europe and America moved to clampdown on dirty car-exhaust fumes – this time for real. When the State of California introduced the Zero Emission Vehicle programme (which gave rise to the ill-fated GM EV1), Toyota was able to move ahead quickly with its all-electric RAV-4 SUV. The RAV4 was a popular and well-engineered electric vehicle, but the futuristic-looking EV1 stole all of the headlines. To Mr Cho's intense annoyance, Toyota was once more cast as the 'fast follower' rather than the innovator.

A New Beginning

In Autumn 1993, US President Bill Clinton announced a new clean-car initiative. America's Partnership for a New Generation of Vehicles would see the government work with the country's 'Big Three' domestic auto-makers – General Motors, Ford and Chrysler – to design and build, in Clinton's words, 'affordable, attractive cars that are up to three times more fuel efficient than today's cars'.

He pledged the full support of his government to help design and build a family car capable of 80mpg (2.94ltr/100km).

Clinton administration aides dubbed this target vehicle the 'supercar' and said it would help reduce America's reliance on oil imports, as well as kick-starting the moribund US auto industry. Clinton told the crowd: 'We do not have the choice to do nothing'.

This sounded alarm bells for Eiji Toyoda, Toyota's chairman, especially when a tentative request to join the White House partnership was turned down flat. If the Americans were going to build a better car, then so was he – and in a far shorter space of time than the 10 years the US had set itself.

Toyota also had an eye on emerging markets. If car ownership in China and India took off, demand for gasoline would send prices to record levels in the first decade of the twenty-first century. As a result of such thinking, the petrol–electric hybrid drive project was bumped to the top of the company's 'to do' list.

The Toyota Prius

Toyota was incredibly ambitious about its hybrid drive. From the beginning, it was decided that the project would be completely in-house. This meant that every facet of the system, the motor, the electrics, the battery and the petrol engine, would be done by Toyota's own designers and engineers. There would be no partners, no sub-contractors and no bought-in 'off the shelf' parts.

About the same time as the hybrid project was getting the green light, Toyoda quietly initiated the G21 (for Global twenty-first century) group. This was a hand-picked team of middle managers who met once a week to examine ways of creating a 'green and environmentally friendly car' capable of beating all existing – and future – emissions' regulations. Unlike the wacky EV1, however, the G21 team's goal was to build a car that still looked, and drove, like an utterly conventional compact family car.

The fate of the project was vested in executive vice president Akihiro Wada. A company man through and through, Wada had worked for Toyota since the sixties and had earned a reputation for getting things done. In 1961, he helped redesign the Crown luxury saloon, rationalizing and standardizing parts, so it could be assembled more efficiently. As the G21 car would have to be the most efficient vehicle the company had ever built, Wada was the right man for the job. He embraced the G21 concept wholeheartedly and quickly realized the concept would only work if it used hybrid technology.

Initially, the project's engineers concentrated on refining existing gasoline engine technology (Toyota was already a world leader in lean burn engines). They believed they could hit a 50 per cent greater efficiency target, but

Incredibly for such a daunting project, Toyota opted to design and manufacture the Prius entirely in-house.

Wada was convinced that other car manufacturers would soon find a way of catching up.

He wanted Toyota to leap a whole generation and truly pioneer a car for the twenty-first century. The car would be named Prius, the Latin word for 'to go before'.

Wada was adamant that he didn't want a more efficient version of what had gone before. 'I don't want to build just another economy car,' he reportedly said. 'We have to rethink development and, if that means building a hybrid car that gets twice the fuel efficiency as another car out there, then that's what we'll do.'

Wada tasked part of the team to press ahead with a hybrid concept car for the 1995 Tokyo Motor Show. The engineers were given free rein to be bold because, they were told, the car would only ever be a concept and wasn't intended for series production. Although it is unclear, it seems likely this was a cunning ruse by Wada to encourage his engineers to design and build a working hybrid in record time.

Toyota had some expertise with hybrids. The company had been developing a hybrid minivan but the vehicle had become bogged down in disagreements between the engineers – who wanted the hybrid – and sales teams convinced they couldn't sell such a radical idea. That vehicle was a series-type hybrid, driven only by electric traction, but the Prius would be a parallel design, using its internal combustion engine and a motor.

The original goal was to build a powertrain that would be one-and-a-half times more efficient than the next best petrol or diesel alternative. However, Wada upped his target to twice the efficiency to force his team to consider radical solutions.

Takeshi Uchiyamada, the chief engineer selected to head the G21 project, admitted later: 'At that moment, I felt he demanded too much'.[37] Uchiyamada was an apparently strange choice to head such a prestigious project because he had no previous experience in product planning or leading a major new vehicle.

However, Wada believed his inexperience would encourage Uchiyamada to 'think outside the box' and break with Toyota's traditionally risk-averse strategy. The chief engineer would later admit that he was given a 'virtual free hand' in the project – a far cry from the usual 'hands-on' management of an important new vehicle.

The team was different in other ways, too. They were relatively young and, in a break with usual Toyota corporate practice, they all shared a single, large conference room, on the sixth floor of the Third Engineering building, isolated from other staff but with a clear view of the Mikawa mountains. By working so closely, the team were able to respond quickly to set-backs and engineering challenges – of which there were many.

The team worked 16h days, testing hundreds of engines in a bid to find the right one for their new car. To save time each engine was run on a computer simulator and, eventually, the long list of eighty possibles was narrowed down to a short list of just four.

Finally, Uchiyamada selected the optimum combination and, in June 1995, approval was given for a full-scale prototype.

Toyota's progress was a cause of some concern to the Americans struggling to meet the terms of the Partnership for a New Generation of Vehicles initiative.

The White House even asked the CIA to compile a dossier on the Japanese project, working from publicly available sources, and at least two such briefings took place – although the US manufacturers could have found out the same information for themselves just by reading the newspapers.[38] In October 1995, their worst fears were realized when Toyota unveiled a Prius concept at the Tokyo Motor Show, where the car aroused a great deal of interest.

As the G21 team hadn't nailed down an exterior design at that stage, the Tokyo concept looked nothing like the eventual Prius. Some of the details were a bit rough (particularly the wing mirrors, which looked very much like an afterthought) but Toyota executives were delighted by the positive reaction to the idea of a hybrid.

However, behind the smiles there was still a huge amount of work to be done before the car, by now given the official code-name 890T, was ready for mass production.

Worse still, when the 'optimum' engine was tested there was a snag – and a pretty big one. The engineers couldn't get it to start and, when they did, the car would only move a few metres before rolling to a stop. Satoshi Ogiso, the team's chief powertrain engineer, recalled in an interview with Fortune magazine: 'On the computer, the hybrid power system worked very well. But simulation is different from seeing if the actual part can work.' It took a month before the glitch was fixed.

Time, however, was a luxury the team did not have. Senior management, excited by the car's potential, repeatedly brought forward the on-sale date. No doubt, they were aware that Honda was also working on a hybrid vehicle and didn't want to finish second again. Eventually, they settled on December 1997 for the Japanese launch – an incredibly tight time-scale for a product that promised to revolutionize the industry.

The powertrain design they settled on was named the Toyota Hybrid System – a carefully integrated package that took up little more space beneath the bonnet than a conventional transverse engine/front-wheel drive transmission. The set-up consisted of a high-efficiency 1.5-litre 4-cylinder internal combustion engine, a compact high-torque electric motor and a separate generator. The

The heart of the Prius was an entirely new driveline, later dubbed the Toyota Hybrid System, which consisted of a high-efficiency 1.5-litre engine, designed according to the Atkinson principle, which leaves the air intake valve open longer, and a high-efficiency electric motor.

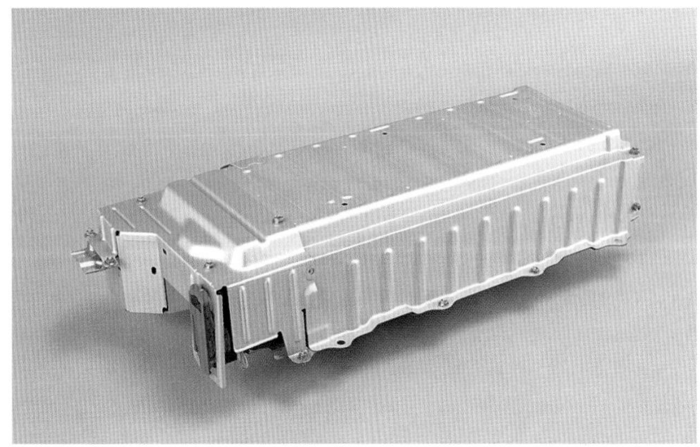

The RAV-4 EV project provided valuable data for the NiMH battery module used in the Prius. However, it was only one tenth the size of the SUV battery pack.

engine was designed on the Atkinson cycle principle, wherein the air-intake valve is left open until the middle of the compression stroke, which achieved greater efficiency than a conventional engine unit.

Although the Atkinson principle was well known (it was invented by the British engineer James Atkinson in 1882), its application in cars had been difficult due to the design's lack of torque. However, a parallel hybrid – where the instant torque delivery of the electric motor could be used to overcome the engine's deficiencies – got over those drawbacks.

Lessons learned on the RAV4 EV project were applied to the bank of nickel-metal hydride (NiMH) batteries, which were housed behind the back seats, and the electric motors. The RAV4 EV had been virtually hand-built and the Prius was destined for mass production, so the batteries could only be one-tenth the size of the SUV's modules and the required power output per volume (20kW) had to be twice the performance of conventional batteries of the time. Unsurprisingly, the first battery pack was so big that it took up all the boot space.[39]

The original design plan had the batteries installed beneath the floor, as in the RAV4 EV, but tests revealed serious over-heating problems. All the team's attempts to solve this were stymied by the battery pack's location. When efforts to use airflow to cool the pack failed, because the air had been pre-heated by the engine, Wada suggested moving the battery module into the boot. Installing them behind the rear seats solved the problem.

The batteries created an 'energy buffer' that was continuously resupplied by the generator driven by the engine. An epicyclic gear-train divided the engine's output between the driving wheels and the generator.

The 1.5-litre, 4-cylinder 16-valve engine was specially developed for the hybrid system and differed from a conventional unit in several respects. Most importantly, it did not need to offer immediate throttle response because the motor could provide an instant power boost as needed. It was therefore designed for maximum efficiency and minimum emissions, assisted by Toyota's new Variable Valve Timing-intelligent (VVT-i) set-up and by a high compression ratio of 13.5:1. Unusually for a petrol engine, the revs did not exceed 4,000rpm.

Keeping the revs down enabled the engineers to make the 4-cylinder considerably lighter with lower internal friction losses than a conventional engine. The engine's maximum output at 4,000rpm was a modest 57bhp and its maximum torque, at the same speed, was 75lb ft (102Nm). The permanent-magnet drive motor provided its maximum torque output of 224lb ft (304Nm) from 0 to 940rpm, and maximum power of 39.4bhp (30kW) from 940rpm to its maximum speed of 2,000rpm. The battery bank, which was much smaller and lighter than in the RAV4 EV, had a capacity of 6.5Ah.

Toyota also brought its electronic expertise to bear on the vehicle, developing a bespoke engine-management system to control the power flow between the mechanical and electric components. Although the engine still did the major share of the driving work, with the motor providing a handy boost for hill climbing or overtaking, the Prius could run in all-electric mode. In normal conditions, the car would start in EV mode before switching to the internal combustion engine as the vehicle picked up speed.

A principal requirement of the drivetrain was that it should be no more difficult to drive than an utterly conventional model, such as the Corolla, and the team worked hard to make the engine/motor switching totally seamless. Their hard work paid off and, at launch, critics praised the smoothness of the drivetrain. *Motion Cars* magazine commented:

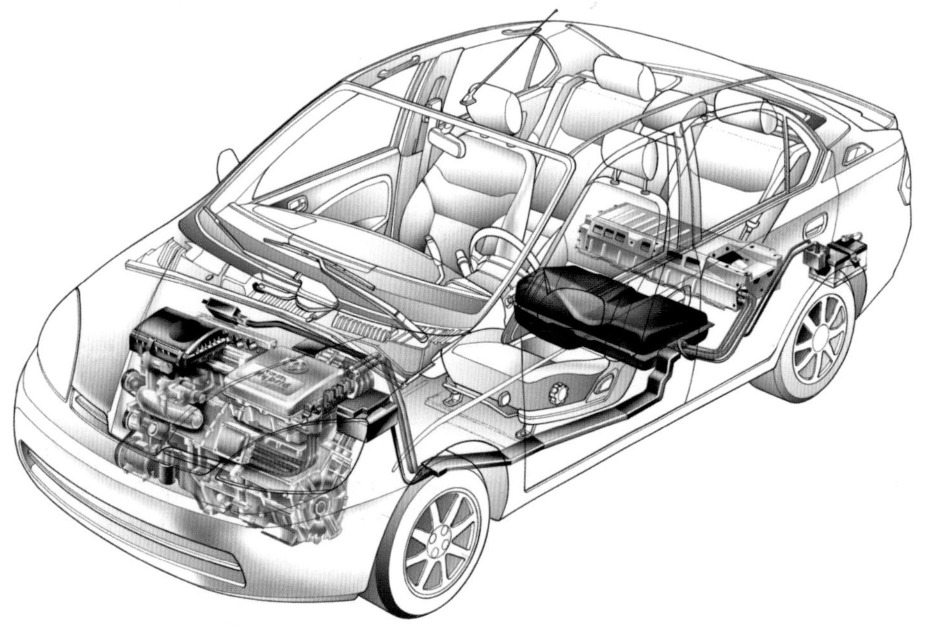

This cutaway shows how Toyota sited the battery module behind the rear seats. Although this reduced luggage space in the boot, it overcame cooling problems and would become the reference design for other hybrids.

Toyota pushed the boat out with a bespoke interior for the Prius. The dashboard's central LCD instruments made conversion from right-hand drive to left-hand drive easier.

> *What's amazing is that you will hardly be aware of which power source is working, or if both are. Operation is utterly transparent, and it's just like you're driving a normal 1.5-litre [car].*

The interior cabin was different in many ways. The main instruments were sited in the centre of the dashboard, approximately 1m from the driver's eye line. Toyota's ergonomic experts decided this was the most comfortable position for a speedometer and it was made possible on the Prius by the car's cab forward design. A 5.8in (15cm) LCD display in the dashboard provided endless hours of entertainment, showing the energy use and recovery of the system. The monitor also served as a general information centre showing the time, the audio selection and warning messages.

About the only conventional thing about the Prius was the way it looked. Although Toyota had invited its in-house styling teams across the world to submit designs, the exterior style that was chosen – supposedly based on a egg squeezed at both ends – seemed disappointingly ordinary. One wonders what would have happened had management taken up Uchiyamada's suggestion that the Prius design brief be opened up to the big European styling studios.

In the event, it was decided to keep the design in-house for fear the hybrid's secrets would be leaked. The shape was based on a conventional three-box design because it was felt a saloon would be more upmarket. Interestingly, the car's success inspired a change of heart: Toyota designed the second- and third-generation Prius vehicles as Euro-friendly hatchbacks.

The press launch of the Toyota Prius, held in a plush Tokyo hotel, was a masterpiece of showmanship. Giant video screens showed looping video of blue skies and birds in flight, while a giant globe rotated slowly on stage. As the globe came to a stop, the expectant audience had their first glimpse of the Prius inside it. When the speeches were finished Uchiyamada, Wada and President Hiroshi Okuda solemnly walked over to the car, got in, turned over the engine, which fired for a second then fell quiet, as they drove smoothly and silently down a ramp and out of the room.[40] As a practical demonstration of the benefits of hybrid drive, it was a superb piece of theatre.

The Prius was also taken to the Kyoto international climate change conference held in December 1997, where lucky delegates were offered test rides. As the world argued over carbon dioxide reduction targets, a car boasting twice the fuel economy and half the exhaust emissions of a conventional vehicle caught the zeitgeist perfectly.

Arguably, the all-electric GM EV1 was a far more advanced concept but the Prius was more appealing to the average driver. The hybrid powertrain suffered no range anxiety issues. It looked, and drove, like an utterly conventional saloon car and asked no compromises of its owner.

The Prius (internal codename NHW10) went on sale on 10 December 1997. Sales were limited to Japan only but, despite a last-minute decision to double production capacity, there were still shortages, as drivers everywhere clamoured to be the first to drive 'the car for the twenty-

The exterior was based on the concept of an egg squeezed on both sides but the result, to European eyes, was disappointing.

Three generations later, the Prius has its own design language, which is celebrated all over the world.

The Prius has grown up and the design is now more visually striking – and European – shifting the Prius from a car favoured by women to a mainstream design with wide appeal to both sexes.

An early shot of the Prius at speed.

The London congestion charge was a boon for Toyota UK when it was introduced in February 2003. Toyota lost no time in capitalizing on the fact that hybrid drivers were exempt.

Toyota Prius Mk I

Type: four-door sedan
Engine: incline 4-cylinder, cast-aluminium block and head
Displacement: 1496cc
Power: 58bhp @ 4,000rpm
Torque: 75lb ft (102Nm) @ 4,000rpm
Motor: three-phase AC permanent magnet
Power: 40bhp @ 940–4,000rpm
Torque: 225lb ft (305Nm) @ 0–940rpm
Batteries: 40 7.2V nickel-metal hydride
0–60mph: 13.7sec

Dimensions:
Length: 168.3in (4,275mm)
Width: 66.7in (1,694mm)
Height: 58.7in (1,490mm)
Wheelbase: 100in (2,550mm)

Chassis:
Suspension F/R: MacPherson strut, coil springs, anti-roll bar/torsion beam, trailing arms, coil springs
Steering: power assisted rack and pinion
Brakes F/R: disc/rear drum, regenerative, ABS
Wheels: 15in cast aluminium
Tyres: 165/65 SR

first century'. In the first month on sale, Toyota dealers received 3,500 firm orders – three times the expected sales target. The Prius was a hit with the critics, too. Motor Trend described it as:

> *...not only a technological marvel, but a truly liveable sedan.... This concept offers every bit the range of a conventional auto, and it works with the existing fuel station infrastructure. And the kicker is, Toyota has already sold more than 25,000 Prius sedans in Japan... securing the title of first mass-produced hybrid.*[41]

The car received the Japanese Car of the Year and New Car of the Year awards, the first time one model had held both accolades at the same time. After its first appearance in the UK, at the 1998 International Motor Show, the Prius won the environmental award category in the IBCAM Institute for Vehicle Technology auto design awards. The following February, Prius won a prestigious AA award in recognition of Toyota's continued efforts to reduce vehicle emissions. 'The Prius already meets known future European emission standards,' said John Maxwell of the AA. 'Our award acknowledges Toyota's commitment to reduce the impact of the car on the environment.'

In June 1999, *Engine Technology International* magazine voted the THS drivetrain, 'Best Eco-Friendly engine of 1999' in its International Engine of the Year Awards. A Royal Society Esso Energy Award followed in October 1999.

The Prius changed the general perception of Toyota from being a follower (albeit a very good one) to a leader in automotive innovation. It also prompted a different mindset within the company. The risk-averse corporate culture was jettisoned and Toyota threw itself wholeheartedly into the development of hybrid technology. It applied the same principles to its up-market Lexus brand, a policy

Keen to cash-in on the move to find a greener way of making energy, Toyota UK held a photo-shoot at one of the country's largest wind farms.

London landmarks were used in the Prius ad campaign to emphasize the fact that the car was exempt from the congestion charge.

The Mark I Prius was one of the most important cars in Toyota's history. It changed the way people thought of the company and nothing was the same again.

Although the saloon profile was not as popular as a hatchback, to European eyes the Prius paved the way for future hybrids.

that paid off by differentiating Lexus vehicles from established German, British and American luxury marques.

The lessons learned were applied in other ways, too. It is now standard practise for product development teams to share a single room and everyone, regardless of their age, rank or specialism, is encouraged to have a say. Every aspect of the Prius project was documented for posterity. The finished 200-page report is still a closely guarded secret.

Toyota, however, could not afford to rest on its laurels. As President Okuda said: 'This is the declaration of an environmental war. We may have woken the tiger that is the global auto industry. The real competition is yet to come.'[42] He was right, of course, but the competition from America and Europe would be a long time coming. Instead, the challenge came from much closer to home.

Seen from the front, the Prius looked like any other Japanese mid-sized saloon.

Honda's Insight

All the major Japanese car companies were actively researching hybrids and electric vehicles during the nineties, partly in response to the Californian Air Resources Board's zero-emissions vehicle mandate but also with one eye on emerging markets.

In 1993, Honda unveiled a fully working concept car (the EV-X) at the Tokyo Motor Show. The company had been encouraged to develop an EV by the success General Motors had enjoyed with its solar racers and, in 1996, it would win the World Solar Challenge outright. Testing of the EV-X began the following year but suffered a setback when early tests showed the vehicle's lead-acid batteries responded badly to heat – not an ideal situation when the southeast region of California has a climate not dissimilar to the Sahara Desert. As a result, Honda became an early champion of the nickel-metal hydride battery.

Its first stab at a production electric vehicle, the EV Plus, was launched in 1997 with an eye-watering selling price of $53,900. Unsurprisingly, the car – an unassuming three-door hatchback – was never actually offered for sale. Owners signed a 3-year lease contract, which cost $455 a month. At the end of the project, in 1999, the cars were taken back and scrapped, just as GM did with the EV-1 (but without the attendant worldwide bad publicity).

Beneath the bland looks, the EV Plus was actually a very sophisticated vehicle. As well as the NiMH battery pack,

The success of the Prius paved the way for Lexus – Toyota's upmarket brand – to adopt the hybrid drive.

The flagship of the Lexus range the new LS460h.

Honda's EV Plus was offered on a lease deal similar to the General Motors EV1.

The EV Plus was a tentative attempt at a full electric car but Honda was planning something much more ambitious with the technology.

it had regenerative brakes, high-intensity discharged headlamps and an electrically heated front windscreen. Additionally, some were fitted with oil-fired heaters for faster cabin warm-up in cold weather.

Although fewer than 400 were made, the experience gained would prove invaluable for Honda's next project.

In 1997, two years after the first Prius concept was unveiled at the Tokyo Motor Show, Honda rolled out the JVX, a sleek-looking 2+2 coupé that employed the company's newly developed Integrated Motor Assist (IMA) system – a small motor/generator installed between the combustion engine and the transmission to provide extra power during acceleration. Honda reckoned the 1.0-litre IMA powertrain could match the performance of a gasoline engine half as big again and was capable of 70mpg (4ltr/100km).

Honda EV Plus

Type: two-door hatchback
Drive: front wheel
Motor: DC Brushless
Power: 66bhp
Acceleration: 4.9sec to 30mph (48km/h)
Top speed: 80mph (130km/h)
Range: 100 miles (160km) under ideal conditions.
Batteries: 24 12V nickel-metal hydride; 288V
Recharge time: 8h with 220V charger, 35h with 110V emergency charger.
Transmission: single speed with reverse
Track front/rear: 59.1in/58.7in (1.50m/1.49m)

Intriguingly, the JVX dispensed with batteries and used an ultra-capacitor to store electrical energy. Although a capacitor would be more reliable than batteries, there were significant drawbacks. As a capacitor discharges very quickly there were safety fears, especially in the event of an accident. Capacitors also have the disadvantage of losing their charge much faster than a battery. An ultra-capacitor would only have been good for quick power boosts, rather than sustained running. Eventually, Honda's designers opted for the battery.

As a concept, the JVX demonstrated other features that would only find their way into production models many years later. The trapezoid exhaust turned up on the Civic, while the vertical rear window design would be referenced on the CRZ hybrid coupé more than a decade later. Other features, such as the air bag seatbelts, which were fitted to bright blue bucket-seats and inflated in the event of crash, never made it to mass production.

The IMA engine concept, however, was very real and when the JVX first went on display in 1997, Honda were racing to bring it to market as quickly as possible. The car that would do that was christened the Insight.

When it arrived two years later, the Insight was, if anything, even more radical-looking than its concept car

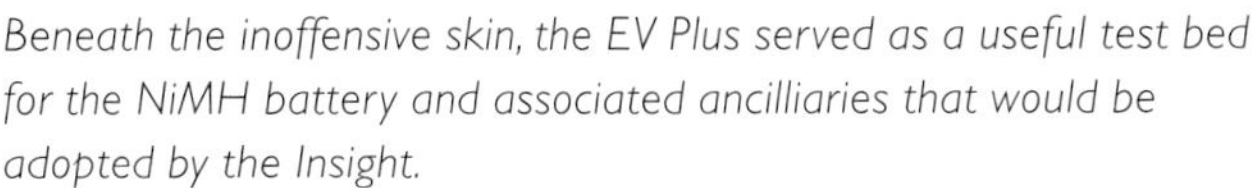

Beneath the inoffensive skin, the EV Plus served as a useful test bed for the NiMH battery and associated ancilliaries that would be adopted by the Insight.

This overhead shot of the Insight reveals the lengths Honda went to in order to maximize the body's aerodynamic efficiency.

An early sketch shows how Honda's designers were thinking of faired in rear wheels from the start.

The Insight's Kamm back can be seen in this photo. The design also harked back to Honda's much-missed CRX small sports coupé.

cousin. Both designs used smooth body panels to cut down aerodynamic drag, but the Insight had fared in rear wheels, rather like the GM EV1, and flat disc-like aluminium alloy wheels.

There were other similarities to the EV1. With the exception of the bumpers, the body panels were fashioned from aluminium for light weight and the body tapered towards the back, in a similar way to the EV1's teardrop shape. The radical body pinch meant the rear track was 4.3in (11cm) narrower than the front wheels. At the rear, the bodywork was abruptly cut off, a design feature known as a Kamm back, in a similar fashion to Honda's much loved CRX sports coupé, because there was no aerodynamic advantage to be gained by continuing the tail section.

Honda worked hard for every small aerodynamic gain and with good reason. At 70mph (113km/h) every 0.01Cd saved is worth 8mpg (35.3ltr/100km). The low, rounded nose was designed to part the air with a minimum of turbulence, louvres in the cooling-air inlets had been carefully designed to cut down aerodynamic drag and the headlights blended smoothly into the contour of the bumper which had large-radius curves in order to smooth the air flowing around them.

To minimize frontal area and drag, the windshield was raked as steeply as possible, and its edges blended smoothly with the sides and cabin roof. The trailing edge of the bonnet was shaped to divert airflow over the windscreen wipers.

The body was different in another way, too. Knowledge gained during the development of the NSX sports car allowed Honda engineers to develop a unique unit-body/space frame construction method that used stressed sheet-metal panels to absorb and distribute loads and extruded frame members for added strength. Using this method allowed Honda's engineers to add strength only where needed, allowing less critical areas to be lighter. The result was a body that weighed 40 per cent less than a comparable Civic hatchback. Honda demonstrated its confidence in the Insight's strength by conducting impact testing at higher speeds than were required to pass US, Japanese and European safety certification.

Beneath the striking bodywork, three plastic resin panels smoothed the airflow below the car. Separate fairings were used to channel air around the exhaust system and the fuel tank. In order to minimize air leakage to the underneath, the lower edges of the sides and rear of the body formed

The frontal aspect was the least radical-looking aspect of the Honda Insight.

Although it looks like a coupé in profile, the Insight was strictly a two-seater.

a strake – similar to the strakes used on supersonic jet aircraft – that functioned as an air dam. The floorpan rose slightly to meet the rear bumper and created a low-pressure area just behind the vehicle that sucked air from beneath the car and reduced turbulence. Honda claimed a world-beating mass production drag co-efficient of just 0.25.

The Insight only seated two people – a consequence of it being 4in (10cm) shorter than the JVX concept. In a bid to make the best of a so-so packaging job, Honda's marketing department coined the term 'personal fit capsule' to describe the cabin's interior dimensions. The company described this as 'a comfortable, relaxing personal space for the driver, with a modern, high-tech and sporty feel that further enhances the car's personal, sporty character'. Reflecting its niche status, every Insight came fully loaded with equipment, including power windows, heat-reflecting glass, an electronic instrument display, fuel-economy computer, power-locking with keyless entry, automatic air-conditioning (although this was an option in some markets), high-back bucket-seats, map lights, a 12V accessory socket and the premium leather-wrapped three-spoke steering wheel, as used by the highly desirable S2000 sports coupé.

The electronic instrument display lacked the 'wow' factor of the Prius but was still a mine of (largely useless) information. The display was divided into three sections. On the left was the gasoline-engine status section, showing engine rpm and coolant temperature, as segmented analogue displays. In the middle was a large digital speedometer, and below it the Insight's lifetime odometer. Along with the lifetime odometer, a lifetime fuel-economy readout and a bar graph that showing an instantaneous fuel readout from 0 to 150mpg (0–1.8ltr/100km) could be displayed.

A button on the left side of the instrument panel, marked 'FCD' (for fuel-consumption display) toggled between the lifetime odometer, two trip odometers and a third mode called the trip-segment mileage display. The two trip odometers, marked A and B, also showed trip fuel economy, as well as instantaneous mpg. The trip-mileage display mode could be used to ascertain an mpg reading for a specific part of a trip, such as motorway fuel economy or fuel economy when accelerating.

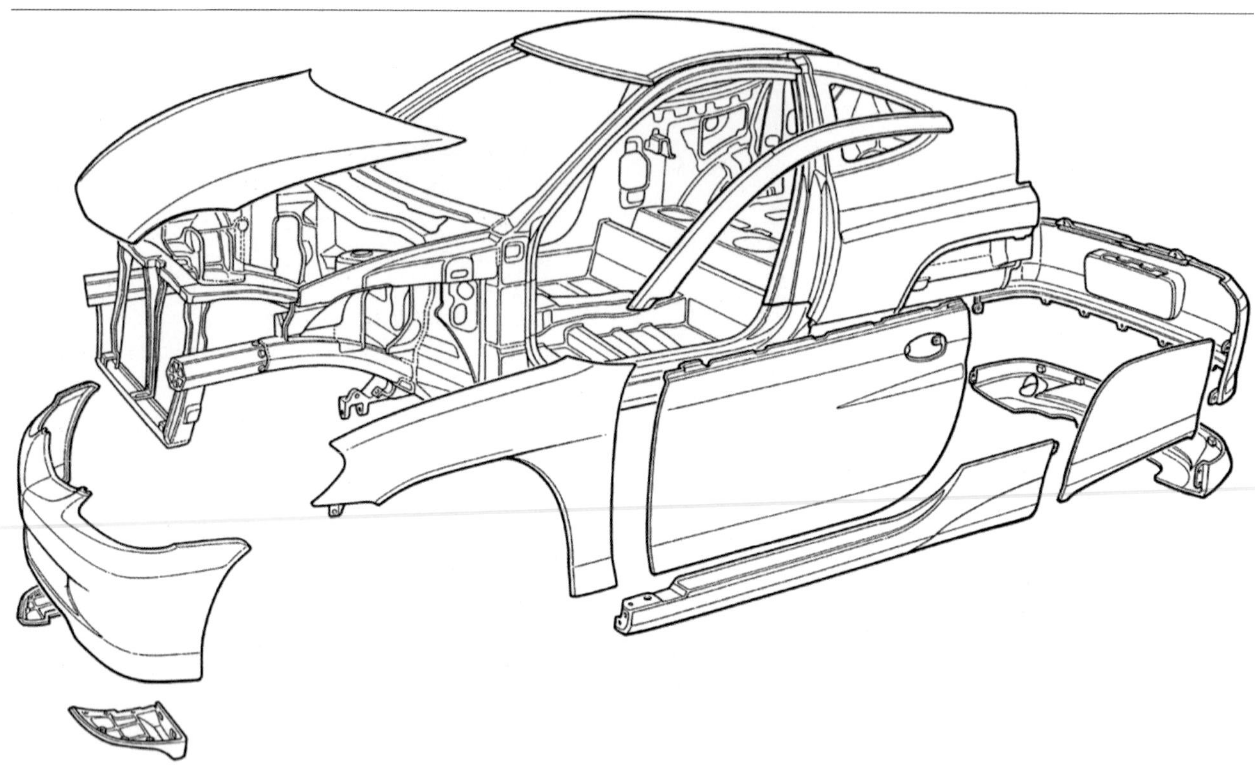

The Insight's body used stressed sheet-metal panels and extruded frame members for added strength. It weighed 40 per cent less than the equivalent Civic hatchback.

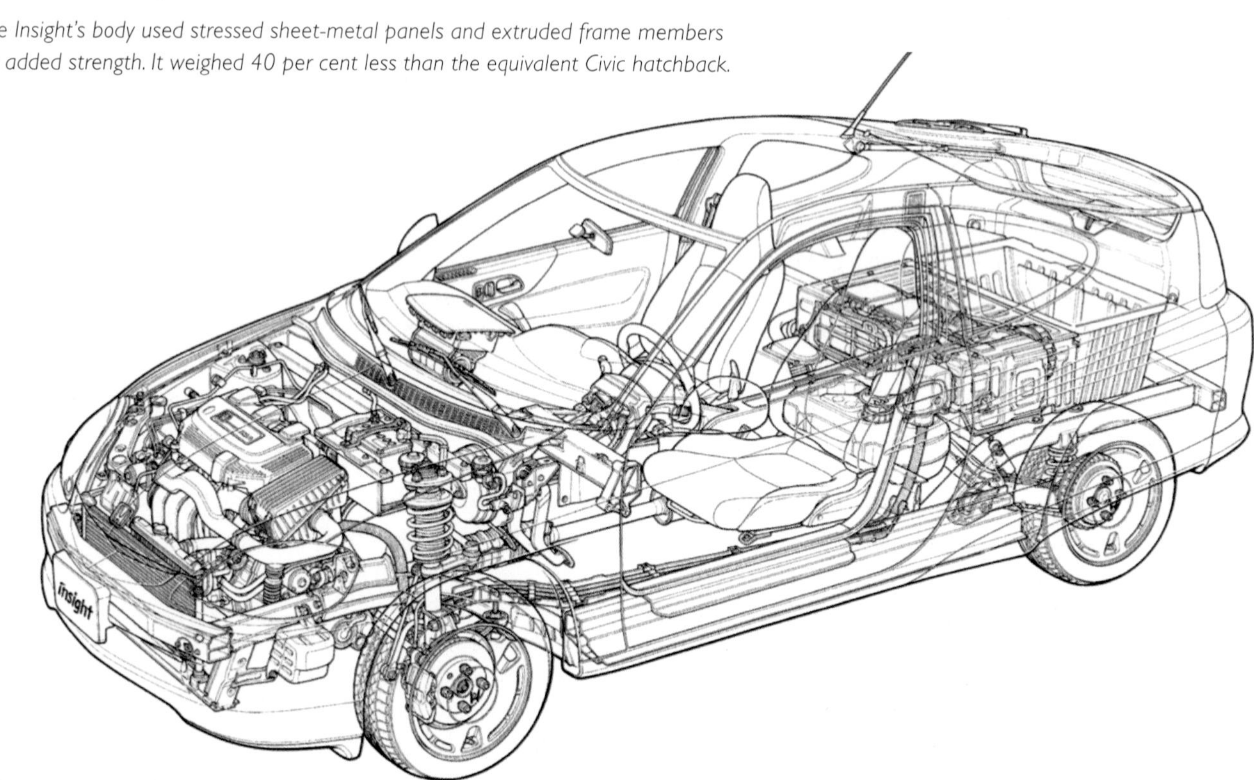

This cutaway shows how Honda tried to pack a quart into a pint pot. Note the size of the battery module behind the seats, which had a significant impact on the Insight's practicality.

The right side of the Insight's electronic instrument display housed the IMA system indicators for fuel level and battery charge, and the IMA Charge and Assist indicator. The Charge and Assist indicator showed whether the IMA system was being recharged or used to supply electrical energy to the IMA electric motor. An economy shift-indicator with arrows for both up and down shift points, was located in the centre of the display.

Sadly, for all its space-age technology and Buck Rogers instrumentation, the Insight was far from practical. As well as only carrying two people, the 5ft3 (1.4m3) cargo area was woeful thanks to the nickel-metal hydride battery pack sitting beneath it. An additional 1.5ft3 (0.4m3) of space was built into the floor but this was only useful for small, fragile items.

But the big scoop was not the radical looks, the cramped cabin or the paltry luggage space, it was the hybrid propulsion system. Although the Honda relied at all times on its 1.0-litre, 12-valve, 3-cylinder, VTEC-E gasoline engine, thanks to its motorcycle division Honda knew all about making lightweight and powerful small capacity powerplants. The Insight's engine was rather special being the world's smallest and lightest 1.0-litre production unit and utilizing advanced materials like aluminium, magnesium and plastics. A permanent-magnet electric motor mounted between the engine and transmission provided extra assistance under certain conditions, such as initial acceleration from a stop. The upside of this design was that, since the electric motor was used only for assistance and not for primary motive power, it could be made smaller and lighter relative to the full-size traction motors in other hybrid systems. As the IMA gasoline engine entered its mid-to-high rpm operating range, the electric motor assistance was switched off and power came from the engine alone operating in its high rpm 4-valve mode.

Power for the electric motor came mainly from the regenerative brakes, rather than from the gasoline engine. When the Insight was coasting, or its brakes applied, with the vehicle in gear, its electric-assist motor became a generator, converting forward momentum into electrical energy, instead of wasting it as heat during conventional braking. If the charge state of the IMA battery fell too low, the motor/generator could recharge it on the move.

The IMA nickel-metal hydride battery pack used technology pioneered in the EV Plus. The batteries were located under the cargo compartment floor, on top of the fuel tank, along with the IMA system's Power Control Unit (PCU). The IMA electric motor also pulled double duty as a high-rpm starter motor.

Honda Insight

Type: two-door coupé
Engine: 3-cylinder, aluminium cast block with off-set crankshaft
Displacement: 995cc
Power: 73bbhp @ 5,700rpm; 67bhp @ 5,700rpm gasoline engine only
Torque: 91lb ft (123Nm) @ 2,000rpm; 66lb ft (89Nm) @ 4,800rpm gasoline engine only
Batteries: 120 D-size nickel-metal hydride; 144V/6.5Ah
Five-speed manual transmission

Dimensions:
Length: 154in (3,940mm)
Width: 66in (1,694mm)
Height: 53in (1,354mm)
Wheelbase: 94in (2,401mm)
Weight: 1,872lb (851kg)

Chassis:
Suspension F/R: MacPherson struts/twist-beam axle
Brakes F/R: ventilated discs/drums
Wheels: aluminium alloy 14x5J
Tyres: 165/65 R 14 low-rolling resistance

Compared to a Honda Civic, the Insight's IMA system was an impressive 24 per cent more fuel-efficient in combined-mode city and highway driving, while also meeting California's stringent Ultra-Low Emission Vehicle (ULEV) standard.

The press were impressed by the Insight's technical merits. *Car* magazine concluded:

> *The Insight is a statement. Not just a green statement by its buyer, but a mighty statement by Honda of its technological muscle and intent.*

The New York Times commented:

> *The Insight drives pretty much like any other car. One difference, which makes the car eerily quiet, is that the*

The Insight used LCD instruments that were a mixture of analogue and digital.

> *engine shuts off when the car is not moving, the shift is in neutral and the foot is off the clutch.*

However it added:

> *The Insight only seats two people. It has only a five-speed manual transmission. Its gas engine is a tiny 1-litre, 3-cylinder, although Honda says that because of the Insight's lightweight aluminium body, aerodynamic design and assistance from its batteries, (it) behaves like a 1.5-litre subcompact. Finally, the aerodynamic design, with its tapered rear end and skirts over the back wheels, will discourage drivers who don't like to be stared at on the road.*[43]

When *Car and Driver* magazine tested the Insight, it recorded 121.7mpg (2.32ltr/100km) in a Honda-sponsored economy run from Columbus, Ohio, to Detroit (chosen, no doubt, to press home the fact that Honda had a hybrid and the US Big Three didn't). However, the magazine couldn't have achieved such a fine return had it not slipstreamed behind a Ford Excursion for most of the 195-mile (314km) route. Two years later, the magazine reported that a long-term Insight had returned a rather less impressive 'real world' fuel consumption of 48mpg (5.89ltr/100km).

The Fight for Hybrid Supremacy

Although the Prius had been first to go on sale, it was beaten to the massively important American market by the Insight. This might seem strange, given that the Prius went on sale in Japan in December 1997 and the Insight wasn't introduced until November 1999, but Toyota felt significant changes, principally more power, were required to make the Prius a success outside of Japan. Toyota announced plans for an export model in July 1998 but, as domestic demand for the car was so strong, the company took its time. Honda, on the other hand, had no such qualms and the Insight went on sale in North America just four weeks after its Japanese debut.

Toyota must have been peeved to see the Insight stealing the hybrid headlines in the United States when the Prius had already been on sale (albeit only in Japan) for two years. Even today, it's a common mistake that the Insight was the first petrol–electric hybrid of the modern era.

Maybe that's why some senior Toyota executives rather sniffily referred to the Prius as 'a real car' – an oblique reference to the Insight's two-seats and rather poor packaging – when the more powerful second-generation Prius (NHW11) finally went on sale in American and European showrooms. The 1.5-litre engine was uprated to 70bhp at 4,500rpm and slightly more torque – 82lb ft (111Nm) at 4,200rpm. The motor also gave slightly more power – 44bhp at 1,050rpm–5,600rpm –and torque – 258lb ft (350Nm) from 0 to 400rpm. Coincidentally, these figures were very similar to the Honda Insight. The NiMH battery was also changed to modular sub-packs that were a packaging improvement over the original steel tube design.

At the same time, the number of modules was reduced from forty to thirty-eight, slightly reducing the nominal voltage from 288V to 273.6V. To distinguish the high power Prius, the front and rear bumpers were given a smoother profile and the black rubbing strip removed. The European Prius also had rear fog lamps and a modest rear spoiler. Toyota's engineers also stiffened up the ride and added a rear anti-roll bar to the torsion beam rear suspension. The rear drum brakes were junked for solid discs and the power steering tweaked to deliver greater feel. *The New York Times*' car critic, Andrew Pollack, wrote:

> *Driving the Prius is like driving a regular car: just press the pedal and the car goes. The switch from electric to gasoline power is... imperceptible. The one difference is*

> *the gas engine's shutting off at a red light, leading novice drivers to conclude, instinctively, that the engine has stalled. It hasn't, of course, and when the accelerator is depressed the car immediately starts up and begins moving.*[44]

In the UK, Toyota sought to overcome baseless fears about resale values by tailoring an exclusive ownership package based on a fully maintained contract hire agreement known as Prius One, which took care of all on-going service and maintenance requirements. The scheme even included a 'relief vehicle' in the event of a mechanical failure, replacement tyres, road tax and European RAC breakdown cover. The company was dismissive of the threat posed by the Insight:

> *As a hybrid, Prius has currently only one rival, the Honda Insight, but beyond the powertrain there are no other comparisons. Prius is a fully practical four-door saloon with a full-size boot. It is also better specified and costs less to buy than the Honda.*

Indeed, Toyota's decision to build a family saloon was looking like a masterstroke as more and more car critics came down against the Insight's quirky style and cramped cabin.

In a three-way test with the Prius, a Honda Civic hybrid and the Insight in 2002, Cheryl Jensen wrote in *The New York Times*:

> *While neither the Civic nor the Prius can match it for economy, the two-passenger Insight is not practical. You'd have a tough time picking up two children from school, for instance, unless one ran alongside. Nor is the Insight comfortable. The ride is much harsher than the other cars', partly because its tyres are very hard, with low rolling resistance for better economy. Because of its very aerodynamic shape, there is virtually no wind noise. But that is more than offset by tyre and road noise.*[45]

The Insight may have had sporty looks but it just didn't have the kind of performance demanded by coupé owners; nor did it have the practicality required by families. It was the non-conformist's choice. As such Honda came nowhere near to achieving the 6,500 annual sales figure it had set itself. In 6 years it managed to sell just 17,020 units. That would have been a sensational figure by the standards of previous hybrids but it was less than the number of Prius vehicles Toyota sold in Japan in its first year on sale. Honda had emphatically lost the war and, as if to acknowledge the fact, it gave the go-ahead for a Civic hybrid in pretty short order.

Based on the seventh-generation of Honda's popular small family car, the Civic hybrid was introduced to the Japanese market in 2001 and America the following year. Honda's engineers found a way to make the Civic IMA system both smaller (by a remarkable 50 per cent) and more powerful (46lb ft torque versus 36lb ft) than its predecessor. There were other innovations, too, most notably the VTEC cylinder cut off system, which switched off three of the 1.3-litre engine's four cylinders during deceleration. The 1.3 was good for 85bhp at 5,700rpm and 87lb ft (118Nm) of torque at 3,300rpm. The brushless permanent magnet assist motor chipped in 13bhp when required and, as with the Insight, was charged via the regenerative braking system. The NiMH battery, consisting of 120 1.2V D-cells wired in series, was located behind the rear seat just like the Prius. Honda claimed its hybrid was 40 per cent more efficient than a conventional Civic.

The hybrid powertrain earned the car city/highway ratings of 46/51 (US) mpg from the Environmental Protection Agency. It was the most fuel-efficient five-seat sedan sold in North America at the time. However, some owners felt the Civic hybrid's real world consumption felt short and filed a class action lawsuit against the company. Honda denied the claims, pointing out many happy owners reported the same – or better – mileage as the EPA figures, and a settlement was reached in 2012. Owners unhappy with their car's fuel consumption received $100. A small claims lawsuit, in which a women was awarded $10,000, was thrown out by the appeals court. Honda was cleared of any wrong-doing.

The Civic may have been something of a stop-gap but it was far more successful than the Insight, proving once and for all that hybrids had struck a chord among environmentally cost-conscious families.

Although the Insight had proved to be a sales disappointment, Honda had been right in believing its integrated motor-assist technology was too good to give up on. As well as a second-generation Civic, it would regroup and return to the market with a new Insight targeted directly at the Prius.

CHAPTER NINE

REBIRTH: NEW HYBRIDS AND THE NISSAN LEAF

The success of the Prius, and the dawning realization that legislators would soon call time on 'dirty' internal combustion engines in some large towns and cities, led to a mad scramble as major industry players raced to catch up with Toyota.

Within a couple of years all the big manufacturers had announced hybrids or electric concepts – but many were destined never to see the light of day beyond international motor show stands and press junkets.

First up were the Americans. The Prius caught US automakers flat footed. Although they were initially dismissive of its power – GM's Ron York told *The Chicago Tribune*: 'I had the uncomfortable feeling I was going to become a hood ornament on a Mack truck' – the truth was clear: the Japanese had achieved what the Americans had been labouring over for years. Having handed over more than c. $1.5 billion since 1995, the White House was understandably rather anxious to see a return on its clean-car investment. Under the terms of the deal, Ford, GM and Chrysler had agreed to design and build concepts by 2000 with a view to having clean cars on sale by 2004.

In October 1999, Ford delivered a hybrid research vehicle (the P2000 LSR) to the US Department of Energy as part of its commitment to the Partnership for a New Generation of Vehicles (PNGV) initiative. The following January, Neil Ressler, Ford's chief technical officer, unveiled the Prodigy concept at the North American International Auto Show. At the time, both vehicles were unusual because they eschewed a small capacity petrol engine for a more fuel-efficient diesel (a decision that would be adopted by the other two PNGV partners as well). Ressler claimed the Prodigy's 1.2-litre powerplant was 35 per cent more frugal than a conventional gasoline engine.

A small electric motor packaged between the engine and the transmission delivered extra power when needed. Altogether the hybrid powertrain was good for 121bhp. Sadly, the three-phase AC induction unit could only produce its maximum 47bhp for 3sec but it could give between 4 and 11bhp for a longer duration. The battery was a 288V, 1.1kWh NiMH pack.

To improve the Prodigy's aerodynamics, Ford engineers removed the wing mirrors and replaced them with side-mounted cameras connected to an on-board monitor – an expensive and largely unnecessary decision.

An automatic louvered engine grille opened only when required and an active ride height system lowered the car at high speed. Extensive use of aluminium helped reduced the curb weight to 2,400lb (1,088kg), about 350lb (158.7kg) less than the donor vehicle, a Ford Contour (also known as the Mondeo in most international markets).

When *Car and Driver* magazine tested the Prodigy[47], it described the diesel engine as sounding 'pretty much like a tow truck' and criticized the way the automatic gearbox short-shifted through the gears for maximum economy (and minimum performance). The magazine concluded that the proposed Ford Escape SUV hybrid, due in 2003, that was set to use the Prodigy's powertrain, would be a better bet.

In 2000, Ford in Europe showed off the E-KA concept, an electrified KA powered by Li-ion batteries, which promised the performance of a petrol engine and a range of 93 miles (150km).

The KA body was put through a weight-reduction programme – trimming 99lb (45kg) – and the battery module was said to be 70 per cent lighter than an equivalent pack using lead-acid technology. The roof and bonnet were fashioned from hylite – an aluminium/polypropylene sandwich – while the wheel rims, rear axle and brakes were

Ford's first stab at a hybrid – built as part of the controversial US Partnership for a New Generation of Vehicles initiative.

Ford's hybrid concept used a Mondeo chassis to save money.

The Ford Prodigy – note the lack of wing mirrors which were deleted to make the body more aerodynamic.

The Prodigy's 1.2-litre diesel was 35 per cent more fuel efficient than a gasoline engine. A small electric motor delivered more power when required.

Tiny CCTV cameras replaced the Prodigy's wing mirrors – an expensive solution.

The Prodigy's interior used LCD screens to project the view from the external cameras – one on each side.

The Prodigy had a conventional large interior, but the trio of screens were unusual.

The Ford Prodigy's central screen was a sophisticated on-board trip computer.

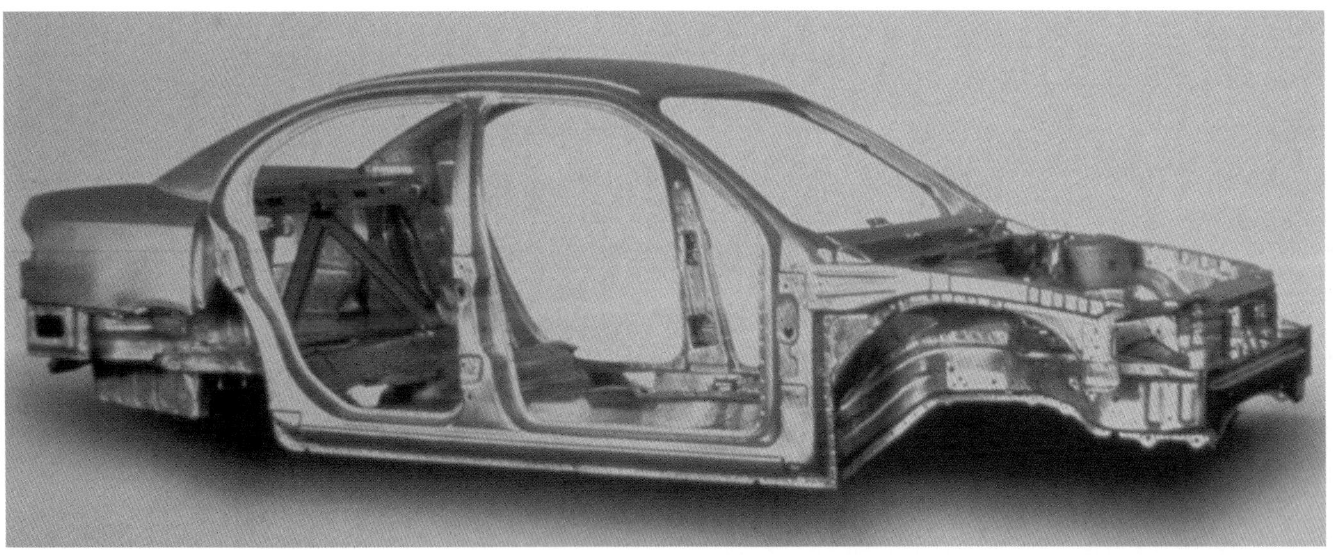

Ford managed to shave 350lb (158kg) off the chassis of the Prodigy's donor vehicle – the Contour.

Ford Prodigy

Engine: 1.2-litre, 4-cylinder in-line direct-injection diesel, aluminium block and head with variable-nozzle turbo-charger
Power: 74bhp @ 4,500rpm
Torque: 113lb ft (153Nm) @ 2,250rpm
Motor: three-phase permanent magnet between engine and transmission
Power: 47bhp @ 4,500rpm
Torque: 207lb ft (281Nm) @ 2,250rpm
Battery pack: 288V, 4.0Ah, 1.1kWh, nickel-metal hydride
Transmission: Ford MTX75 five-speed automatic
Performance:
0–60mph: 12sec
Body: aluminium unit body
Wheelbase: 109.5in (2,781mm)
Length: 192.8in (4,897mm)
Width: 69.1in (1,755mm)
Height: 55.9in (1,420mm)
Curb weight: 2,400lb (1,080kg)
Brakes: F/R: ventilated disc/drum
Tyres: Goodyear Integrity, P195/60R-17

The E-KA concept helped popularize electric cars in Europe but never made production.

Ford allowed selected journalists to test-drive the E-KA concept – but one test ended in embarrassment.

A charge indicator replaced the E-KA's rev counter.

Beneath the bonnet, the KA's asthmatic 1.3-litre OHV engine was replaced by an electric motor.

aluminium. As a result the E-KA could reach 62mph (100km/h) in 12.7sec and had a maximum speed of 80mph (130km/h).

Ford claimed a full charge took 6h from fully discharged. Two independent cooling systems kept the battery pack and the drive system cool. The E-KA was also an early recipient of electric power steering, which saved weight and was more compact.

Ford produced two E-KAs and even allowed journalists to drive one. Embarrassingly, when BBC Top Gear's Phil Salcedo drove the vehicle, it broke down on the German autobahn. Despite that faux pas, Salcedo wrote:

> *Ford's foray into electric is a revelation. There's ample power for overtaking, the smoothest of smooth acceleration... and a ride so quiet you have to be aware of hapless pedestrians completely oblivious to your imminent arrival.*

Yet, despite calls to put the E-KA into production, the concept was never destined for the showroom floor because the use of exotic materials and the cost of the Li-ion batteries would have made it prohibitively expensive.

The Chrysler ESX Concepts

As signatories to the PNGV initiative, DaimlerChrysler and General Motors were also under pressure to come up with their own low-emissions concepts.

The first attempt by Chrysler, an impressive-looking series hybrid called the Intrepid ESX, was shown in 1996 and was powered by a 1.8-litre 3-cylinder turbo-diesel. Two oil-cooled electric motors drove the wheels. After a couple more years' experimentation, Chrysler returned with the ESX II, a radical reinterpretation of the concept which utilized a parallel hybrid layout – a 1.5-litre diesel and a 20bhp AC-induction electric motor – in an aluminium spaceframe body clothed by plastic panels.

DaimlerChrysler's final effort – the Dodge ESX3 – stuck with plastics instead of sheet metal for light weight. Despite being a full-sized sedan capable of seating five adults, it actually weighed less than a Toyota MR2. The ESX3 was designed to fit together from just a dozen large mouldings, rather like an Airfix model kit. Opting for plastics not only made the Dodge 46 per cent lighter, but, in a handy coincidence, 15 per cent cheaper to build.

Unveiling the ESX3, Tom Gale, the company's executive

The Chrysler Intrepid ESX used a 1.5-litre diesel and a modest 20bhp motor but looked considerably faster.

The ESX used partly faired rear wheels for better airflow and a cut-off boot.

From the front, the Chrysler ESX looked almost conventional.

The ESX looked considerably sportier than the drivetrain allowed.

The ESX 1.5-litre diesel engine – not a popular choice for American drivers.

The Chrysler ESX's interior included an interface terminal for a hand-held computer. The Hewlett Packard 620LX sat on a docking station, where the audio head unit would normally be fitted. Unlike the ESX, the HP 620LX did at least go on sale.

Just like Ford, Chrysler ditched the wing mirrors on the ESX3.

The use of plastic allowed the ESX 3 to weigh less than a Toyota MR2.

Chrysler's claim that the ESX3 would only cost $7,500 more than a comparable gasoline-powered car seems optimistic, to say the least.

Dodge ESX3

Engine: 1.5-litre, 3-cylinder in-line, direct-injection diesel, variable nozzle turbo-charger, aluminium block and head, front-wheel drive
Power: 74bhp @ 4,200rpm
Torque: 122lb ft (165Nm) @ 2,200rpm
Motor: three-phase permanent magnet between engine and transmission
Power: 20bhp @ 2,200rpm
Torque: 98lb ft (133Nm) @ 0–1,100rpm
Battery pack: 165V, 6.0Ah, 1.0kWh, lithium ion
Transmission: six-speed dual-clutch semi-auto manual
Performance:
0–60mph: 11sec
Body: injection-moulded thermoplastic with tubular aluminium reinforcement
Wheelbase: 118.1in (3,000mm)
Length: 192.8in (4,897mm)
Width: 74.2in (4,897mm)
Height: 55.3in (1,405mm)
Curb weight: 2,250lb (1,013kg)
Brakes: F/R: vented disc/disc
Tyres: Goodyear Eagle LS P175/65R-18

vice president (product development and design), took a pot-shot at the other two PNGV concepts. 'At Daimler-Chrysler, we have our eye on the consumer,' he said. 'While we've achieved tremendous gains in fuel efficiency with the ESX3, we've put that technology in a dynamic design that is clean and safe, that has the comfort, utility and performance consumers demand – and is closing in on affordability.'

Chrysler estimated that the ESX3 would cost about $7,500 more than a comparable gasoline-powered car – about half the premium its predecessor, the 1998 ESX2, would have commanded.

The hybrid powertrain was another diesel-electric lash-up, this time a 1.5-litre 3-cylinder direct-injection job with a variable geometry turbo-charger. The Delphi air-cooled electric motor was shoe-horned between the crankshaft and the six-speed semi-automated dual clutch manual trans-axle. DaimlerChrysler chose the then unusual lithium-ion battery technology for the 165V, 1.0kWh motor. Bosses called it a mild hybrid (or a 'mybrid') and claimed the ESX3 was good for 72mpg (4ltr/100km) – a mere 2mpg (14ltr/100km) better than the ESX2 and still some way short of the US Government's target of 80mpg (3.5ltr/100km)).

When it was unveiled, the company made encouraging noises about putting an 'affordable' hybrid on sale within 3 years. Bernard Robertson, senior vice president (engineering technologies), pledged: 'Our concept cars aren't just interesting exercises for our engineers. We work hard to get exciting new technology off the shelf and into the showroom as quickly as possible.'

Controversy surrounds the ESX3 and its predecessors. Evan Boberg, a highly experienced engineer who worked at Chrysler for 12 years, including 3 years at the company's advanced research group (known internally as Liberty), claims in his book, Common Sense Not Required, that none of the hybrid concepts achieved the performance requirements set out for them. Sadly, as all three were only ever concept cars, the general public never got the chance to find out for themselves.

The General Motors Precept

General Motors' interpretation of the PNGV was the most radical of the trio. It was called the Precept and looked like a nightmarish collision between a Citroën CX and the original EV-1. Memorably, *Car and Driver* magazine described the styling as looking 'like Han Solo's toaster'.

Mindful of the sensational aerodynamic drag figures achieved by the EV-1, the GM team went all out for slipperiness. The engine (a 1.3-litre direct-injection turbo-diesel borrowed from GM's Asian affiliate Isuzu) was moved to the back of the car so the nose and engine compartment could be sealed up for maximum airflow efficiency. The rear wheels were partially enclosed and, just like the Ford Prodigy, the mirrors were deleted in favour of side-mounted cameras linked to LCD screens. The door handles were also removed. Airflow through the rear-mounted radiators also reduced drag by reducing the low-pressure area immediately behind the car. All this resulted in a drag coefficient that was even more impressive than the EV-1.

At a claimed 0.163 it was 20 per cent better than the EV-1 (0.19) but without mirrors and door handles it was

Described by *Car and Driver* as looking like 'Han Solo's toaster' the GM Precept was the most ambitious of all the hybrids from America's 'Big Three'.

Rear-mounted radiators and partly-enclosed rear wheels boosted air-flow and created a low-pressure area behind the GM Prodigy.

The Prodigy used twin LCD screens for satellite navigation and the major instrumentation.

The Prodigy's interior was every bit as complex as its exterior.

GM moved the Isuzu engine to the back of the car for maximum aerodynamic gain.

The Prodigy's length is clear from this photograph.

GM claimed the Prodigy was capable of 0–60mph in a shade over 12sec.

never going to pass type approval for general sale. Nor were the lightweight front seats, which appeared to be made from fish netting, the last word in style or comfort.

The Isuzu diesel was mated to a 13bhp electric motor that acted as starter, powered the air-conditioning, charged the nickel-metal hydride batteries and assisted the engine during full throttle acceleration. In the front engine bay sat a liquid-cooled 34bhp electric motor (essentially the same unit as the EV-1), which drove the front axle.

This powertrain made the Precept the most ambitious design of the three PNGV cars but also, by far, the most complex.

It was a technological tour-de-force but hideously complex. To get the show on the road, the Precept required three powerplants, sixteen radiators, three separate electrical systems and dozens of microprocessors. The chances of it ever going into production were virtually nil (although GM did produce a version of the Precept that used a fuel cell some time later). Indeed, at launch, Robert Purcell, executive director of GM's advanced technology vehicles, admitted as much, when he said: 'Eighty miles per gallon really pushes you to the edge of the envelope. Pieces of what we have got in Precept could find their way into production vehicles.'

Unlike the others, the Precept could run in all-electric mode. The diesel took over for steady cruising. When maximum power was required, both motor and engine could power the car. GM claimed the Precept could go from 0 to 60mph in 12.2sec.

Car and Driver found GM's concept the most interesting of the PNGV trio but criticized the fish net-style front seats and the LCD displays, which all but disappeared in direct sunlight – something of a problem for drivers in sunny southern California. The magazine concluded:

> *The Precept is too wonky and makes too many sacrifices for its 79.6-mpg combined [fuel consumption] rating and will likely never make production. In fact, it looks doubtful that we'll see an 80-mpg supercar in 2004 priced at less than an F-16 if the Precept is any indication of what it takes.*[48]

The magazine was correct. Behind the scenes, the US auto-makers were telling their PNGV political partners that the technology they had developed was just too expensive to go on sale. Building a couple of concept cars was one thing, they argued, but gearing up for mass production would cost hundreds of millions of dollars with no realistic prospect of making a profit. They pointed to the huge popularity of gas-guzzling pickups and SUVs as evidence that American drivers had no appetite for small, economical cars using costly and unproven hybrid technology. Environmentalists, too, were suspicious of the project. Some believed the use of diesel engines would only add to America's pollution problems. Strangely, this view ignored evidence to the contrary from Europe and Japan, where particulate traps meant diesels were now cleaner than petrol engines.

In the end it didn't matter. The project was dealt a fatal blow when Al Gore, Bill Clinton's Vice President and the man who had been the driving force behind the PNGV project, lost the 2000 Presidential election. The incoming President, George Bush, was a former oilman with no interest in 80mpg (3.5ltr/100km) diesel-electric hybrid cars. A few months after the change of administration, the new Energy Secretary, Spencer Abraham, told reporters that, after consulting with car makers, he was 'refocusing' the programme because buyers weren't interested in

GM Precept

Engine: rear-mounted 1.3-litre, 12-valve, 3-cylinder direct-injection diesel, aluminium block and head.
Power: 54bhp @ 2,500rpm
Torque: 125lb ft (169Nm) @ 2,000rpm
Motors: Motor: three-phase permanent magnet between front wheels; rear between engine and transmission
Power (F/R): 34bhp @ 8,200rpm; 13bhp @ 3,500rpm
Torque (F/R): 81lb ft (110Nm) @ 0–3,050rpm; 111lb ft (150Nm) @ 0–900rpm
Performance:
0–60mph: 12.2sec
Body: aluminium space frame with aluminium and plastic panels
Wheelbase: 111.8in (2,839mm)
Length: 193.1in (4,905mm)
Width: 68in (1,727mm)
Height: 54.4in (1,382mm)
Curb weight: 2,600lb (1,170kg)

sedans. They wanted fuel-inefficient SUVs instead.

The PNGV programme – and its goal of selling diesel–electric hybrids by 2004 – was quietly shelved. It was replaced by the FreedomCAR project focusing on hydrogen fuel cells, which (in theory) would supply electricity for a new generation of EVs. However, as with the PNGV project, the auto-makers and politicians gave themselves plenty of leeway. The US Energy Department said it would take between 20 and 35 years before hydrogen fuel cell vehicles were on widespread sale (interestingly, Honda did it in less than 10).

FreedomCAR was a bargain-basement project, it didn't have the funding and certainly didn't have the political clout of its predecessor, and it laid down no firm timetable for when fuel cell vehicles would be ready. In short, it looked like a classic political fudge.

GM's First Production Hybrid: the Silverado

In 2004, GM introduced its first ever hybrid. It wasn't a child of the exciting Precept. That car was gathering dust in a museum somewhere. Instead, the world's largest car manufacturer produced a hybrid pickup: the Chevrolet Silverado.

Drivers who remembered the EV-1 were appalled. The Silverado wasn't even a hybrid in the traditional sense. The electric motor in the transmission housing merely provided juice to start the 5.3-litre V8 petrol engine, charge the batteries and power the various electrical ancillaries. The system did allow the engine to shut off when coasting down hills or braking to a stop and applied torque to smooth take-offs, but that was it.

Unsurprisingly, the Silverado (and its sister pickup the GMC Sierra) showed little improvement over its conventional cousin's pitiful 16mpg (17.9ltr/100km) and 21mpg (13.5litr/100km) on the highway – just a mere 2mpg (142ltr/100km) improvement in city traffic.

Motor Trend magazine's tester Neil Chirico noted:

> *Though I applaud the General for putting something on the road while other automakers just talk about it. I don't see many buyers flocking to the Silverado hybrid because of improved fuel economy or the way it drives. The power flow is infested with surges, sags, bumps, dips and wobbles....*[49]

The magazine's long-term tester could only manage 1–1.5mpg (189ltr/100km) more than the conventional competition.

Green car enthusiasts were bitterly disappointed by the Chevrolet Silverado.

The Chevrolet Silverado – despite its hybrid claims, the electric motor did little more than start the engine and charge the battery.

The Silverado's 5.3-litre V8 engine was as thirsty as you would expect.

The Chevrolet Silverado may have pandered to American consumers' tastes, but any claims that it was a pointer towards a greener future were ludicrous. And while the Americans vacillated, Toyota was pressing home its advantage.

Prius 2: Toyota's Home Run

First up was a four-wheel drive hybrid. The Estima (Previa in the UK) people carrier showed the Americans that it was possible to create a serious hybrid from a large car. It featured a 2.4-litre, variable valve timing internal combustion engine and a 17bhp electric motor to power the front wheels and a 24bhp electric motor powering the rears.

During normal driving the petrol engine did the work but, when required, all three could be used for maximum acceleration. At urban speeds, the petrol powerplant cut out entirely and the two electric motors propelled the car almost silently.

The Estima was an impressive addition to Toyota's line-up but claims of 50mpg (5.7ltr/100km) economy were wide of the mark. When *Auto Express* tested one it could do little better than half that figure. The magazine blamed the extra weight of the hybrid drive but Toyota engineers countered that the vehicle had been designed with Tokyo's dense stop-start traffic in mind. In those conditions it was capable of doubling the fuel consumption of a standard Estima MPV. Unsurprisingly, the Estima hybrid was not exported to Europe or America. Japanese drivers also saw a mild hybrid version of the Crown saloon but these were merely warm-ups for the big act – a new Prius.

Six years after the launch of the original Prius, and with more than 130,000 examples sold worldwide, Toyota unveiled an even more advanced version of the world's most successful petrol–electric hybrid. Toyota hailed the second generation Prius as: 'A blend of futuristic design and technology that offers D-segment levels of space, comfort and performance with B-class economy'. In other words, it was as big as a Ford Mondeo and as frugal as a Fiesta.

Actually, Toyota claimed 56.5mpg (5ltr/100km) on the urban cycle, which was better than every B-segment car on the market by a considerable margin. So, if anything, it was playing down its claims for the new car.

Even more impressive were the exhaust emissions. Hydrocarbon and nitrogen oxides emissions were 80 and 87.5 per cent lower than the tightest European regulations for petrol engines (regulations the majority of diesel

Six years after the original, Toyota returned with a second-generation Prius that was bigger and better.

The second-generation Prius wasn't far off the Ford Mondeo in terms of size.

The switch to a more conventional hatchback was done with one eye on the European market, which had proven more resistant to the Prius's charms than Japan or America.

engines could not meet). Indeed, the Prius 2 was capable of breaking the psychologically important 100g/km barrier for CO_2 exhaust emissions on the extra-urban cycle.

How did it do this? A more powerful 1.5-litre petrol engine worked together with a smaller, more efficient electric motor to deliver better performance. The electric motor alone was more powerful than most 1.0- and 1.2-litre internal combustion engines and, at 295lb wt (400Nm) of torque from 0 to 1,200rpm, the Prius had more pulling power than a modern V6 diesel.

As a result, the car despatched the 0–62mph benchmark in 11sec – almost 3sec faster than the first-generation model – which was comparable to a 2.0-litre turbo-diesel engine. Toyota proudly claimed that the new hybrid synergy drive system had more new patents (530) than the first one (a 'mere' 300).

The bodyshell was re-examined for weight loss because less mass meant lower fuel consumption and the Cd figure of 0.26 was class leading.

Although the family resemblance to the first-generation Prius was clear, the second model was considerably larger. At 174in (4,450mm) it was 5in (135mm) longer than its predecessor and had a 6in (150mm) longer wheelbase at 105in (2,700mm). Despite this increase in size, the new

The engine had more power and the motor was more efficient. Toyota claimed this combination could give a V6 diesel a run for its money.

The second Prius was 5in (135mm) longer than its predecessor and had a 6in (150mm) longer wheelbase at 105in (2,700mm).

Toyota kept faith with the central colour monitor screen inside.

The screen on the Prius mark two had a real-time readout of energy consumption.

car was 15 per cent more fuel efficient than the first model.

The second-generation Prius was every bit as much a technological showcase as its ground-breaking predecessor. The hybrid driveline may have been the car's unique selling point but there were other headline-grabbing gadgets and gizmos. Wherever possible Toyota's engineers sought for do away with inefficient mechanical linkages – the throttle, brakes and transmission were all electronic. Black box technology also governed the anti-lock brakes, stability control and the brakeforce distribution system, which varied the amount of braking applied to each wheel in an emergency situation to maximize the car's stopping power.

Voice recognition – which allowed drivers to operate some of the vehicle's ancillary systems without taking their hands from the wheel – was a sure-fire showroom winner. Controlling an audio system by voice command seemed impossibly futuristic when the best the Prius's rivals could offer were switches and buttons on a steering wheel. The Prius had these, too, but voice control gave better bar-room bragging rights.

Reflecting Toyota's determination to build the brand by offering excellent value as well as class-leading performance, every Prius was generously equipped. Electric windows and mirrors, climate control, remote central locking, a CD player with six speakers and an alarm/immobilizer were all fitted as standard.

The critics were impressed. *Auto Express* ran one as a long-term test car and found: 'It [was] simplicity itself to drive, with the smooth CVT automatic gearbox and silence at idle, courtesy of the electric motor, making journeys stress-free'.[50] When it tested the car a couple of years later it wrote: 'The Prius is one of the cleverest cars you can buy. High list price apart, it's hard to fault the cost of running a Prius.'

Autocar argued that the Prius made economic sense despite its high price. In February 2004, the magazine wrote:

> *Prices start at a fairly serious £17,495 but hybrid power means company car drivers would pay tax on just eleven per cent of the purchase price, while drivers commuting into the capital would be exempt from the Congestion Charge. Factor in the £1000 Government 'Powershift' grant, strong fuel consumption, group seven insurance and the lowest road tax possible and that case looks strong. Whether it's strong enough to persuade most buyers to pick the Toyota over an Accord CDTi, or any of the other highly talented and more dynamically satisfying turbo-diesel rivals remains to be seen. But one thing is clear: hybrid power is a seriously viable alternative.*

As if to rub in its advantage, the Lexus RX450h showed what was possible if Toyota built a hybrid SUV – in marked contrast to the Chevrolet Silverado.

Hybrid power and Lexus were a natural fit. Buyers loved the smoothness and refinement.

By the RX450h Toyota's engineers were expert in packaging the hybrid drive line and its battery module.

The RX450h boasted every conceivable luxury.

The latest RX450h has 295bhp when required, thanks to a more powerful inverter and twin electric motors.

The interior of the current RX450h shows a move away from woods to brushed metals as trim materials.

Of course, not everyone was impressed. The BBC *Top Gear* programme handed a Prius over to Jeremy Clarkson in December 2004 and the controversial presenter concluded that the only upside of Prius ownership was its quietness at speed. He criticized the quality of the cabin plastics and felt the low-rolling resistance tyres were dangerous. If you want to save the world, Clarkson decided, the best way to do it was in a Volkswagen Lupo.

In America, however, the Prius had become the darling of Hollywood. Environmentally aware stars such as Leonardo DiCaprio and Cameron Diaz used them as everyday vehicles and the car was given starring roles in several TV shows including *The West Wing* and *Six Feet Under*. As a result, sales in North America went through the roof and in pretty short order the Prius became Toyota's third best-selling model behind the Camry and the Corolla. Initial sales estimates of 36,000 for the US were revised upwards to 100,000 and then higher still.

Flushed with success, Toyota declared that it would press ahead with a hybrid for all its major models, starting with a Lexus SUV. In Europe, Lexus would position itself as the 'green' luxury alternative to Jaguar, BMW and Mercedes.

The RX 400h, a crossover SUV introduced in 2004, showed what was possible with a hybrid drive and a V6 engine. It shamed the GM Silverado's atrocious fuel-consumption, giving the same (or better) performance as a petrol V8 with vastly improved economy and lower emissions. The public agreed. In 2006, Lexus sold over 108,000 examples in the United States, making the RX the best-selling luxury vehicle in America.

By 2012, the Lexus RX had gone through three generations – each more powerful and fuel efficient than the last – and showed no signs of fading popularity.

The current RX450h has a revamped 3.5-litre V6 engine boosted to 295bhp when required, thanks to a more powerful inverter and twin electric motors. A drive-selectable EV mode allows the car to travel for short distances on electricity.

In a sign of the RX's growing sophistication, and recognition that most will never venture off-road, the MacPherson strut rear suspension has been replaced by a double-wishbone set up for tighter handling and better luggage space.

In Europe, the Lexus range encompasses a small premium hatchback (the CT200h), the GS 450h premium saloon, the LS 600h luxury saloon and, of course, the RX

Lexus hopes to crack the European market with the CT200h premium hatchback – a contender for the segment currently ruled by the Audi A3.

In 2012, the GS450h revealed a more overtly sporty design language for Lexus.

The Yaris Hybrid was the cheapest petrol–electric car on the market in summer 2012.

Toyota Yaris Hybrid

Four-door supermini.
Engine: 4-cylinder, 1497cc, petrol, plus electric motor
Power: 98bhp combined
Torque: 82lb ft (111Nm) petrol; 125lb ft (169Nm) electric
Performance:
0–62mph: 11.8sec
Top speed: 103mph (165km/h)
Wheels: 15in (381mm) alloy
Tyres: 175/65 R15
Price in UK: £15,895

450h – giving Toyota an unbeatable range of hybrids in the luxury car market. Every Lexus is a full hybrid, meaning they can be driven by just the electric motor alone, with a computer selecting the most appropriate power source.

In 2012, having notched up more than 3 million hybrid sales, Toyota introduced its most important new hybrid since the MK1 Prius.

The Yaris Hybrid was special not just because it was the cheapest petrol–electric car from a major manufacturer, but because it also undercut many turbo-diesels in the supermini segment as well.

There were other notable achievements: with a CO_2 emissions figure of just 79g/km the Yaris became the cleanest car not running on pure electricity available in the UK and the battery pack was small enough to fit beneath the back seats without compromising boot space. The hybrid powertrain weighed just 442lb (201kg) – 92lb (42kg) less than the system used in the larger Auris hatchback – thanks in part to reducing the number of cells in the nickel-metal hydride battery pack from 168 to 120. Charging efficiency was improved, however, by revised electronics.

The Yaris used a revised version of the Mk2 Prius's 1.5-litre Atkinson-cycle petrol engine mated to a revised Hybrid Synergy Drive offering three modes: Normal, Eco and EV. The latter was rather less exciting than it sounded – the small battery pack meant the Yaris could only run on electricity for short bursts. Nevertheless, Toyota claimed a combined fuel consumption figure of 80.7mpg (3.5ltr/100km). *Autocar* said: 'If your head rules you, the Yaris Hybrid will be one of the most rational purchases you ever make. It is efficient, it will be cheap to run and it is very well equipped.' However, the magazine criticized the supermini's 'lack of sex appeal'.

The interior of the Yaris Hybrid is typical of Toyota's attention to detail.

Electric Supermini: the G-Wiz

Around the same time as Mk2 Prius sales were going stratospheric, a strange-looking pure electric vehicle appeared in a handful of select London showrooms.

Conceived by a Californian engineer called Lon Bell, and manufactured in India by a joint Indian-US partnership, the G-Wiz was a small 2+2 seater powered initially by a DC drive (an AC drive followed in 2005).

Bell's concept was simple: he aimed to develop the perfect city car by stripping away anything that wasn't absolutely necessary and powering it by electricity. The batteries were located beneath the front seats and the motor could produce a maximum of 17.6bhp.

Controversially, the G-Wiz was exempt from UK crash test rules because it was classed as a quadricycle rather than a passenger car. When BBC *Top Gear* tested it anyway the results made grim viewing if you were a G-Wiz salesman. The show 'crashed' a G-Wiz into a suspiciously sturdy kitchen table and the results were wince-inducing: the table was hardly damaged, while the G-Wiz was a write-off. It was a cheap shot filmed for laughs but GoinGreen, the car's importer, didn't see the funny side. It refuted the test results as well as pointing out that, as a predominantly urban car, the G-Wiz was less likely to be involved in a high-speed crash anyway.

Top Gear also gave the G-Wiz a pasting for the way it drove. The programme-makers put it in a drag race with a Renault Alpine sports car and, when it lost that, the little electric car was pitched against the kitchen table, which was carried by four burly men. The G-Wiz looked to be on a winner against the table until it conveniently ran out of power and the four men walked past it to the finishing line. Jeremy Clarkson concluded: 'If you want to get to work on time – get a table'. He continued: 'The G-Wiz has no redeeming feature. It has no head room, it has no leg room, it has no space for a passenger alongside me and God has not yet created a creature that would fit in the back. The EU does not class this as a car – it's a quadricycle – and I can see why. It just isn't one.' Ouch.

When the UK Department of Transport Research Laboratory did get around to testing it – 3 years after it went on sale – the testers wrote of their 'serious safety concerns' after the vehicle fared badly in the off-set barrier test.

Despite this, several thousand G-Wiz vehicles have been sold – and by far the majority to satisfied owners in

G-Wiz

Two-door, 2+2 seater hatchback
Motor: AC induction motor, three-phase, 6kW continuous driving the rear wheels
Performance:
Top speed: 51mph (82km/h)
Torque: 38lb ft (52Nm)
Range: 40–48 miles (64–77km)
Body: tubular steel space frame with side-impact beams, energy-absorbing bumpers and collapsible steering column
Wheelbase: 66.9in (1,699mm)
Length: 102.3in (2,598mm)
Width: 51.1in (1,298mm)
Height: 62.9in (1,598mm)
Brakes:
F/R: disc/drum
Tyres: 13in energy-saving low-rolling resistance tubeless

The G-Wiz was an unexpected hit with Londoners looking to avoid the congestion charge.

London was such a big market that a special edition G-Wiz celebrated the UK's capital city.

Not everyone wanted to put the G-Wiz on a pedestal. BBC Top Gear *excoriated the car.*

This shot demonstrates the compact dimensions that made the G-Wiz so popular in congested cities.

the UK, where the G-Wiz – with upgraded safety – has become something of a cult among trendy London suburbanites. Indeed, for a time the G-Wiz had the lowest depreciation of any car, including Porsches and Mercedes, as demand outstripped supply and there was a 5-month waiting list.[51] G-Wiz even introduced a 'London' special edition to cash in on its popularity. Celebrity owners included Jonathan Ross, Jerry Hall and Kirstin Scott Thomas, who said: 'It's such fun to drive, easy to park and nippy. Children laugh when I go by.' So did *Top Gear* presenters.

The G-Wiz did notch up one notable achievement, however. By public demand, several London councils installed charging points in car parks and on the streets – putting in place the first rudimentary infrastructure for electric vehicles in Britain's capital since City and Suburban's seven-storey Denman Street electric car emporium a century earlier.

The success enjoyed by the G-Wiz did not go unnoticed. By 2006, several car manufacturers had quietly begun preliminary work on small electric cars. Even Norbert Reithhofer, the CEO at BMW, talked about a G-Wiz type of electric city car and one manufacturer already had a serious development programme well underway – one that would lead to the first true electric vehicle of the twenty-first century.

Nissan Goes for Broke

Although Toyota stole the headlines with the Prius, Nissan had a longer history of producing electric vehicles. The Tama Electric Car company had been swallowed up by Nissan in 1968 and the company had toyed with EVs ever since. So imagine how galling it must have felt when, in 2007, Nissan was forced to purchase a hybrid drivetrain from Toyota in order to build the Altima hybrid sedan.

As long ago as 1970, Nissan had exhibited an electric city concept (the 315X) at the Tokyo Motor Show and two years later built the EV4 pick-up. It also produced an electric version of the popular Laurel. Since 1990 it had been quietly working on a pure EV in collaboration with Sony. The partners examined possible automotive applications for lithium-ion (Li-ion) battery technology, which offered higher density, and greater power, than conventional nickel-cadmium (NiCd) and nickel-metal hydride (NiMH) batteries. When the preliminary work produced promising results, and with the Californian clean-air mandates looming, spending on EV development was increased by 30 per cent.

'We had a huge number of engineers dedicated to the project,' remembered Minoru Shinohara, vice president of Nissan's technology development division. 'It was the largest scale engineering focus we've ever had on a single technology outside of engine design.'

The Nissan FEV (Future Electric Vehicle) could be fully recharged in 15min from a high-energy power source.

Nissan's FEV II was a more conventional-looking vehicle but was the company's first car to utilize lithium-ion batteries.

In 1991, the company claimed it had developed the world's first 'super quick charge' battery that could achieve a 40 per cent recharge in a remarkable 6min. The Nissan FEV (Future Electric Vehicle) could be fully recharged in 15min from a high-energy power source. The car had a top speed of 81mph (130km/h) and a cruising range of 100 miles (160km) at 45mph (72.4km/h). This was followed a couple of years later by the FEV-II, which looked like a collision between a Volkswagen Beetle and a Micra but utilized Li-ion batteries.

But Masato Fukino, the senior project engineer at Nissan's Vehicle Research Laboratory, cautioned that there was still a long way to go before an EV was viable. In an interview with *The Day* newspaper, in 1991, Fukino acknowledged the lead GM held with the Impact. Asked if Nissan could overhaul GM, he just smiled and said: 'Yeah... in the near future'.[52]

That future was nearer than anyone thought. In 1995, Nissan unveiled the FEV II, which was powered by Li-ion batteries, and the year after the Prairie Joy EV, the world's first electric car with Li-ion batteries. Based on a conventional Prairie people-carrier, the curiously named Joy EV was used as something of a mobile test bed for the new Li-ion battery technology. As Hideaki Horie, expert leader at Nissan's EV technology development division, recalled:

> *The majority of the industry, even our colleagues, were sceptical about the Li-ion system. We chose the Li-ion battery because we believed in its potential and possible applications for vehicles, much higher than the nickel hydride batteries that were common at that time.*

Although the Prairie EV was limited to fleet sales, around thirty units were actually sold. It also endured one of the most extreme tests for any battery-powered car – as a support vehicle for the Japanese National North Pole Exploratory Team at their research station in Ny-Alesund, Svalbard, Norway – which at 79°N is the world's most northerly settlement. The team used a Prairie EV as their daily transportation for 6 years, driving from the base research station to the town and airport and, most importantly, while conducting meteorological observations. The Nissan was the perfect choice because, as a zero-emissions' vehicle, the scientists could be sure it would not contaminate the research data with CO_2 emissions. 'The Nissan EV became a symbol of our pledge at the International Arctic Research Village that the environment would not be damaged by the execution of research activities,' explained Dr Hajime Ito, of the Japanese National Institute of Polar research. 'VIPs visiting our village were welcomed at the airstrip by the Prairie EV, which transported them to town without the slightest noise or exhaust gas. It was also an excellent vehicle for scientific purposes, such as the observation of wild animals, which you could approach without sound or smell.'

The car gave sterling service for six years. When it failed to start Nissan shipped the vehicle back to Japan where it was stripped down. Incredibly, despite the freezing temperatures the batteries had operated in, the problem was traced to a simple disconnected condenser. The part was replaced and the car restarted immediately. Tests on the batteries showed no unexpected deterioration caused by the cold.

A year after the Prairie Joy EV, Nissan followed up with an award-winning battery-powered minivan, the Altra EV (called the R'nessa EV in Japan), which was sold in the United States and Japan mainly to utility companies. Nissan achieved high power (83hp) with low weight by using a neodymium alloy magnet – the strongest known – for the motor. The twelve-module Li-Ion battery was fitted beneath the passenger compartment floor – an essential move to avoid compromizing the luggage compartment (which would have been the kiss of death for a SUV like the Altra). Nissan reckoned it could power the car for 120 miles in ideal conditions (more like 80 miles in the real world). Other refinements included a four-wheel anti-lock braking system (ABS), regenerative braking, a 75mph (120km/h) top speed and an 800lb (360kg) passenger/cargo capacity. Air-conditioning, power windows and door locks, a premium audio system and dual supplemental air-bags were all standard. Charging was by a user-friendly inductive battery charging system through an electromagnetic paddle inserted into a charge port in the front grille, rather like the GM EV-1.

Customers included the Southern California Edison Company, the Pacific Gas and Electric Company and the Los Angeles Department of Water and Power. They were even used as parking enforcement vehicles by the Santa Monica Police Department and around 200 were built.

While these extended real world trials were going on, Nissan planners were busy figuring out what urban motorists would be driving in the twenty-first century. At the 1999 Los Angeles Motor Show, the company took the wraps off the Hypermini, an ultra compact EV designed for making short trips with a maximum of two people.

Once again the usual figures were trotted out to overcome initial range anxiety fears. Nissan's press release said:

> *Traffic survey data indicates that approximately ninety per cent of all passenger cars are driven less than forty-two miles a day and that roughly ninety per cent of compact vehicles carry only one or two occupants. Designed with these trends in mind, Hypermini's interior has ample room to accommodate two people in complete comfort, while a rear cargo compartment provides enough space for everyday items such as groceries, sporting equipment and luggage.*

Seen today, the Hypermini looks uncannily similar to the Smart fortwo and the Toyota iQ. Back in 1999 it was a radical reinterpretation of the accepted commuter car-design language with its large glass area, tallboy body proportions and massive headlights. The car was light thanks to its aluminium spaceframe construction and plastic panels. The battery modules were positioned beneath the floor in order to avoid the car toppling over on smartly driven bends. A large, liquid crystal display (LCD) positioned in the centre of the instrument panel enabled the driver to see essential information, including air-conditioning and stereo status, at a glance. The air-conditioning system could be programmed to cool down or heat up the interior before the car was driven (the LEAF has a similar system) ensuring the ambient temperature was always perfect.

Also like the LEAF, the Hypermini communications system offered up traffic information, charging locations and satellite mapping displayed on an LCD monitor. Nissan claimed the Li-ion batteries were good for an 80-mile (128km) range and a top speed of 60mph (95km/h). Once again, the Li-ion battery pack was charged via an inductive paddle. Nissan also claimed the Hypermini was 90 per cent recyclable by weight.

Although the Hypermini was, once again, an ultra low-volume car that was virtually hand-built, it still won Nissan the fourth annual New Energy Grand Prize from Japan's Ministry of International Trade and Industry. A small fleet of Hyperminis was used by the local authority in Tokyo and, in Yokohama, it was even possible to rent a Hypermini for a short commute. Nissan North America leased thirty Hyperminis to Californian utilities and state municipalities for $99 a month. In addition, eleven were evaluated by the US Department of Energy between January 2001 and June 2005. Its testers concluded that the

The Hypermini, unveiled in 1999, was Nissan's idea of an electric city car.

Ahead of its time, visually, at least, the Hypermini shares much in common with the Toyota iQ.

urban electric vehicle concept had commercial potential thanks to emissions' cleanliness, low operating costs and the convenience of home-charging.

Nissan also gave selected journalists and opinion-formers brief drives (in a brilliant bit of product placement the car even appeared in a Hollywood movie called Sleepover in 2004). Paul Hudson, writing in *The Daily Telegraph*, said:

> *If electric vehicles conjure up images of milk floats, think again. The Hypermini, designed for use in traffic clogged Japan, is a thoroughly modern vehicle.... Driving its simplicity itself – select Drive, press your right foot and the Hypermini picks up with surprising panache. Acceleration tails off on inclines, but Nissan's claimed maximum of 60mph is no idle boast. The electronically-assisted steering is ideal for urban driving and the Hypermini feels stable, despite its short wheelbase.*[53]

Auto Express was rather less convinced. 'Could this be the future of urban motoring in Britain? Probably not,' it wrote. 'The Hypermini is undoubtedly a clever piece of engineering, but question marks remain over its potential in the UK. The driving experience is flawed, the interior packaging ineffective and its limited range of only 70 miles reduces its appeal.' The magazine criticized the car's interior quality and the cabin's lack of space.

Ford has a Re-TH!NK

Ford had actually beaten Nissan to an electric city car by several years but, once again, the Americans somehow conspired to throw away their advantage, although the car itself refused to die. Pivco was a Norwegian company founded in Oslo in 1991 to design and build small commuter cars. The company used an aluminium chassis clad with plastic panels and NiCd batteries to power a three-phase AC induction motor, which turned the front wheels.

After a couple of small-scale concepts, Pivco turned to Lotus, in Norfolk, to help design a true production model. The roof was fashioned out of ABS plastic and the chassis became a cheaper steel/aluminium mix. Pivco claimed its new baby – christened the TH!NK – had a real world range of 50 miles (80km) and a top speed of 56mph (90km/h) – perfect for urban commuting. Unfortunately, the company ran short of funds but a saviour appeared in the form of Ford, which bought the company (and the TH!NK) during one of its expansionist phases.

It would seem Ford bosses had big plans for the brand. As well as the TH!NK city car, Ford also announced the four-seat TH!NK Neighbor and a couple of two-wheeled EVs, the Th!nk bike fun and the TH!NK bike traveler. The TH!NK bike fun had a rigid frame, whereas the bike traveller had a compact folding frame, which made it simple to store and transport. The fun was powered by a 24V 400W motor and the traveller a 24V 250W motor.

The TH!NK city provided comfortable transportation for two adults and was designed for the cut 'n thrust of urban driving. The motor was liquid cooled for greater efficiency, as were the nineteen NiCd batteries, which generated approximately 11.5kWh of electricity. The car utilized a conductive charging system. After an overnight charge of eight hours, the car would be ready for action. Owners reported the batteries could reach 80 per cent in four to six hours, depending on the ambient conditions.

To build public acceptance, Ford based fleets of TH!NK city cars at major stations, including Grand Central Station, in New York, where they could be used by environmentally conscious commuters. But 2 years later production ceased after a mere 1,005 units had been manufactured. At the time, Ford said it was more interested in fuel-cell technology. It sold out to an Indian businessman and development was halted.

However, in March 2006, a Norwegian investment group – which included Jan Otto Ringdal, one of the brains behind the original concept – acquired the company, which was renamed THINK Global. In 2008, the company showed off a revamped TH!NK city – now in its sixth generation – which was powered by Li-ion battery technology.

The new TH!NK city was a thorough update. As well as the batteries, THINK Global made good use of modern telematics. The car could send text messages to mobile phones, updating owners on how close the batteries were to a full charge, and an 'assist' button alerted a call centre should the car run out of juice. But all that technology didn't come cheap. The TH!NK city cost £14,000 plus £100 per month battery rental and Auto Express warned: 'Making that pay is likely to be tough, even with estimated energy costs of only £110 per 10,000 miles – fuelling a Toyota Aygo over that distance is roughly £800'.[54]

Still, the improved batteries and the 40bhp motor gave the TH!NK a top speed of 65mph (105km/h) and it accelerated from 0 to 30mph (48km/h) in a smart 6.5sec –

Ford had big plans for the TH!NK city car but its confidence seemed to waiver after a small-scale trial.

Under new owners, the TH!NK went into production – and into UK showrooms.

TH!NK cars emerge from the production line – the car's gestation was troubled but it refuses to die.

London is one of the TH!NK's key European markets.

although 50mph (80km/h) took a yawn-inducing 16sec. The little car could cover 126 miles (203km) on a full charge. The company claimed the city was the world's only crash-tested and highway-certified electric vehicle. Richard Blundell, managing director of Think UK (the company's British importer) said:

> *Unlike the lower-range, electric quadricycles that have had limited success in the UK, the TH!NK city is a real car which provides a realistic option for those motorists who want to drive a true zero emissions car. Driving a silent car will give urban motorists a totally new experience. The TH!NK city produces no waste heat and no pollution. Critically for London and many other urban markets it beats the congestion charge. Moreover, the TH!NK city is fun to drive, cheap to run, great to look at, generates incredible mileage figures and is extremely kind on the environment. This is a proposition that we believe will interest many drivers who are re-thinking their approach to motoring.*

Standard equipment included power-steering, central-locking, an electric heater and electric windows and mirrors.

Thanks to substantial American investment, and a strategic partnership with General Electric, THINK was able to increase production capacity at its factory, in Aurskog, just outside Oslo, to 10,000 vehicles per year, and make plans for new assembly plants in America, Europe and Asia. The company also showed off concepts for an open-top sports version and a five-seater called the TH!NK Ox.

Unfortunately, the banking crisis and subsequent global recession – plus the cost of developing the new car with the help of Porsche – left the group critically short of money and on 15 December 2008, production halted again. The following year the company restarted operations after another injection of capital. Production also began at a new factory in Valmet, Uusikaupunki, Finland. The company was as good as its word on international expansion and, in December 2010, the first cars rolled off the production line of THINK's newest factory in Elkhart, Indiana. The deal was sweetened by the state of Indiana, which was the factory's first customer. THINK CEO Barry Engle hailed the deal as 'part of a larger effort to help transform the US light-duty vehicle fleet from one that is most dependent on imported oil, to one that is fuelled entirely by domestically produced electrical energy'.

In October 2010, THINK reached something of a production landmark with the completion of the 2,500th city. Sadly, in March 2011 THINK's global operations ground to a stop once more. The company filed for bankruptcy in June the same year – the fourth time it had collapsed in 20 years. As of the time of writing, THINK's assets have been bought by another company – Electric Mobility Solutions – headed by the Russian entrepreneur Boris Zingarevich, who has plans to restart production yet again with a seventh-generation TH!NK city on the cards.

Back to the Future: the Nissan LEAF

In August 2009, Nissan's chief operating officer Carlos Ghosn unveiled a car at a ceremony to dedicate Nissan's new headquarters in Yokohama. Ghosn, the former boss of Michelin who had brought Nissan back from the verge of bankruptcy, was the most powerful figure in the automotive industry who publicly supported electric cars. Thanks to his success, when Ghosn spoke, people listened and he was in no doubt that EVs were the future. He outlined his concerns at the Los Angeles Motor Show in November 2008. 'In China there are fifty cars for every thousand people – in the US there are 800 cars for every thousand people,' he told journalists. 'We will need another planet if China catches up to the US.' During a speech to the University of Pennsylvania's Wharton School of Business he summarized his view of what was needed: 'If you are going to let developing countries have as many cars as they want – and they're going to have as many cars as they want one way or another – there is absolutely no alternative but to go for zero emissions. And the only zero-emissions vehicle available today is electric.'

The car Ghosn unveiled in August 2009 was a game-changer. It was called the LEAF (which, thanks to the Japanese love for acronyms, stood for Leading, Environmentally friendly, Affordable, Family car) and it was to be the world's first purpose-designed zero-emission electric vehicle from a major manufacturer to be mass-marketed globally. At a stroke, Nissan had taken a huge stake in an all-electric future.

The same month Ghosn revealed the LEAF, Nissan set up a website where potential buyers could register for

Carlos Ghosn unveils the ground-breaking LEAF – and changes the way the world thinks about electric cars.

August 2009: Carlos Ghosn poses with the LEAF. Nissan was taking a huge gamble on an electric future.

The LEAF was a clean-sheet design that showed what was possible when a major manufacturer took electric vehicles seriously.

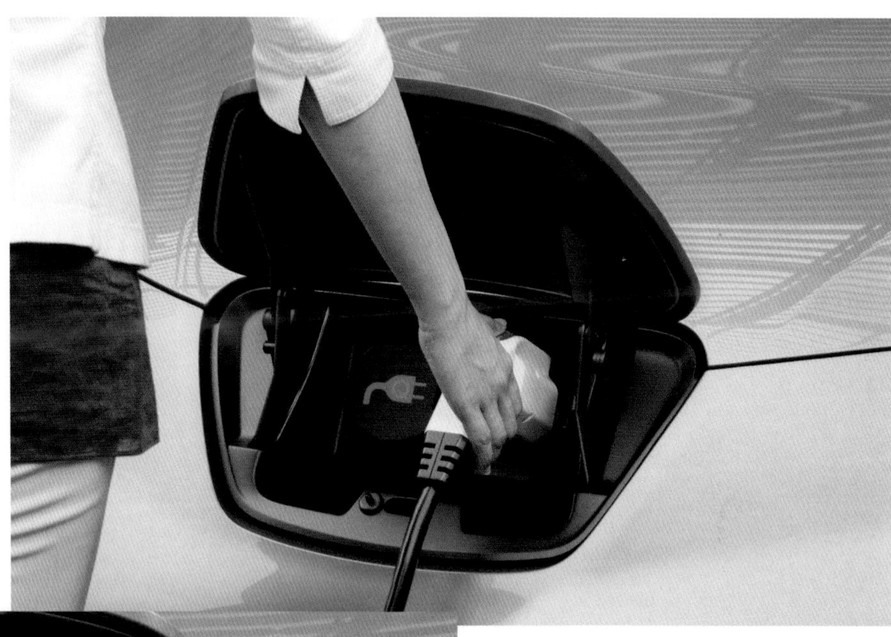

The Li-ion battery module was charged via a socket on the LEAF's nose.

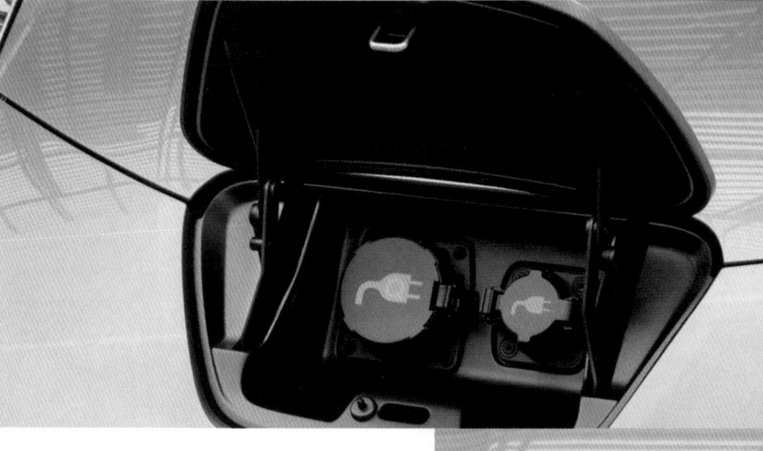

Nissan deliberately styled the charging port to look like a fuel filler flap.

With the flap closed, the charging socket integrated neatly into the car's nose.

The interior of the Nissan LEAF. Every journey was a special experience – the car even played a little welcome jingle.

The instruments were designed to mimic mobile phone ergonomic thinking. The speedo was in the driver's sight line.

more information. Nissan's marketing people wanted to gauge how much publicity the LEAF was generating. Within 12 months 175,000 people had left their details as anticipation began to build.

The LEAF wasn't just another EV. It wouldn't be hand-built and sold in tiny numbers. It wouldn't be a lease-only proposition and Nissan wouldn't snatch them back for the corporate crusher when it grew tired of EVs. It wasn't a conversion of an existing petrol-powered model or a city-based quadricycle. It wasn't even a hybrid like the Prius. It was a clean sheet design built to be manufactured and sold in huge numbers just like any other mass-production car. Put simply, it was the beginning of a new era.

To test the electric drivetrain, and the laminated lithium-ion batteries it used, Nissan's engineers had converted a couple of quirky right-hand-drive Cube hatchbacks (EV-01 and EV-02). Their biggest breakthrough was the laminated Li-ion battery, which had a power output of more than 122bhp. On the LEAF the forty-eight module battery was mounted under the seats and floor. It was produced by the Automotive Energy Supply Corporation (AESC), a joint venture set up by Nissan, the NEC Corporation and NEC Tokin Corporation, to mass-produce Li-ion batteries for automotive applications. The partners had invested more than £80m in AESC – much of it building a production facility in Japan capable of producing 65,000 units a year. As part of Nissan's global ambitions for the LEAF, battery plants were also set up in America, the UK and Portugal. Using a DC 50kW quick-charger, the battery could be charged to up to 80 per cent of its capacity in under 30min. A domestic 220–240V supply recharged the pack in 8h – more than sufficient for an overnight top-up. The recharging socket for normal charging and quick charging was conveniently located on Nissan LEAF's nose under a 'fuel filler flap' adorned with the Nissan logo.

Mark Perry, Nissan's chief product planner for North America, admitted in an interview with The Wall Street Journal that the sophisticated battery cost Nissan around $18,000 to produce – meaning the early cars would actually be sold at a loss.[55] The company's production plan pegged the point at which the LEAF moved into profitability as year three.

Business Secretary, Peter Mandelson, dedicated himself to bringing the Nissan LEAF to Britain. In the event, Nissan awarded its Sunderland plant the European construction contract and a new battery plant.

Nissan invested more than £400m in its British plant to gear up for LEAF production.

In a bid to allay any qualms the public might have had about having to replace such an expensive part, Nissan claimed the battery would retain between 70 and 80 per cent of its original capacity even after 10 years.

Built on a new platform, the LEAF provided generous seating for five adults. Power came from an in-house developed compact electric motor driving the front wheels. The AC motor developed 109bhp and 207lb ft (280 Nm) of torque, enough for a maximum speed of more than 90mph (140km/h).

Despite the improved energy density of the Li-ion battery, the LEAF's potential range was still pegged at 100 mile (160km). Pierre Loing, vice president, product and advance planning, said:

> *One of our jobs is to prove to every potential customer that the present range is adequate for their needs and to make them understand that the genuine benefits of EV travel more than outweigh the perceived problem.*

> *[The LEAF] is a real car, a roomy five-seater hatchback, offering a level of performance similar to other cars in its class. But best of all, there are no tailpipe emissions at all. Against a backdrop of climate change that alone marks it out as a car of the future.*

Governments around the world agreed. Politicians were desperate to be photographed with the new electric car. In Britain, the Labour Government assiduously courted Nissan for first the battery plant and then the contract to build LEAFs for Europe in Sunderland. Business Secretary Lord Mandelson committed £20.7m under the UK's Grant for Business Investment scheme to secure the deal. The European Investment Bank also pledged £197m. Both grants were dwarfed by the £420m figure Nissan planned to invest in its UK factory to gear up for full scale production.

The car made its European debut at the 2010 Geneva Motor Show. Unveiling it, Pierre Loing said:

The world is changing and Nissan is a catalyst for that change. The Nissan LEAF is the world's first mass-produced mainstream electric vehicle from a mainstream manufacturer. It is a serious car, a real car, and the right car for the times.

Deliveries to customers in America and Japan began in December. Drivers in Europe had to wait until the following Spring. Customers who registered their interest online were given priority. In the first year, Nissan sold 22,000 LEAFs, including 10,000 in the US alone. That figure was small by global standards, where best-selling cars sell in their millions, but it was comfortably more than any other EV in history.

Just as the Toyota Prius proved there was pent up public demand for a petrol–electric hybrid, the Nissan LEAF demonstrated that an all-electric car could be successful. It did so at exactly the right moment, too, as turmoil in the Middle East sent oil prices rocketing to a new high.

The LEAF may have been first – but it certainly wouldn't be the last. One hundred years after it was almost wiped out, the electric car was back.

Nissan LEAF

Four-door family hatchback
Motor: AC induction three-phase driving the front wheels via CVT automatic
Power: 107bhp @ 2,730–9,800rpm
Torque: 206lb ft 279Nm) @ 0–2730rpm
Performance:
0–62mph: 11.9sec
Max speed: 90mph (144km/h)
Length: 173in (4,445mm)
Width: 69in (1,770mm)
Height: 60in (1,550mm)
Wheelbase: 105in (2,700mm)
Kerb Weight: 3,447lb (1,567kg)
Gross Weight: 4,323lb (1,965kg)
Service interval: 18,000 miles (28,800km)
Warranty: 3 years
Warranty: 60,000 miles (96,000km)
Price in UK: £30,990 before government cash incentives.

CHAPTER TEN

FROM COMMUTER CARS TO SUPERCARS – ALL THE WORLD LOVES AN ELECTRIC CAR

Thanks to the success of the Toyota Prius, and the ambition demonstrated by the Nissan LEAF, electric vehicles are more popular today than they have ever been. Almost 100 years since the golden age of the electric vehicle, the global motor industry – for so long a staunch supporter of the internal combustion engine – has finally woken up to the benefits of using electric propulsion.

Not counting the Renault Twizy quadricycle, at the time of writing there are seven full electric models from major manufacturers on sale in the UK. In 2012, the LEAF was joined by the Renault Fluence, the Mitsubishi i-MiEV, the Citroën C-Zero and the Peugeot iOn – although the Citroën and the Peugeot were essentially rebadged versions of the Mitsubishi (itself an electric version of the Mitsubishi i kei car). Then there are the Vauxhall Ampera and the Chevrolet Volt.

The Mitsubishi i-MIEV went on sale in Britain in 2011.

Spot the difference – the Citroën C-Zero was a lightly modified Mitsubishi as was...

The Peugeot iON. Customer indifference led to production of both the French cars being suspended in August 2012.

GM's Shocking New Direction

Walking around the stands at the 2006 Detroit Motor Show, General Motors' vice chairman Bob Lutz paused to look over a two-seater roadster. The car was being developed by a fledgling Silicon Valley start-up called Tesla Motors. Lutz – the car-crazy former marine who had given the green light to the preposterous Dodge Viper and the insane 1,000bhp Cadillac Sixteen – was no fan of green vehicle technology. Most memorably he once described global warming as 'a crock of shit' and rejected the Toyota Prius as a PR stunt. Unsurprisingly for someone who had a V16 engine on display in his office, he was also a persistent critic of attempts by American legislators to set a corporate average fuel-economy standard for US domestic auto-makers.

But the Tesla Roadster – named after Nikola Tesla, the electrical pioneer who developed the modern alternating current supply system – was different. For a start, it was an electric car unashamedly aimed at petrol heads. It used a chassis engineered by Lotus, which once belonged to GM. The body panels were made in France and assembled at the Lotus headquarters in Hethel, Norfolk. North American Roadsters were shipped to California for final assembly, while Roadsters destined for Europe were finished in Britain. The Lotus connection gave rise to the common misconception that a Tesla was merely an electrified Elise. In fact, although it shares some components (the windscreen, the dashboard and the steering wheel), fewer than 7 per cent are interchangeable.

The Roadster also had a longer wheelbase than the Elise and a redesigned tub that used the 1,000lb (454kg) battery pack, which contained 6,381 Li-ion cells, as a stressed member. The Roadster's side-rails were lower than the Elise, so drivers didn't have to drop their backsides into the seats before lifting their legs into the footwells. The battery's extra weight required new suspension and a new rear subframe, too.

Tesla chose a very powerful electric motor: an air-cooled, three-phase, four-pole induction motor capable of producing 248bhp and generating 200ft lb (271Nm) of torque. A sport model introduced in 2009 used a higher

The Tesla Roadster showed that EVs need not be boring.

density stator that was hand-wound to bump power up even further to 288bhp. This was mated to a BorgWarner single speed gearbox, selected after a Magna two-speed transmission proved unsuitable.

Unsurprisingly, the Tesla was no shrinking violet and could scorch through the 0–60mph benchmark in less than 4sec and cover a quarter mile in 12.6sec. The top speed was electronically limited to 125mph (201km/h) but few who drove the Roadster doubted it could go faster. Just as surprising was the claimed range – 244 miles (393km) – although this would prove to be a source of controversy.

When BBC *Top Gear* tested it in 2008, the Roadster was shown apparently running out of power in a race. The commentary said: 'Although Tesla say it will do 200 miles we have worked out that on our track it will run out after just 55 miles.' Tesla sued, claiming the show had misrepresented the car's range, but lost. Judge Mr Justice Tugendhat said: 'A manufacturer's statement about the range of a [car] is always qualified by a statement as to the driving conditions under which [it] may be expected. But such statements are rarely, if ever, given to the public by reference to racing on a test track.'

Back in 2006, Lutz, the vice chairman of the biggest car company in the world, which had built – and scrapped – the EV-1, was stunned by the Tesla Roadster. Suddenly his eyes were opened to the possibilities of an electric vehicle. He told *Newsweek* magazine: 'If some Silicon Valley start-up can solve this equation, no one is going to tell me anymore that it's unfeasible'.

Lutz returned to Detroit and pulled together a team of engineers to work on an electric car. Originally, he believed GM needed a twenty-first century successor to the EV1 but was convinced by Jon Lauckner, GM's vice president for global vehicle development, that the long-standing battery problems couldn't be licked sufficiently to overcome range anxiety or the problem of a charging infrastructure that was still on the drawing board. What Lauckner proposed was a 'range extender' – a battery pack that could be recharged by a small internal combustion engine driving a generator. This would differ from the Toyota Prius and the

Tesla has ambitious plans for a family of sporting EVs.

Honda Insight by virtue of the fact that the gasoline engine would not drive the wheels, merely the generator, so the GM vehicle – which was internally nick-named the iCar in a nod to Apple's famous iPod music device – would be a true all-electric car. In the event this would not prove possible. In some high-speed conditions the internal combustion engine still directly drives the wheels in conjunction with the generator/motor. GM claims this 'combined mode' improves efficiency by around 15 per cent.

There was another reason why Lutz was suddenly seized by the potential of an electric car – and it was far more hard-nosed. 'We saw Toyota getting highly beneficial rub-off from their Prius success, which permitted them to cloak themselves in the mantle of total greenness,' he remembered. 'This was starting to hurt because it was one reason for a sudden surge in Toyota's market share.'[56]

Given a commercial imperative, work proceeded on a concept car and the first Chevrolet Volt prototype was unveiled at the following year's North American International Auto Show – a remarkably speedy turnaround time for a project that only got the green light the previous year.

The engineers who worked on the concept had come up with the first modern series plug-in hybrid driveline, which they dubbed E-Flex and then Voltec, when the Volt name was approved by the GM board. Early test mules – with the E-Flex powertrain installed in a Chevrolet Cruze body – had been encouraging. Depending on how the car was driven, a series plug-in hybrid could return astonishing mpg figures. This would give rise to some controversy in 2009 when GM claimed the production Volt was capable of 230mpg (1.23ltr/100km). Early adopters soon discovered that this was only achievable if the Volt's petrol engine was used as sparingly as possible and the batteries were recharged from the mains supply every day. Once the batteries were exhausted – usually around the 30-miles (48km) mark – the petrol engine would be needed to generate electricity and it had a 'real world' mpg average of about 37mpg (7.64ltr/100km) – a far cry from GM's claims. The problem wasn't GM, it was the testing methodology. Using the same standards, Nissan was able to claim the LEAF would achieve a ludicrous 367mpg (0.77ltr/100km).

Arguably, such fantasy figures did both vehicles more harm than good by raising expectations among the buying public to unrealistic levels.

Indeed, the disparity was so great that the US Environmental Protection Agency had to come up with a new way of measuring the fuel consumption of electric vehicles like the Volt and the LEAF. Using a hideously complex formula that equates 33.7kWh of electrical energy to one US gallon of gasoline and how many kilowatt-hours would be needed to cover just 100 miles (160km), it came up with an 'mpg-e' figure. The Volt notched up a creditable (and far more believable) average of 93mpg-e.

Low and sleek, with a high waistline, shallow glass area and enormous alloy wheels that filled every inch of its swollen wheel arches, the original Volt concept was a show-stopper alright. Sadly, it was also far from production-ready, a fact even GM had to admit.

The drag coefficient of 0.43 was laughably poor for a car that was supposed to be ultra fuel-efficient and the Li-ion battery technology the Volt needed was not yet available (although GM was working with two partners on evaluating two competing types of battery chemistry). Bob Lutz was in bullish mood, however. At the car's unveiling he predicted that for the 78 per cent of US commuters whose round trip to work was 40 miles (64km) or less, a production Volt wouldn't burn 'a drop of petroleum' and that even on a longer 60-mile (96km) trip the car would be good for 150mpg (1.88ltr/100km).

Tony Posawatz, an engineering manager on the Volt programme, told *The New York Times* that a Volt owner would save about 500 gallons (2,275ltr) of gas every year (assuming an annual mileage of 15,000 miles/24,000km) equating to $900, even taking into account the cost of electricity.[57] GM vehicle development chief Jon Lauckner said: 'This program is not a public relations ploy. We are dead serious about taking this technology into high volume production'. This, some critics pointed out, seemed to contradict GM's previous stance that it would prefer to focus on developing hydrogen fuel-cells.

Nevertheless, the Volt was a resounding hit. *The Detroit News* splashed on the Volt's unveiling with the headline: 'GM Powers Up' and the company's stock price – which had been looking shaky on rumours of a debt mountain and poor sales – crept up a bit higher.

Almost overnight the Volt had gone from a concept car pipe-dream to a symbol of hope for the ailing car giant. Even as the US economy seized up and the banking crisis pitched GM into bankruptcy, the embattled company kept faith with a production Volt. The car became the poster child for politicians seeking a new beginning for the crippled American auto industry.

As the recession dragged down America's 'Big Three' (now the only three of any note), the Volt became a symbol of the rebirth of the US auto industry. Incredibly, the Volt project even turned Bob Lutz into something of an evangelist for EVs. In 2009, he told US motoring journal-

The original Chevrolet Volt concept was a statement of intent – but totally unsuitable for production.

The Volt became the poster child for hopes of a renaissance for the American car industry.

GM claimed the average Volt owner would save $900 per year even taking into account the car's high price.

The Volt used a 1.4-litre petrol engine to provide power for the 71bhp electric motor and charge the battery pack.

The Volt had an interior every bit as futuristic as its exterior.

This cutaway shows the Volt drivetrain, including the battery module down the spine of the car.

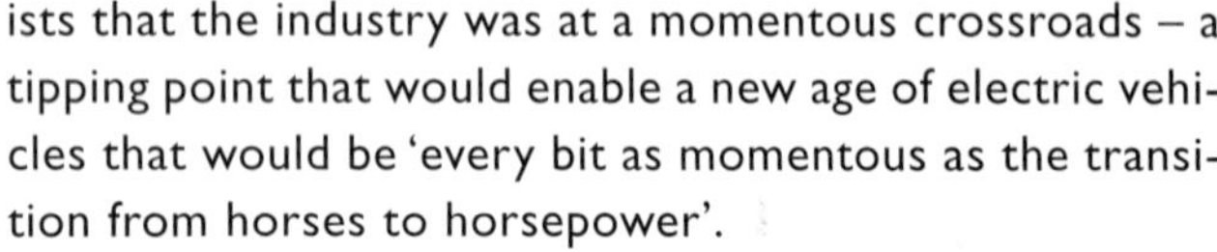

ists that the industry was at a momentous crossroads – a tipping point that would enable a new age of electric vehicles that would be 'every bit as momentous as the transition from horses to horsepower'.

The first pre-production Volts took to public roads in 2009. GM built around eighty mules for testing and validation purposes, as well as de-bugging the vehicle software and ironing out the controls. Lutz had pledged the Volt would be capable of travelling 40 miles (64km) on a full charge and the design team made his claim a key performance parameter. This required a Li-ion battery pack with a storage capacity of 16kWh as a minimum. To avoid premature battery failure, the cells would not be allowed to go completely flat. When they dropped to a pre-determined level – around the 45 per cent mark – the 1.4-litre engine would run the generator to maintain the battery until a charging point could be found. By preventing a total discharge, GM's engineers reckoned the costly battery would be good for a 10-year service life. The pack would recharge from a normal 13A domestic socket in around 6h.

The original concept car featured a 3-cylinder 1.0-litre range extender engine. The production version, first shown in September 2008 as part of GM's centennial celebrations in Detroit, used a 1.4-litre, 4-cylinder petrol engine to provide power for the 71bhp electric motor/generator and maintain a minimum battery charge. An 8-gallon (35ltr) petrol tank was shoehorned behind the battery pack – big enough for a 300-mile (483km) range. The main motor, the generator and the petrol engine were connected to the Volt's front wheels via a planetary gearbox and a system of electronic clutches.

Thanks to knowledge gained on the EV1, GM knew weight was the Volt's greatest enemy. As a result, the Volt featured a new dual pinion electro-mechanical power steering system, cold-formed front suspension springs, which made them shorter and smaller, and a lightweight premium hi-fi system, designed and built by US audio specialist Bose, which was 50 per cent more efficient than a standard set-up. The T-shaped Li-ion battery pack ran up the transmission tunnel. This layout meant the Volt could only seat two adults in the rear but at least it had a minimal impact on the car's luggage capacity.

On 30 November 2010, GM held a special ceremony at its Hamtramck assembly plant, in Detroit, to hail the first Volt off the production line. Ironically, it was never sold. A driver took it from the line and it was driven straight to GM's Heritage Center Museum in Michigan. The second production Volt was put up for public auction with the money going to schools in Detroit. It was sold for $225,000.

Initial production estimates were fairly modest: just 10,000 in the first full year of production and 45,000 thereafter. Production was set to expand when the car launched in Europe (as the Vauxhall/Opel Ampera). In May 2011, GM raised its sales estimate to 16,000 for 2011, before being forced into a humiliating climbdown 6 months later when officials admitted they wouldn't even achieve the original 10,000 figure.

The Vauxhall/Opel Ampera launched the Volt in Europe.

Vauxhall had high hopes for the Ampera. The company needed a halo car to boost its image.

On the road, the Ampera looked every inch the sporty family car.

For 2012, GM merely said production would depend upon worldwide demand although the Volt plant has a theoretical maximum annual capacity of 60,000 vehicles.

The Volt's press reception was generally favourable. *Car and Driver* wrote:

> *With the possible exception of a fairly cramped back seat and an undersized cargo hold, the Volt checks all the boxes, plus it outdrives the hybrid competition. This is without doubt the most important new car since the advent of hybrids in the late '90s, and GM has nailed it. Is this the handing off of the Prius's very illustrious torch?*[58]

Autocar said of the Volt's sister car, the Vauxhall Ampera: 'As an electric car that can be your only car, theAera has no peers'.[59]

Not everyone was impressed, however. Perhaps the EV-1 débacle was still on people's minds or maybe GM's publicity ahead of the Volt's launch had been a bit too good and the final product just couldn't measure up to the ballyhoo. Whatever the reasons, Edward Niedermeyer, editor of the website The Truth About Cars, was asked to evaluate the Volt by *The New York Times*. He wrote:

> *General Motors introduced America to the Chevrolet Volt (in 2007) as a... car that would someday be the future of motorized transportation. It would go 40 miles on battery power alone, promised GM, after which it would create its own electricity with a gas engine. Three and a half years – and one government-assisted bankruptcy later – GM is bring a Volt to market that makes good on those two promises. The problem is, well, everything else.*

Niedermeyer pointed out that the Volt had benefited from billions of taxpayer dollars to help fund its development but what GM came up with, he said, was a vehicle that cost $41,000 but offered the performance and interior space of a $15,000 economy car. The article was headlined: 'GM's Electric Lemon'. Ouch.

Honda Goes to Work

Honda moved quickly to catch up with Toyota. The integrated motor assist hybrid-electric system was applied to a range of vehicles, including a new Insight, but buyers who

Honda returned with an Insight that was far more conventional-looking than its predecessor.

The Mk2 Insight used a 1.3-litre engine with a 13bhp motor directly connected between it and the constantly variable transmission gearbox.

Unlike its predecessor, the Insight seated four people.

loved the original Insight were disappointed when its successor was unveiled.

It may have been the world's cheapest hybrid at launch in 2009, undercutting the Prius by several thousand pounds, but the radical aerodynamics and two-seater coupé style had gone, replaced by an unassuming Toyota clone with seating for five and a big hatchback boot.

Worse still, it wasn't particularly green and it wasn't until the second set of engine revisions, in 2012, that CO_2 emissions dipped below the psychologically important 100g/km barrier. This also meant the Insight qualified for a free road fund licence in the UK. The Mk2 Insight used a 1.3-litre engine with a 13bhp motor directly connected between it and the constantly variable transmission gearbox. A mild hybrid system, the Insight could not run on electricity alone but the motor's instant torque did provide a useful low revs boost.

Ironically, the new Insight sold in far greater numbers than its avant-garde predecessor. Honda hybrid sales topped 800,000 in 2012 – more than 200,000 of them sold in the previous 12 months – but the company was still a long way from Toyota with more than 3 million hybrid sales. As for the Insight, *Autocar* said: 'The Insight is better, but still not good enough'.

Those buyers disappointed by the blandness of the Insight were more excited by Honda's other hybrid. The CR-Z (for Compact Renaissance Zero) made its debut as a concept at the 2007 Tokyo Motor Show. An exciting-looking sports coupé, Honda CEO Takeo Fukui confirmed the car was slated for production in 2009 and promised it

Honda Insight 1.3 IMA HS

Front engine, front-wheel drive, five-passenger, four-door compact hatchback
Engine: 4-cylinder, 1339cc, petrol plus integrated 13bhp electric motor
Power: 87bhp @ 5,800rpm plus 13bhp
Torque: 89lb ft (120Nm) @ 4,500rpm plus 53lb ft (72Nm) electric
Economy: 65.7mpg (4.3ltr/100km]
CO_2: 99g/km
Kerb weight: 2,728lb (1,240kg)
Price in UK: £20,335

The Honda CRZ concept appeared at the 2007 Tokyo Motor Show.

The CR-Z had hints of the CRX sports coupé just like the Mark One Insight.

The cockpit of the CR-Z concept.

Honda held on to the coupé concept for the production CR-Z.

would be sporty and innovative, as well as more efficient than Honda's current hybrid line-up.

Although the CR-Z would be based on the second-generation Insight, chief chassis engineer Terukazu Torikai had the Lotus Elise in mind when he designed the new car. The Insight chassis was stiffened to the same level as the highly acclaimed Civic Type R and, at key stages of development, CR-Z mules were flown to Europe and tested on some of the continent's most demanding roads to ensure they gave the correct feedback and excellent handling.

Norio Tomobe, the CR-Z project leader promised the car would provide 'exhilarating driving pleasure' and promised a guilt-free 2+2 sports car.[60]

At launch, magazines praised the handling but criticized the lack of power from the 1.5-litre iVTEC SOHC inline 4-cylinder engine (sourced from the Jazz hatchback) and its integrated motor. The system delivered a combined peak output of 122bhp at 6,000rpm – with the internal combustion engine contributing 111bhp. The electric motor was fed by nickel metal-hydride batteries housed under the boot.

Car magazine wrote:

> *As you run the engine out to the redline the noise – like a Civic Type R at two-thirds volume – is great, but not matched by much forward progress. There also isn't the low-end torque-thump you'd hope for from an electrically-assisted drivetrain... so rather than being the expected party-piece, the drivetrain is a little underwhelming.*[61]

The magazine went on to describe it as 'exactly the kind of oddball, flawed, contradictory car that Japan occasionally, inadvertently produces...'. The CR-Z was capable of handling much more power, however.

The CR-Z's 1.5-litre engine was criticized for its lack of power.

Honda entered two CR-Z Racers in the 25-hour Thunderhill endurance race at Willows, California, packing 200bhp thanks to turbo-charging and a modified electric motor. One car qualified on pole and during the race the other finished second in the Endurance three class despite a near ten-lap deficit caused by refuelling difficulties. Heavily modified versions of the CR-Z have appeared at the Specialty Equipment Market Association (SEMA) show, held in Las Vegas, with up to 533bhp.

In 2011, Honda answered calls for a more powerful production CR-Z by turning to the race tuning expertise of Mugen Motorsports. Set up in 1973 by Hirotoshi Honda, the son of Honda Motor Company's founder Soichiro Honda, and Masao Kimura, Mugen enjoys a close relationship with Honda. Despite the family ties, Mugen (which means 'Without Limit' in Japanese) has never been owned by Honda, although it specializes in tuning the company's engines. In many ways, Mugen is to Honda what AMG is to Mercedes (although AMG is now a wholly owned subsidiary of the German car giant).

Mugen's engineers took an unusual route to boost the power of the CR-Z. They retained the Jazz engine but added a supercharger and re-mapped the engine-management system, upping the power to 197bhp and 158lb ft (214Nm) of torque. To cope with the extra performance, the CR-Z chassis received five-way adjustable dampers, a wider front track, bigger more powerful brakes (320mm vented discs with four pot calipers on the front) and a carbon fibre bonnet and doors. The front seats were swapped for sports buckets and the rears

Honda CRZ Mugen

Front engine, front-wheel drive, two-passenger, coupé.
Engine: 4-cylinder, 1497cc, hybrid, supercharged
Power: 197bhp @ 6300rpm
Torque: 158lb ft (214Nm) @ 5,000rpm
0–60mph: 6.6sec
Top speed: 145mph (232km/h)
Kerb weight: 2,526lb (1,148kg)
Price in UK: Approx £23,000

Honda answered criticism of the CR-Z's performance with a Mugen version. Power was upped to 197bhp – the same as a Civic Type R.

Mugen fitted an impressive-looking spoiler to the CR-Z's hatchback.

The Mugen CR-Z interior.

The Honda NSX showcases Honda's hybrid technology.

were removed altogether in the name of weight-saving.

The Honda CR-Z Mugen made its public debut at the 2011 Goodwood Festival of Speed. A production version, fettled by the Northampton-based Mugen Euro performance tuning division, is due to go on sale in 2013, costing approximately £23,000 in the UK.

By the following year, Honda had wholeheartedly embraced the hybrid concept. As well as the Insight, the Civic and the CR-Z, the company also offered the world's first hybrid supermini in the Jazz and was preparing a hybrid supercar. The latter – almost certain to wear an NSX badge – is the most exciting of all, promising superb performance from a powerful mid-mounted V6 engine, all wheel drive and electric motor assist.

The NSX concept that was unveiled by CEO Takanobu Ito at the Detroit Motor Show in 2012 had two small electric motors driving the front wheels. This layout enabled Honda to drive each wheel independently, tightening the car's cornering line, as required, and vectoring torque across the front axle. A third IMA-style motor was fitted to the NSX gearbox and boosted the V-6 engine's power. The engine and the battery were both mid-mounted for excellent handling and Honda promised it would follow the original NSX's formula of power allied to lightweight materials.

Company bosses believe the NSX will be the perfect hybrid halo car for the Honda range and work has already begun to build anticipation. The car was Tony 'Iron Man'

The view most drivers will have when the Honda NSX goes on sale in a few years' time.

Stark's personal wheels in *The Avengers* – one of the biggest blockbuster movies of summer 2012.

In North America, Honda also offered pure electric vehicles, including the Fit EV – a battery-only version of the European Jazz. The Fit EV's 20kWh Li-ion battery delivered a claimed driving range of up to 120 miles (193km) and could be recharged in just 3h on 240V power using the onboard charger. However, recharge time via the typical US household 120V supply was a more wearisome 15h.

The claimed mpg-e figure of 116 (2.4litr/100km) was slightly better than the (larger) Nissan LEAF. However, the Fit cost $575 more than the Nissan. Initially available on a lease scheme, the car was rolled out to California and Oregon, before reaching six East Coast markets in early 2013.

Even more promising, however, was the FCX Clarity – a hydrogen-powered fuel cell vehicle. Hand-built at the former NSX dream car factory at Toshigi, in Japan, the FCX Clarity was based on the original FCX concept car (itself a product of a family that originated with the FCXV2 in 1999). Launched at the Los Angeles Motor Show in 2007, it was the world's first commercially available fuel-cell vehicle. Electrical power was generated by a 100kW vertical flow hydrogen fuel-cell stack. The cell combined hydrogen, stored in an onboard fuel tank, with oxygen and the resulting chemical reaction created electricity to power the motor, which drove the front wheels. Water vapour and heat were the only by-products.

Honda's fuel cell was made up of a thin membrane wedged between two electrode layers in-between two separators. Several hundred layers were connected in series. The hydrogen fuel was fed into the fuel cell's anode where, with the help of a catalyst, it was split into electrons and protons. The electrons were channelled through a circuit to create electricity and the protons passed through the polymer electrolyte membrane. Oxygen entered the cathode and combined with the electrons and protons to form water.

A Li-ion battery beneath the rear seats helped supplement the fuel cell's output and stored electrical energy harvested via regenerative braking. A high-output, compact motor drove the front wheels and the car could manage 60 miles (95km) per kilogram of hydrogen.

Of all the future technologies, hydrogen fuel-cells offer perhaps the most realistic prospect of mass production. Although the FCX Clarity is still very much a niche vehicle (only a few hundred have been made to date), as a practical demonstration of the possibilities of fuel-cell

Honda's FCX Clarity offered a tantalising glimpse of a fuel-cell future.

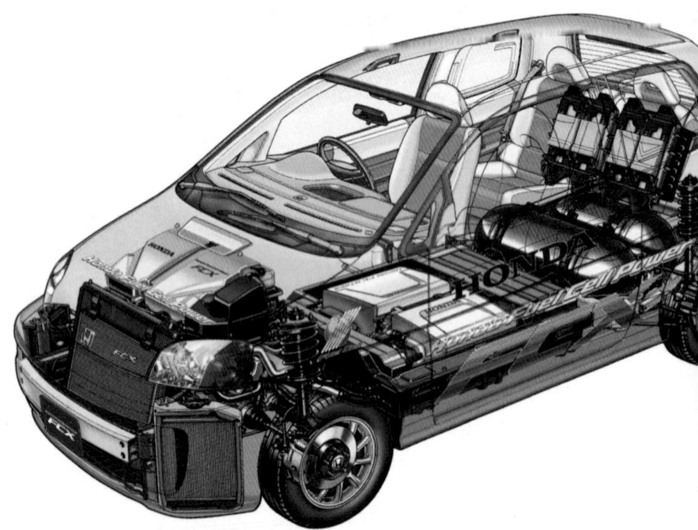

The Clarity's predecessor was the unassuming FCX hatchback – note the twin tanks beneath the boot.

For such a radical reinterpretation of the motor car's power source, the FCX look disappointingly humdrum.

The FCX Clarity took the hydrogen fuel-cell conept of its predecessor and wrapped it up in a slinky coupé-esque body.

The interior of the Clarity was production ready.

technology it is hugely important.

Auto Express magazine wrote:

> *Honda wants to bring this car, or something very much like it, to our showrooms with a price tag of around £50,000. For some, that can't come soon enough.*[62]

Car and Driver was rather more pessimistic:

> *Plated with platinum catalysts and lined with exotic membranes, fuel cells are still NASA-priced. The Clarity is a money-losing experiment at encouraging hydrogen infrastructure development, the company says. Be part of it or don't. Chances are, you'll never get the choice.*[63]

Battery Blues

The Honda FCX Clarity offered a tantalizing glimpse of one green future but what of the battery-powered pure electric vehicle?

Having nailed his colours firmly to the mast, Carlos Ghosn, head of Nissan and Renault, was pressing ahead – but there was a snag. A year after the LEAF went on sale, the industry received a nasty shock: electric cars weren't selling anywhere near as many units as expected. The combined sales of the Nissan LEAF and the Chevrolet Volt were shockingly poor. Together they accounted for just 0.1 per cent of the North American new car market. The trend was repeated around the world.

UK sales of electric vehicles fell 50 per cent in the second quarter of 2011, despite government grants and lots of good publicity. Just 215 vehicles were sold between April and June, a massive drop on the 465 sold in the first 3 months.

Reluctant buyers cited the cost of the cars – even with grants they were substantially more expensive than a petrol or diesel alternative – and the hassle of paying for home-charging equipment.

The UK's poor on-street charging infrastructure was also a sticking point because, as many inner city homes had no driveway, access to a household electric socket was a challenge.

British drivers also faced an insurance shock. Several companies refused to provide cover for EVs and those that did demanded a substantial premium over a conventional car. The industry cited uncertainties over battery replacement and disposal costs, lack of historical data, the notional accident risk of silent electric motors and even 'tripping hazards' due to charging leads on the pavement. Continued reluctance among insurers to provide cover for EVs may force car companies to come up with their own policies – a move Honda has already taken with the Fit EV in North America.

Renault's Shock Move

In early 2012, Renault took the axe to its range in the UK. Out went the once popular, but now lacklustre, Laguna family car, the pretty but slow-selling Laguna Coupé, the intriguing but pointless Wind small coupé, the Modus mini MPV, the Kangoo van, the Espace MPV and the entire Gordini sports range. In came the biggest range of EVs yet seen from a major manufacturer.

Renault had tested the market with an electric version of the Kangoo van in 2011. It was manufactured on the same production line in northern France as internal combustion-powered Kangoos. The 22kW Li-ion battery was located in a central position beneath the floor, enabling the EV version to boast the same luggage capacity as its conventional cousin. It was powered by a 70bhp electric

Renault Kangoo Van ZE

Motor: synchronous electric motor with rotor coil
Power : 44 70bhp
Torque: 167lb ft (226Nm)
Transmission: direct drive with reducer
Battery: lithium-ion
Range: 100 miles (160km)
Top speed: 81mph (130km/h)
Length: 164in (4,213mm)
Width: 83in (2,133mm)
Unladen height: 71in (1,818mm)
Wheelbase: 105in (2,697mm)
Weight: 3,102lb (1,410kg)
Carrying capacity: between 105 and 122ft3 (3 and 3.5m3)
Payload: 1,430lb (650kg)
Number of seats: 2

Faced with collapsing sales, Renault drastically trimmed down its range in the UK – at the same time as boosting its number of EVs. The first was the Kangoo EV van.

December 2011: Renault hands over the first electric Kangoo van to a retail customer. The first retail sale of a Renault EV in Britain.

motor, which revved to 10,500rpm and delivered peak torque of 167lb ft (226Nm). Renault claimed a range-to-empty of 100 miles (160km). The first UK example was delivered in December 2011.

The Kangoo ZE (zero emissions) was only the beginning. Renault was preparing to embrace electric cars with an enthusiasm unmatched by any other mass manufacturer, including its sister company Nissan. Chairman Ghosn explained:

> *The automobile industry contributes to the problem of climate change. It generates 12 per cent of the CO_2 emissions that result from human activity and accounts for 25 per cent of the world's oil consumption. At Renault, therefore, we have decided to be part of the solution.*
>
> *The stakes relating to the introduction of widely affordable electric vehicles call for far-reaching changes to our industry so that the automobile is once more perceived as a means of progress, both for mankind and for the planet. The aim is to integrate the automobile more fully in its environment and make our towns and villages greener, quieter and more pleasant to live in.*

By 2012, the French giant had a strong EV line-up consisting of three new models: the Fluence ZE C-segment saloon, the Zoe supermini and, most daring of all, the Twizy city car.

The Fluence ZE became the second of Renault's electric vehicles introduced to the UK on 1 March 2012. Developed from the petrol/diesel-powered Fluence saloon (itself based on the Megane hatchback), Renault claimed electrification did not compromise the car's accommodation or equipment. This wasn't quiet true: an extra 5in (130mm) had been added to the vehicle's length to allow for the Li-ion battery to be installed between the rear seats and the boot. This required a subtle redesign of the boot; while at the front, recharging points were added to both front wings. Renault engineers also had to pay careful attention to the car's weight distribution as the 95bhp electric motor was lighter than a petrol or diesel powerplant.

With a fully charged battery Renault gave an official driving range of up to 115 miles (184km). In town, where the electric system was at its most efficient, this could be extended to 125 miles (200km). However, high-speed cruising reduced the range-to-empty to a less impressive

The Fluence ZE was a direct competitor for the Nissan LEAF but wasn't built on a bespoke platform. It borrowed liberally from the Renault Megane.

Inside the Fluence ZE's cabin was typical 2012 Renault, soft plastics, a Tom, Tom colour satellite navigation system and quality a notch below the VW Golf.

60 miles (96km). A full recharge took between 6 and 8h using a fast-charge wall box installed in the customer's home. A 3h charge, using a conventional 240V household socket, was sufficient for 25 miles (40km). Additional instruments fitted to the ZE included a charge gauge and an econometer, which told the driver how the car's energy was used. The econometer was divided into three colour indicators: light blue for normal running, dark blue for optimal performance and red for wasting energy. An on-board computer displayed the range (in non-UK friendly kilometres), battery capacity, average and instant energy consumption.

To help overcome the high purchase cost of EVs, Renault came up with a battery rental scheme, the cost of which was linked to the vehicle's annual mileage. The cost, at the time of launch, was from £76 for 36 months with an annual mileage limit of 6,000 miles (9,600km). Renault claimed renting the battery for a monthly fee: 'Gives total peace of mind should any problems arise with the unit and also covers all matters concerning recycling'. To sweeten the pill, Renault included a full recovery package – including retrieval, should a driver run the car's battery flat.

Autocar magazine found the Fluence to be something of a curate's egg – good in parts. Although it handed out praise for the ride, the magazine criticized the 'lifeless' steering and the abrupt way the Fluence slowed down when the driver lifted off the accelerator. It reserved its biggest criticism for the car's battery, however.

> *Renault does point out that the range can drop as low as 50 miles in 'extreme conditions' but I'd hardly call traffic in west London last night and this morning 'extreme', nor the -1°C temperatures we tested the Fluence in. From being fully charged, around an eighth of the electric range was used for every five miles travelled. That makes even the 50 miles worst-case scenario seem optimistic.*
>
> *A big heavy saloon doesn't really seem the ideal starting point for a company hedging its bets on electric cars taking off. If electric cars are indeed to play a role in the future of motoring, then it's a shame this particular one looks so much like the present.*[64]

The latter criticism could hardly be aimed at the next electric Renault to emerge – as the eye-catching Twizy two-seater was pretty much unique.

The 95bhp motor gave the Fluence ZE a useful turn of speed.

The rev counter was dispensed with for a charge remaining indicator.

Renault's most daring EV was the Twizy. So much, in fact, that it wasn't even classed as a car. Legislators labelled it a quadricycle – bringing back memories of the Sinclair C5.

The Twizy was marketed as the perfect city commuter.

Doors were an option on the Twizy and full-sized windows weren't available at any price.

Renault Twizy

Price: £7,400 (+£45/month)
Top speed: 50mph (80km/h)
0–28mph: 6.1sec
Kerb weight: 1,045lb (475kg)
Engine type: electric asynchronous
Installation: mid, transverse, RWD
Power: 17bhp
Torque; 42lb ft 57Nm) at 2,100rpm
Gearbox: none
Battery: 6.1kWh lithium-ion
Boot: 1,891in3 (31ltr)
Wheels: 13in (330mm) alloy;
Tyres: 125/80 R13(F) 145/80 R13(R)

Renault priced the Zoe aggressively. In the UK it cost £12,340 less than the LEAF. The sting was in the monthly battery rental of £70.

A functional around-town runabout, the Twizy looked as if it had driven off the set of a Hollywood science fiction blockbuster. It didn't even call itself a car. Despite having four wheels and two seats, Renault described it as a 'quadricycle'. The stripped down body was barely larger than a motorcycle and the car didn't even come with doors as standard (they were a £545 option) and there were no windows at any price.

The powertrain was as basic as it was possible to get, a 6kWh Li-ion battery running down the central spine of the car powering a rear mounted AC motor. The power output looked nothing special but thanks to 42lb ft (57Nm) of torque, the lightweight Twizy was quick off the mark. A full charge took just three-and-a-half hours and the car was good for 60 miles (96km) – a practical maximum for a car designed around the urban commute to work. The price was £7,400, making the Twizy easily the cheapest EV available from a mass market manufacturer, albeit one even Renault couldn't describe as a car, plus £45 per month battery rental.

Unlike the Fluence car, critics showered the Twizy with praise. *Autocar* declared 'it's fabulous', *The Daily Telegraph* praised the 'spectacular' cornering ability and T3 magazine declared 'as a gateway to the future, and opening up the possibilities of electric cars, we're intrigued'.

The Zoe ZE fell somewhere between the bland Fluence and the jaw-dropping Twizy. A concept vehicle first

The interior of the Zoe, with its neatly integrated colour monitor screen, looked more contemporary than the Fluence.

Renault took the brave decision to charge a rental fee for the Zoe's battery module – thereby reducing the entry point cost.

Renault Zoe

Price: £13,650 (including the UK Government electric car grant of £5,000)
Engine: electric motor
Power: 88bhp
Torque: 162lb ft (220Nm)
Transmission: single-speed, front-wheel drive
0–62mph: 13.5sec
Top speed: 84mph (134km/h)
Range to empty: 130 miles (208km)

emerged at the Frankfurt Motor Show in 2009, when it was hailed as Renault's vision of a supermini EV. It was powered by a 95bhp motor and used a Li-ion battery pack beneath the seats. This powertrain would be largely carried over to the production Zoe but, in almost every other way, the Frankfurt concept was a flight of fancy. The tear-drop shaped body featured a transparent solar panel roof and there were Lamborghini-style gull wing doors. The French cosmetics company L'Oreal had a hand in the Zoe's climate control system, which sprayed perfume into the cabin to mask nasty smells.

Renault returned to the Paris Motor Show a year later with a substantially different Zoe, described as a 'near definitive' interpretation of the car that would go on sale in 2012. The wacky looks had been toned down, as had the electric motor's power output (from 95bhp to 79bhp) and the top speed (84mph/134km/h vs 90mph/144km/h). There were no solar panels fixed to the roof or crazy gull wing doors. The Zoe was now a perfectly ordinary-looking four-door supermini, although the L'Oreal Biotherm climate control system did make the cut.

More importantly, the Zoe was Renault's first fully developed electric-only car platform (Twizy quadricycle aside) and was therefore designed with perfect weight distribution and cabin space. Renault even talked about making a 'hot' Renault sport version for performance-minded environmentalists.

The Zoe was also priced to sell. In the UK, Renault said it would charge £13,650 (£12,340 less than the LEAF), making the Zoe comfortably the cheapest 'real' EV available to British drivers in 2012. Of course, there was the inevitable battery rental fee: the power pack cost at least £70 per month. The Zoe was also the first EV with a universal charger – capable of accepting any power input. Plugged into a fast charger, the Zoe would be ready to go after just half-an-hour. A conventional home socket, however, required a charge time of 9h. Renault claimed the car would travel up to 130 miles (208km) under ideal conditions. The electric motor gave 88bhp (20bhp less than the larger Nissan LEAF) and the top speed was 84mph (134km/h). As usual, the battery pack was mounted under the floor helping reduce the car's centre of gravity.

In a bid to convince sceptical journalists of the Zoe's usefulness, Renault arranged a demonstration in the toughest conditions imaginable: on a frozen lake north of the Arctic Circle, near the town of Kiruna, in Sweden. Although the punishing temperatures meant the Zoe's range dropped to just 60 miles (96km), the demonstration appeared to do the trick.

Auto Express magazine wrote: 'First impressions are very good'. It praised the soft suspension, acceleration and braking, adding: 'Not only is it the most affordable electric car, it's also practical, simple to use and attractive. It demands fewer compromises than any other EV on sale – the Nissan Leaf included.' However, the thorny problems of range and inadequate infrastructure prevented the magazine delivering a ringing endorsement. 'Its success depends on whether customers can live with its limited range,' the article concluded.

More than a century after the twin problems of battery range and recharging issues prevented the EV consolidating its early lead in the automobile industry, the same difficulties lay ahead.

Supercar Salvation

It's ironic, given their environmentally friendly image, that hybrid drivetrains are set to dominate the future supercar sector.

Traditionally, supercar manufacturers such as Jaguar have focused on making their cars lighter – and faster – through the use of exotic lightweight materials like carbon fibre composites, titanium and magnesium. But future

The use of high-output electric motors helped Jaguar extract supercar performance from a 1.6-litre 4-cylinder petrol engine.

The C-X75 originally used gas turbines to charge the battery modules but they were ditched for production.

Porsche promises crushing performance for the 918 hybrid, here painted in the iconic Martini racing livery.

CO_2 emissions' standards have forced a re-evaluation of hybrid technology.

Although batteries and extra motors add weight – the mortal enemy of supercar designers – the benefits of an electric motor's ability to deliver its maximum torque at any speed are enough to overcome the drawbacks. Many of the next generation of supercars will use smaller, more fuel-efficient engines and electric motors.

Ferrari claims the HY-KERS drivetrain that will be used in its Enzo replacement, the F150, cuts emissions by up to 40 per cent, while still delivering devastating performance, and Jaguar believes the CO_2 emissions of its C-X75 will be less than 98g/km.

The British car was perhaps the most interesting. The Ferrari still uses an old-school 800bhp, 7.3-litre V12 albeit supplemented by 115bhp from an electric motor mounted at the end of the car's seven-speed gearbox and engaged via a clutch. As Ferrari chief executive Amedo Felisa says: 'We sell performance, not CO_2'.

Jaguar turned to Williams, the legendary Formula One racing outfit, to help develop the C-X75 from a gas turbine concept car into a production-ready supercar. It chose an unusually small (by supercar standards) 1.6-litre, 4-cylinder, twin-turbo petrol engine. Working together, engineers from Jaguar and Williams achieved a reliable 313bhp per litre from the engine giving a staggering overall output of 500bhp from a mere 1600cc.

The C-X75 engine will power the rear wheels assisted by electric motors on each axle. In the original C-X75 concept, a pair of gas turbines charged the battery modules and drive was by the electric motors alone. But the harsh realities of production – even for a car limited to just 250 units – meant the turbines had to go.

The Li-ion battery pack runs down the spine of the car and weighs around 506lb (230kg). Drivers will be able to drive in all-electric mode for around 30 miles (48km).

Jaguar claims the performance of the C-X75 will equal the Bugatti Veyron – the undisputed king of the current generation of supercars. Sadly, Jaguar cancelled the C-X75 in late 2012. Only five test-beds will be built and none will be sold.

Not to be out done, Porsche is scheduled to begin production of its 918 Spyder in September 2013.

The eagerly awaited successor to the Carrera GT, the 918, uses a mid-mounted dry-sump V8 that's good for more than 500bhp and a pair of electric motors – one on each axle – adding 'at least' 218bhp. In total this drivetrain will deliver more than 700bhp yet, thanks to a pure EV mode that will allow the 918 to travel 16 miles (25km) on battery power alone, the 918 will return 94mpg (3.01ltr/100km) and just 70g/km of CO_2.

Performance should be startling. Porsche engineers confidentially predict a 0–62mph of less than 3sec and a top speed of 201mph (322km/h) – a far cry from

The Lotus Esprit is enduring a troubled gestation. If the car reaches production, a hybrid is likely. Sports car manufacturers cannot afford to ignore the benefits of electric motors any more.

Porsche 918 Spyder

Body: two-seater Spyder
Drivetrain: parallel full hybrid; 4.6-litre V8 mid-engine with dry sump lubrication; hybrid module with electric motor and decoupler; electric motor with decoupler and gear unit on front axle; electrical system recuperation; four cooling circuits for motors, transmission and battery; thermal management
Engine Power: more than 570bhp (V8 engine)
90kW (hybrid module on rear axle)
80kW (electric motor on front axle)
more than 770bhp (combined)
Brake system: high-performance hybrid brake system with adaptive recuperation; ceramic brake discs (PCCB)
Energy supply: lithium-ion battery with 6.8kWh capacity (BOL nominal), 202kW maximum power and mains compatible plug-in charger
Performance:
Top speed: 201mph (325km/h); purely electric: 93mph (150km/h)
Acceleration: 0–62mph in less than 3sec
Consumption: 94mpg (3.0ltr/100km)
CO_2 emissions: 70g/km
Range: more than 15 miles (25km) on batteries alone

Ferdinand Porsche's first hybrid car, the Semper Vivus, 113 years earlier. The top speed on purely electric power is 94mph (150km/h).

To keep the Li-ion battery pack cool, the exhausts are integrated into the body – exiting behind each seat via separate bulkheads. The chassis will be made from carbon fibre reinforced plastic for stiffness and light weight. First deliveries are due in 2014 and the car will cost £678,000.

Ferrari's bitter F1 rival, McLaren, is said to be planning to incorporate hybrid technology in the successor to its MP4-12C supercar. The new model, due in 2013, will use KERS (kinetic energy recovery system) power-boosting technology, using an electric motor/generator. This will provide an extra 100bhp at the touch for a button – perfect for overtaking when 750bhp from the 3.8-litre twin turbo V8 just isn't sufficient.

It's not just the money-no-object hypercars that will benefit from electric motor assistance. Even junior supercar manufacturers, such as Honda (NSX) and Lotus (new Esprit), are planning to use hybrid technology as a means of making their sports cars more exciting to drive and kinder to the environment.

History has come full circle. Soon electric cars will once more be the fastest in the world.

THE MORE THINGS CHANGE, THE MORE THEY STAY THE SAME

A century after they almost died out, electric cars, in one form or another, are finally here to stay.

As of 2012 there are four competing technologies:

- The all-electric vehicle, which uses an electric motor(s) for its propulsion with one or more storage systems.
- Hybrid: a vehicle where drive to the wheels can be supplied by an electric motor and an internal combustion engine together. Usually a larger internal combustion engine does most of the work via a mechanical transmission, with a small electric motor helping out.
- Plug-in hybrid: A development of the hybrid design which has a plug for recharging batteries from the mains. These are an improvement on the simple hybrid concept having greater storage capability, a charger and improved energy management. They can usually drive on all-electric power at lower speeds and for short distances.
- Extended range electric vehicle, which functions like an all-electric vehicle but has an auxiliary energy supply (usually in the form of a small engine) that kicks in when the battery is feeling a bit run down.

Manufacturers have embraced the hybrid concept like an old friend. Toyota, Honda, Peugeot and Citroën already have hybrids on sale. By the middle of this decade, virtually every other manufacturer will have at least one hybrid offering in their line-up. Many of these will allow all-electric drive for short distances, too.

According to research by the Boston Consulting Group, hybrid sales could command almost 18 per cent of the European new car market by the end of this decade. However, in most cases, plug-in hybrids do not offer full electric performance capability. The only way for them to do this would be to add more batteries but this, in turn, would lead to unacceptable weight and cost increases.

True, the 2012 Toyota Prius Plug-In Hybrid, which uses a 4.4kWh Li-ion battery pack, is capable of up to 62mph (100km/h) for 14 miles (24km), but this is currently an exception.

The industry has responded with range-extending technology, which offers full electric running at all speeds with no need for an internal combustion engine until all the on-board electrical energy has been expended. In short, buyers who want to do their bit for the environment can enjoy all-electric motoring without the nagging worry that they might be stranded with a flat battery.

Given the public's acceptance of the Vauxhall/Chevrolet Ampera, several manufacturers are investigating second generation range extending technology but sluggish sales are making them cautious. Instead, plug-in hybrids seem to be the electric car technology most likely to gain significant market share in the medium term.

Looking further ahead, third-generation range extenders will integrate the various systems in the name of simplicity and efficiency.

The future of the pure electric vehicle is harder to predict.

For all its clever technology and ease-of-use, the Nissan LEAF is still hobbled by range limitations. It will take a monumental effort to persuade the majority of the driving population that a car that can't travel more than 100 miles (160km) in ideal conditions is practical enough to be a family's sole means of independent transportation; the early signs aren't good. Sales of the LEAF fell by a quarter in the first half of 2012, compared to the previous year.

The price of petrol and diesel, plus the continued financial patronage of governments worldwide, will be crucial factors in the success (or otherwise) of the pure electric car. According to Boston Consulting, if a barrel of oil breaches the $180 mark, EV penetration would increase to 12 per cent of the European market (5 per cent in the United States and 8 per cent in Japan). A reduction in the cost of batteries would also help.[65]

Not everyone shares that view. J. D. Power expects hybrids and EVs to make up a mere 7.4 per cent of global sales by 2020. It believes the cost of batteries and the complexity of electric cars will hobble EV production in favour of traditional (and cheaper) internal combustion competition.[66]

But why all the interest in EVs and hybrids after all these years? Because car manufacturers know electric vehicles will make an enormous contribution to their overall corporate average fuel economy. In America, for instance, major manufacturers must achieve an overall mpg of 35.5mpg (6.63ltr/100km) by 2016, as mandated by federal regulations and the regulations in Europe are even tougher.

After car makers failed to comply with 2008 European Union tailpipe targets, the European Council of Ministers formally approved a shift to mandatory standards. In 2009, these were set at 42mpg (5.6ltr/100km) – 130g/km of CO_2 – to be phased in by 2015 and 57.6mpg (4.1ltr/100km) – 95g/km of CO_2 – by 2020.

Electric vehicles are essential to meeting these targets because upstream electricity emissions from power stations, etc., are not counted. In addition, electric vehicles are given 'super credits' until 2015.

But there are other obstacles standing in the way of success.

How long will it take before a viable fast-charging infrastructure is in place? Can governments afford to continue to hand out generous EV subsidies or tax credits? Will the next generation lithium-oxygen batteries offer greater performance and/or range? And, most importantly, are EVs really the 'green' option or will ultra-efficient, small capacity internal combustion engines reclaim the moral high ground?

After more than a century of struggle between internal combustion and electricity, the battle, it seems, has only just begun.

REFERENCES

1. Piccolini, M. 'Animal Electricity and the Birth of Electrophysiology: the Legacy of Luigi Galvani' (Brain Research Bulletin, Vol. 46, No.5, July 15, 1998, pp.381–407)
2. Stock, J. B. *Amazing Iowa* (Rutledge Hill Press, 2003)
3. Rubenstein, J. M. *Making and Selling Cars* (John Hopkins University Press, 2001)
4. *The Electrical World* (August 1898)
5. *The Horseless Age* (August 1897)
6. Munro, Bill, *London Taxis: A Full History* (Earlswood Press, 2011)
7. Munro, Bill, *London Taxis: A Full History* (Earlswood Press, 2011)
8. Rae, J. B. 'The Electric Vehicle Company: a Monopoly That Missed' Business History Review (December 1955)
9. Nevins, A. *Ford: The Times, The Man, The Company* (Scribner, 1954)
10. Mom, G. *The Electric Vehicle: Technology and Expectations in the Automobile Age* (John Hopkins University Press, 2004)
11. *The Evening Post* (6 November 1926)
12. *The Ohio Plain Dealer*, 3 November 2008
13. Ford, H. and Crowther, S. *Edison as I Know Him* (Cosmopolitan Book Co., 1930)
14. Mom, G. *The Electric Vehicle: Technology and Expectations in the Automobile Age* (John Hopkins University Press, 2004)
15. Handy, Galen, website www.earlyelectric.com
16. English, 'A. 'Lohner Semper Vivus Review' Daily Telegraph (4 May 2011)
17. Anderson, C. D. and Anderson, J. *Electric and Hybrid Cars: A History* (McFarland, 2010)
18. Mom, Gijs *The Electric Vehicle: Technology and Expectations in the Automobile Age* (John Hopkins University Press, 2004)
19. *The Iron Age* [magazine] (2 November 1922)
20. *The New York Times* (10 August 1920)
21. Kirsch, D., *The Electric Vehicle and The Burden of History* (Rutgers University Press, 2000)
22. *Time* (October 1953)
23. www.intrepid-travelers.com
24. Georgano, N. *Electric Vehicles* (Shire Publications, 1996)
25. *New Scientist* (3 October 1974, p.47)
26. McCahill, T. 'GM's Mini-Mini Cars', *Mechanix Illustrated* (October 1969, p.76)
27. Barret, R. 'Plugged in Early: Briggs had a Hybrid in'70s', *Milwaukee-Wisconsin Journal Sentinel* (10 March 2008)
28. MacDowall, R. and Burke, A. 'Performance Testing of the Ford/GE Second Generation Single-Shaft Electric Propulsion System', US DOE (June 1993)
29. 'After 40 years, GE's father of EV R&D finally sees tipping point', GE Reports (4 November 2010)
30. Dale, R. *The Sinclair Story* (Gerald Duckworth, 1985)
31. Meiners, J. 'Remnants of the evil past', *Car and Driver* (June 2011)
32. Witzenberg, G. 'At Witz' End – EV1 – The Real Story', Autobloggreen (August 2008)
33. Dean, P. and Reed, M. 'An Electric Start: Media, Billboards, web Site Herald Launch of the EV1', *Los Angeles Times* (6 December 1996)
34. *Imagine the Impact*, GM promotional short (1990)
35. 'Democratic Convention Features High Tech', ABC News (www.abcnews.go.com, August 1997)
36. Taylor, M. 'Owners Charged Up Over Electric Cars, But Manufacturers Have Pulled the Plug', *San Francisco Chronicle* (22 April 2005)
37. Taylor, A. 'The Birth of the Prius', *Fortune* (March 6, 2006)
38. Roe, S. 'Supercar: the Tanking of an American Dream', *Chicago Tribune* (2003)
39. Shitazaki, H. *The Prius That Shook The World* (Nikkan Kogyo Shimbun Ltd, 1999)
40. Thornton, E. 'Japan's Hybrid Cars', *Businessweek* (15 December 1997)
41. Bartlett, J. *Motor Trend* (August 2005)
42. Shitazaki, H. *The Prius That Shook The World* (Nikkan Kogyo Shimbun Ltd, 1999)
43. Garrett, J. 'Behind The Wheel: Honda Insight', *New York Times* (4 June 2000)
44. Pollack, A. 'Toyota Prius: It's easier to be Green', New York Times (19 November 2000)
45. Jensen, C. 'On the Town in Three Green Machines', *New York Times* (14 April 2002)
46. Hirsch, J. 'Attorneys General Win More Time to Ponder Honda Civic Settlement', *Los Angeles Times* (14 February 2012)
47. Robinson, A. 'The Green Brigade', *Car and Driver* (May 2001)
48. Robinson, A. 'The Green Brigade', *Car and Driver* (May 2001)
49. Chirco, N. '2004 Chevrolet Silverado Hybrid – One Year Test Update', *Motor Trend* (February 2005)
50. Hope, G. 'Toyota Prius', *Auto Express* (November 2004)
51. Boxwell, M. *The Electric Car Guide – G-Wiz* (Greenstream Publishing, 2010)
52. Biers, D. 'Japan's Car Makers Are Thinking Electric', *The Day* (18 July 1991)
53. Hudson, P. 'Brief Drive: Nissan Hypermini', *The Daily Telegraph* (10 October 10 2000)
54. Gibbs, N. 'First Drive: TH!NK City', *Auto Express* (April 2008)
55. Ramsay, M. 'Nissan says LEAF Electric Will Be Profitable wth US Plant', *Wall St Journal* (13 May 2010)
56. Naughton, K. 'Bob Lutz: The Man Who Revived the Electric Car', *Newsweek* (December 2007)
57. Brooke, L. 'All the Technology Needed for 100mpg (Batteries Not Included)', *New York Times* (7 January 2007)
58. Vanderwerp, D. '2011 Chevrolet Volt Full Test', *Car and Driver* (October 2010)
59. 'VauxhallAera Road Test', *Autocar* (28 March 2012)
60. 'Honda CR-Z "Inspired by Lotus"', Autocar (20 January 2010)
61. Oliver, B. 'First Drives', *CAR* [magazine] (May 2010)
62. 'First Drives', *Auto Express* (November 2007)
63. Robinson, A. '2009 Honda FCX Clarity', *Car and Driver* (March 2008)
64. 'Fluence First Drive', *Autocar* (7 February 2012)
65. Devineni, A. and Dinger, M. *Powering Autos to 2020: The Era of the Electric Car?* (Boston Consulting Group, July 2011)
66. Omotoso, M. *Drive Green 2020 – Alternative Powertrain Forecast* (J. D. Power and Associates, 2010)

INDEX

1,000 mile endurance run 48–49, 56

Adraktas, Konstantine 80
AeroVironment 120
American Association of Licensed Automobile Manufacturers 29
American Battery Company 12
American Motor Car Manufacturers Association 30
Amilcar Compound B38 63
Anderson, Robert 8–9
Andretti, Mario 97
Arbel 67
Astor, John Jacob 24
Atkinson cycle 143
Atkinson, James 143
Audi A1 112
Audi A3 112
Audi Duo 110
Audi Duo Mk 2 110–111
Audi duo Mk 3 111
Audi e-tron 112, 114
Audi e-TRON Spyder 113
Audi Q5 Hybrid 112
Audi R18 e-tron Quattro 114–115
Audi R8 e-tron 112
Auto-Mixte 46
Automobile Club de France 13
Automotive Engery Supply Corporation 191
Ayrton, William 11

Baker 33
Baker Electric Brougham 38
Baker Motor Vehicle Company 36
Baker Torpedo 36–38, 40
Baker Torpedo Kid 38
Baker, Walter C. 36
Barthmuss, Dave 134
Battronic Truck Corporation 72, 74
BBC Top Gear 163, 177, 179, 196
Beaumont, Bob 90–92
Beaumont, W Worby 17
Becker, Christopher 9
Bedford 82–83
Begley, Ed jnr 132
Bersey cab 20–21
Bersey, Walter 20
Bose 200
Botting, Nicholas 105
Briggs & Stratton 96–97
British Electromobile Company 20
British Leyland 82
British Motor Corporation 78
Buchanan Report 74
Buchanan, Sir Colin 74
Bugatti Veyron 218
Buick Skylark 69

California Air Resources Board (CARB) 84, 123, 136, 139
Cars for Cities study group 74
Carter Coaster 78
Carter Engineering 78
CGE-Tudor 63–64
Chalker, Lynda 105
Chanteloup hill climb 13
Charles Caffrey Carriage Company 19
Chasseloup-Laubat, Count Gaston 13, 14
Chevrolet S-10 Electric 129, 132
Chevrolet Silverado 170–171
Chevrolet Volt 6, 194, 197–202
Chevrolet Volt Concept 198
Chicago World's Fair 1893 12
Cho, Fujio 140–141
Chrysler EPIC 139
Chrysler Intrepid ESX 163–164
Chrysler TEVan 139
CitiCar 90
Citroen AX Electric 118
Citroen Citela 116–117
Citroen C-Zero 194
City and Suburban Electric Carriage Company 33–34
Clarkson, Jeremy 177, 179
Clinton, Bill 141
Columbia 23–24
Columbia Electric Motor Carriage 24
Consumers Association 106
Co-Op Dairy 67
Crompton-Leyland Electricar prototype 82
Crossland, Leonard 79
Cuntz, Herman F. 28
Curry, Chris 100

Davidson, Robert 8
Day, Harry 61
DeLorean 103
Desbarats, Gus 103
Detroit Electric 49–51, 55
Diaz, Cameron 177
DiCaprio, Leonardo 177
Dodge ESX 3 163, 165–166
Donington Park race circuit 83

Edison nickel-iron battery 48, 49
Edison, Thomas 12, 39, 48
Edison-Ford electric car 51–52
Electra King 90
Electraction 92
Electraction Tropicana 92
Electric Mobility Solutions 187
Electric Storage Battery Company 22
Electric Vehicle association of America 58, 61–62
Electric Vehicle Company 22–25, 28–31, 59
Electrically Assisted Pedal Cycle Regulations 100
Electrobat 12, 19, 24
Electromobile cab 20–21, 34
Elwell, Paul 11
Enfield 465 80
Enfield 8000 80–82
Engle, Barry 186
Environmental Protection Agency 198
ETX-I 98
ETX-II 98
Eureka Williams 68
Exide Ironclad batteries 58

Faraday, Michael 8
Featherstone, Andrew 38
Feldmann, C.Russell 68
Ferdinand, Archduke Franz 43
Ferrari F150 218
Fiat X1/23B 94–95
Flowers, Frank 92
Ford Australia Sunchaser 121
Ford Comuta 78–80
Ford E-KA 158, 161–163
Ford P2000 158
Ford Prodigy 158–161
Ford Ranger EV 136, 137, 139
Ford TH!NK 184–185
Ford, Henry 7, 29–31, 39
Fukui, Takeo 203

Galvani electric locomotive 8
Galvani, Luigi 8
GE 100 97
GE ETV-1 97
General Electric Delta 87
General Motors EV1 84, 120, 124–129, 141
General Motors EV1 recall 132
General Motors EV1 second generation 129–134
General Vehicle Company 61
Genestatom nuclear-powered car 67
Ghosn, Carlos 7, 187, 212
Gibson, Mel 132
GM Electrovair 84–86
GM Electrovan 85–86
GM Electrovette 92–93
GM Heritage Center Museum 200
GM iCar 197
GM Impact 122
GM Precept 166–169
GM XP512E microcar 86–87
GMC 92, 94
Goodwood Festival of Speed 2011 207
Great Horseless Carriage Company 20
Gregoire, Jean-Albert 63
G-Wiz 179–181

Hall, Jerry 181
Hanks, Tom 136
Harrods department store 63
Hart, E.W 41
Hautier Cab Company 38–39
Haynes, Roy 92
Helmer, Jean 107
Henny Kilowatt 68–71
Henny Motor Co. 68
Heyman, HW 74
Honda Civic hybrid 157
Honda Civic Type R 204
Honda Compact Renaissance Zero concept 203
Honda CRX 152
Honda CRZ 203–205
Honda CRZ Mugen 205–207
Honda EV-Plus 149–150
Honda EV-X 149
Honda FCX Clarity 208–210
Honda FCX hatchback concept 208
Honda Fit EV 208
Honda Insight Mk 1 150–157, 197
Honda Insight Mk 2 201–203
Honda Integrated Motor Assist 150
Honda Jazz hybrid 207
Honda JVX 150
Honda NSX 207
Honda, Hirotoshi 205
Honda, Soichiro 205
Horton, Peter 132
hydrogen fuel cells 208

Imperia 46
Imperia GP 47
Indianapolis raceway 71
Industrial Light and Magic 131
Issigonis, Sir Alec 78

Jaguar C-X75 217–218
Jeantaud world record holder 14

Jeantaud, Charles 12
Jellinek, Emil 43
Jenatzy, Camille 13, 14, 16
Jersey RAV 4 EV experiment 135–136

king of Siam 36
King, Bob 97
Kirsch, David 62
Krieger Hybrid 46
Krieger, Louis 41
Kuhlman, Jeff 132
Kyoto international conference on climate change 145

La Jamais Contente 15, 17
La Rochelle electric car experiment 118–119
Lauckner, Jon 196, 198
Lexus 147, 149
Lexus CT200h 177
Lexus GS450h 177
Lexus LS 600h 177
Lexus RX400h 177
Lexus RX450h 175-177
Locomomotive (Roads) Act of 1865 11
Lohner, Jacob 40
Lohner-Porsche 40, 42
Lohner-Porsche Mixte 43
Loing, Pierre 192
London Electric Taxicab Company 20
London to Brighton Emancipation Run 20
Lotus 184, 195
Lotus Elise 195, 204
Lowenthal, Alan 132
Lunar Rover 87-89
Lutz, Bob 195

Mandelson, Peter 191, 192
Maples, Ernest 74
Mars II 71
Maxim, Hiram Percy 23, 24
Mazda RX2 69
McLaren 219
McMullan jnr, Morrison 69
Meinl Julius 41
Mercedes Mixte 46
Meyan, M Paul 13
Michelotti 82
Milburn Light Electric 52–55
Milburn, George 52
Milde-Krieger 65
Milk floats 72–73
Milwaukee-Wisconsin Journal Sentinel 97
Mini Traveller 76, 78
Mitusbishi i-MiEV 194
Model T Ford 52, 60
Morris, Henry 12, 18, 24
Morrison, William 12
Mugen Motorsports 205

Nader, Ralph 132
NASA 87–89
National Union Electric Co 69, 70
NEC Corporation 191
Nevins, Allan 31
nickel-iron batteries 51, 58
Niedermeyer, Edward 202
Nissan 315X concept 181
Nissan Altima hybrid 181
Nissan Altra EV 182
Nissan Cube EV-01/02 191
Nissan FEV II 181–182
Nissan Future Electric Vehicle 181–182
Nissan Hypermini 182–184
Nissan LEAF 6, 187–193, 197
Nissan Prairie Joy EV 182
Nissan-Hitachi prototype 95
Northern Coach-Builders 72
Ogle Design 100, 102
Ohio Electric 52
Oldham 80
Oldsmobile Aurora 131
Owen Magnetic Model 60 48

partinium 17
Partnership for a New Generation of Vehicles 141, 143, 158, 169
Paul, Alexandra 132
Pedestrian-Contolled Electric Delivery Trusk 67
Peel Engineering Trident 76–77
Peel, Sir Robert 8
Perry, John 11
Peugeot 106 Electric 116, 118
Peugeot 205 Electric 107
Peugeot 3008 Hybrid4 65, 67
Peugeot iOn 194, 195
Peugeot Voiture Kogoro de Ville 64–65
Pieper, Henri 46
Pitts, Michael 105
Pivco 184
Plante, Gaston 11
Pope Manufacturing Company 23
Pope, Colonel Albert Augustus 23
Pope-Waverley 36
Porsche 918 45, 218
Porsche Cayenne hybrid 44–45
Porsche Panamera hybrid 45
Porsche, Ferdinand 40, 44
Posawatz, Tony 198
Prius One service plan 157

Queen Alexandra 33

Rauch and Lang 33, 38
Reagan, Ronald 84
Reithhofer, Norbert 181
Renaissance Cars 92
Renault 5 83
Renault Dauphine 68–69, 71
Renault Elektro Clio 116
Renault Fluence 194, 212–213
Renault Kangoo ZE 211–213
Renault Twizy 194, 213–215
Renault Zoe ZE 215–217
Renault Zoom concept 115–116
Rice, Isaac 22
Riker Electric Vehicles 26–27
Riker Torpedo 26
Riker, Andrew 25
Ringdal, Jan Otto 184
Roberts, Clive 123
Roosevelt, Franklin 28
Ross, Jonathan 181
Rothschild, Baron Nathan 41
Royal Mail electric vehicles 62
Rutherford, Johnny 97
Ryan, Thomas F. 23

Salom, Pedro 12, 18, 24
Samuel, Sir Jon 80
Scottish Aviation Scamp 75–76
Selden patent 28
Selden, George 28
Semper Vivus 41–43, 219
Sinclair C1 100
Sinclair C10 102
Sinclair C15 102, 103, 104
Sinclair C5 99, 102–107
Sinclair X-1 107
Sinclair Zike 107
Sinclair, Sir Clive 99, 101, 107
Smith Delivery Vehicles 71–74
Smith, Roger 120, 122
Specialty Equipment Market Association (SEMA) 205
Steinmetz 33, 61
Steinmetz, Charles Proteus 61
Stempel, Bob 123
Stevens, Brooks 96
Stratingh, Sibrandus 9–11
Studebaker 34–35
Sturgis, Harold 12
Subaru Electro-wagon X1 95
Sunraycer 120–121

Tama Electric Car Company 66, 181
Tesla 136, 195–196, 197
Tesla Roadster 195–196
Tesla, Nikola 195
TH!NK Ox 186
Tomobe, Norio 204
Torikai, Torukazu 204
Toujours Vitesse 17
Toujours-Contente, Le 41
Toyoda, Eiji 141
Toyota Century hybrid 141
Toyota Crown hybrid 171
Toyota Earth Charter 140
Toyota Environmental Action Plan 140
Toyota Estima 171
Toyota G21 project 141
Toyota Prius 6, 142–147, 156–157, 197
Toyota Prius 2 171–174, 177
Toyota Prius international awards 147
Toyota RAV4 EV Mk 1 134–136, 141, 143
Toyota RAV4 EV Mk 2 136
Toyota S800 hybrid 141
Toyota Yaris Hybrid 177–178
Triblehorn 33
Trojan Electrojan 71
Trouve, Gustave 11
Truth About Cars website 202

Uchiyamada, Takeshi 142
UK Electricity Council 76, 80, 101
University of Groningen 10

Vanguard Coupe 90
Vauxhall Ampera 194, 200–202
Volta, Alessandro 7
Voltaic pile 8
VW CitySTROMer 108, 109
VW Elektro-Hybrid Golf 108, 110
VW Jetta CitySTROMer 108, 109

Wada, Akihiro 141
Wagoner, Rick 120
Wall Auto Wheel 96
Wall, Arthur 96
Watson, Dr WG 75
Whitney, William C. 23
Williams Grand Prix Engineering 218
Wills, Barrie 102
Wilson, Woodrow 52
Witzenburg, Gary 123, 124, 125, 131, 134
Wood Rogers, Tony 100
Woods dual power car 48
Woods Motor Vehicle Company 35
World Solar Challenge 120, 149
Wouk, Victor 69

Zero Emission Vehicle Programme 141
Zingarevich, Boris 187
Zwerner, John 121, 129